# A GHOST UPON YOUR PATH

# A GHOST UPON YOUR PATH

## JOHN McCARTHY

## BANTAM PRESS

LONDON · NEW YORK · TORONTO · SYDNEY · AUCKLAND

TRANSWORLD PUBLISHERS
61–63 Uxbridge Road, London W5 5SA
a division of The Random House Group Ltd

RANDOM HOUSE AUSTRALIA (PTY) LTD
20 Alfred Street, Milsons Point, Sydney,
New South Wales 2061, Australia

RANDOM HOUSE NEW ZEALAND LTD
18 Poland Road, Glenfield, Auckland 10, New Zealand

RANDOM HOUSE SOUTH AFRICA (PTY) LTD
Endulini, 5a Jubilee Road, Parktown 2193, South Africa

Published 2002 by Bantam Press
a division of Transworld Publishers

A catalogue record for this book is available from the British Library.
ISBN 0593 048849

'In Memory of My Mother' (p.97) from Patrick Kavanagh's *Selected Poems*,
edited by Antoinette Quinn (Penguin Books), is reprinted with the permission of
the Trustees of the Estate of the late Katherine B. Kavanagh, through the Jonathan Williams
Literary Agency.
'The Two Trees' by W.B. Yeats (pp.111-12), is reprinted by permission of
A.P. Watt Ltd on behalf of Michael B. Yeats.
Frank O'Connor's translations of 'I am a ghost upon your path' by Donal IX MacCarthy Mór
and of 'No Help I'll Call' by Egan O Rahilly (p.259) are reprinted by permission of PFD on
behalf of Frank O'Connor. © Frank O'Connor.

Typeset in 12/16pt Granjon by
Falcon Oast Graphic Art Ltd.

Printed in Great Britain by
Mackays of Chatham plc, Chatham, Kent.

1 3 5 7 9 10 8 6 4 2

For my brother Terence

# ACKNOWLEDGEMENTS

THE LIST OF PEOPLE WHO HAVE GIVEN ME HELP AND ADVICE IN writing this book is long and I fear I cannot honour all my debts here.

From the outset my wife Anna has encouraged and supported me and provided valuable guidance and criticism.

Family plays an important role in the following pages. Without the genealogical skills and memory of my brother, Terence, much of the book would not have existed. My newly discovered family, the 'long-distance cousins', played a vital part in helping me understand my heritage and the warmth of Irish hospitality. Special thanks to Jean MacCarthy, Mike and Eileen Kennedy and Justin of Clash.

Writing a book set in a community would have been impossible without the cooperation and support of that community and so I offer heartfelt thanks to all the people of Inch and the surrounding area for making me so welcome. Maureen Fitzgerald, Bridey Flynn and Florence O'Sullivan were particularly generous with their time, giving me much information on Kerry past and present.

Not only did they open their doors to me, but many opened their hearts in friendship. There couldn't be kinder landlords than Phil and Mike Courtney. All the Foleys made me feel a part of their family and showered me with hospitality, advice and insight. Many thanks to Pat and Máire. Fidelus and John were the absolute constants of my stay: from my very first visit to Foley's Pub until the day of my return to England, their door was always open to me and I will never forget their generosity of spirit.

The team at Transworld, my publishers, have been as enormously supportive as always. I owe special thanks to Patrick Janson-Smith, who first helped me plot an Irish path, and to the editorial team: copy-editor Jane Heller, Deborah Adams and the proof-readers, and also Vivien Garrett and Linette Gray.

But for the gentle guidance and good humour of my editor, Bill Scott-Kerr, I would never have managed to pull together the threads that make up this book. Thank you, Bill.

# PROLOGUE

WE LOOKED AT EACH OTHER AND SMILED, ONE OF THOSE 'HERE we go, let's be brave' smiles. My brother, Terence, and I were surrounded by cardboard boxes that we'd just brought out of storage. As best as we could remember, they contained a whole swathe of family mementos, photographs, letters, school reports and some papers on our family history.

After my father's death we'd skimmed through all these while sorting out his house before selling it and moving on to our own homes. The process of going through the accumulated belongings of our parents' and our own lives was exhausting physically and, though we often laughed at the sheer volume of things we'd hoarded down the years, the experience had been emotionally draining. It felt almost like a betrayal of our parents, of us all, to throw away even the smallest souvenir. We seemed to take forever to decide that the humble little pot that one of us had bought for our mother on a holiday thirty years before really should go to the jumble. I think it was the feeling that we were losing touch, or letting go, not just of our father and mother, not just of the house and the belongings, but of the whole sense of us as the tight family unit that we had been, that was so difficult and upsetting.

1

It wasn't until we had at last cleared everything, and the removal men had come, loaded their trucks and set off, that the reality finally hit us. We stood in the drive and hugged and sobbed, knowing that we had to close the door on our family home. As I drove away towards my new place I continued crying and although my thoughts and emotions were confused, I knew that life would never be the same again and that somehow I was now really on my own. Had I broken some special link that had allowed me to keep in touch with my parents?

Although in the end we'd managed to be quite ruthless in our clear-out, there were some things we hadn't been able to fit into our new homes and these had gone into storage. Family papers and mementos fell into this category not so much because of their bulk but because we wanted to go through them properly when there was more time and when we felt emotionally stronger.

Now we felt ready to take the plunge and, what's more, since my marriage to Anna, our immediate family had expanded from just the two of us to three so that there was someone else to share the experience with. Anna hadn't known my parents and as we went through the boxes we found ourselves talking about people and events in more detail than we might have done had we been alone. There were papers and photographs of the houses we'd lived in and although it seemed easy enough to talk about them, I felt myself becoming anxious as memories, or rather snatches of memories, flashed through my head. It might have been a recollection of us all working together in the garden at our first home, which my parents built. It was to be years before the field was tamed into a more formal garden and the main summer occupation was cutting the wild grass that grew beyond the raised lawn which marked the edge of cultivation. My father had a thoroughly lethal cutter and the rest of us would follow him with rakes and a barrow to cart the hay off to the growing bonfire. In these memories the summers seem to have been always hot and sunny but now I started feeling cold and realized then that I was uncomfortable thinking about my parents, my mother especially. The old photographs in particular brought on feelings of confusion. When we found a picture of my parents on their wedding day we told Anna of what I'd said years later when our parents had been showing us their wedding photos themselves. My mother had explained that of course that was before Terence and I had come along. Unable to bear the thought that we had missed this great event, I had remonstrated, 'We *were* there, I was standing on Terence's head in Mummy's tummy!'

While some photographs weren't emotionally charged - although it was a surprise that we really did wear flares and grow our hair like that — the ones that kindled the warmest memories also upset me most. It wasn't just that they were often poorly composed and rather blurred.

'It's strange,' I said, 'it's almost as if I don't know these people. I mean, I know who they are of course, but it's as if somehow I don't really recognize them.'

Terence nodded his head. 'Yes I know,' and he went on, quoting, ' "The past is a foreign country: they do things differently there." '

The saying, from L. P. Hartley's *The Go-Between*, summed up my alien feelings exactly.

And yet the past was a country that we, especially Terence, had explored extensively. Along with my father he'd researched our family tree, tracing us back to the west of Ireland more than a thousand years earlier. Most of the fruits of that labour were in the boxes we were going through and the majority related to work done twenty years before. It had culminated in a family holiday in Ireland, in Dublin and then in County Kerry on the west coast.

One photograph, taken on that trip, captured the sense of dislocation that I'd been feeling as we rifled through the boxes. It has that typical look of a family holiday snapshot, capturing the whole scene but not quite doing justice to any of the components. The mountains in the background which should look majestic, rippling like a wrestler's shoulder muscles as the clouds pass over them, seem hazy and two-dimensional and there is too much weed-strewn field in the foreground. The two figures leaning against a rock at the heart of the picture aren't quite in focus. My mother's smiling face is nevertheless immediately recognizable and after a little careful scrutiny with a magnifying glass, the other face proves to be mine.

At that time I'd left home and was living and working in London. The holiday had been just as much fun as all the others in preceding years but the other photos from the trip interested me where this one upset me. Looking at pictures of Terence and even of my father was fine, though I was sad that he was no longer with us. It was this one of my mother and me that caused a lump in my throat. The vagueness of the image echoed the vagueness of my feelings, and I feared that she, and our relationship, would forever be out of focus.

The rock we were leaning against was clearly the reason we were in the middle of this field in an otherwise nondescript landscape. There were marks carved on it, and we remembered that it was called an Ogham stone. Ogham had been an ancient Irish language of some sort. Although we couldn't be sure of its precise location, Terence and I both thought it was at a place called Ardcanacht, a small area of farmland in County Kerry where our family had once lived. I stared at this photograph for some time– my mother, the Ogham stone and me – sighed and put it back in the box.

# CHAPTER ONE

THE DANCE FLOOR OF PADDY MURPHY'S BAR IS DESERTED BUT A few elderly couples sit at its side looking very satisfied with themselves as they enjoy a few late-night drinks. Businessmen are settled among holidaying families and couples in the pools of light near the bar. A mournful Irish lament issues from the PA system, blending with their quiet chatter, while other solitary characters, like me, sit silently at the fringes of the saloon reading by the light of the dim table lamps or else looking out through the distortion of rain-spattered windows to the dark sea beyond.

These lamps would look at home in a suburban bedroom but, like the pot plants which also grace the establishment, they seem incongruous when Paddy's Bar lurches suddenly and an increased hum of engines announces the start of the passage of the car ferry *The City of Cork* from Swansea to the city it was named for.

I need time to sit quietly and gather my thoughts. The drive to Swansea for this, the last sailing of the season in November 2001, was a journey one wouldn't want to repeat; gridlock in London meant that I didn't check in at the terminal until more than an hour after the final deadline.

A drink is definitely on my agenda but asking for one reveals further incongruities on board; the bar staff aren't Welsh or Irish, or even English – it turns out that the crew of *The City of Cork* is mainly Polish. Stranger still, Paddy Murphy's has no Guinness, even in cans, just a few tins of Heineken and some small bottles of wine.

Sipping at a glass of lukewarm white wine as the ship heads out across Swansea Bay and begins to roll a little, I reflect on my reasons for making this journey across the sea to Ireland.

My mother died in 1989 and my father in 1994. While I'd thought I'd come to terms with their loss, over the past year or so I've been feeling an increasing desire to spend some time alone thinking about them and our life together. There seem to be some loose ends in desperate need of retying.

Whenever I look at my mother's face in the old photographs I begin to feel uneasy, uncertain and guilty. And there is a whole folder full of letters from her, written when I was away at school and university, that have much the same effect. Many times since coming home from my five-year sojourn in Lebanon I have wanted to read them but have never been able to. Just looking at the familiar, sloping handwriting has made my chest tighten. Rather than confront these confused feelings, and deal with them, it has seemed easier to put everything – photos, letters and emotions – back in the boxes.

When I think of my mother I often imagine her greeting me after I'd been away from home for a while. I see her coming towards me, taking small quick steps, her body rounded forward as if she is holding, containing something. And she is; just as we meet she opens her arms and a flood of warm love surges from her body, from her smiling eyes, as she hugs me close saying, 'My darling John, it's so lovely to see you!'

Soon we are laughing and exchanging stories.

'Did I tell you what happened with Mrs Stephens and the cat?' And she begins telling her tale, stopping every now and then. 'Oh no, I've got to go back a bit, you see Mrs Stephens, you know she used to have that high-powered job working as a secretary in the city, well, she thought that when Julia Browne said that about the typewriter she was saying . . .' The story goes on; some of the details I can't really follow but it doesn't matter as I'm laughing, carried along by her delight in the life around her.

But the image always fades away as I walk into the cold, hard fact that she will never hug me again. The one time we most wanted, most needed to hug, on my return from Beirut, she wasn't there. She'd died two years before, three years after my capture and without ever having had any real concrete evidence that I was safe and well. I learned of her death a year after the event and at that time tried to grieve but I couldn't cry even though I wanted to. Maybe something within me warned that I could tip myself over into a deeper depression in what were already miserable circumstances. It was difficult to take in; of course I had no contact with the outside world, so my whole life beyond the cell was lived in the imagination. I consoled myself with the fact that I'd been so used to 'spending time' with her in my daydreams that I felt I'd somehow established a happy relationship with her without a physical presence. Our relationship, though frozen in time, was alive. It was a strange form of self-delusion which made the reality, when I had to face it, even more painful.

I had been aware, from seeing videos of appeals for my release that she'd made on the news, that her health was failing. The cancer we'd all hoped she'd defeated in the 1960s had reappeared in the month or so before I went to Beirut, and I couldn't bear to think how much her physical suffering was being exacerbated by the emotional trauma of my disappearance. Although I despised my captors, who showed the videos and said how nice she looked, for not simply sending out a photograph of me, I was preoccupied with my own guilt for putting myself in such a dangerous situation by going to Lebanon in the first place. I wanted to hug her and say I was sorry. I still do, but in some irrational way I suppose I'm frightened that after so much pain she'd find it hard to forgive. She died well over ten years ago yet I'm still stuck with a need to be in touch with her. That's the way it works, of course; loved ones may be gone but we keep talking to them.

When I got back home I learned from my brother Terence and my father just how much she had suffered, and they, too, alongside her. I remember talking late one night with my father. He'd been telling me that the doctors couldn't understand how she'd kept going for so long. The cancer was so advanced, they'd said, that she should have died months earlier than she did.

'You see, John, she just wouldn't give up. She was going to be there to welcome you . . .' He wasn't able to finish the sentence. I couldn't let my own feelings go even though I was now safe at home. It was still so soon after my release that I couldn't face trying to deal with her loss as I attempted to get my feet back on the ground in the real world. It was easier to retreat into the safe place I'd built where she was still the living but fantasy figure I'd had with me in the year before I knew of her death. While I knew my father only wanted to show how brave and strong my mother had been and that having me back in the family was the most important thing to her, my feelings of guilt became more entrenched, and so they remained until my departure for Ireland.

My father had been just as brave when he, too, succumbed to a second bout of cancer a year after my return. I was glad to be able to be at home then, and in the three years between my return and his death we became very good friends, closer in many ways than we'd been before my kidnap. We spent a lot of time together and Terence and I lived at his house for some of the time, especially during his last year. We had arguments, often quite angry ones, about politics and I found this stimulating, and I enjoyed sharing his intelligence and humour. We came to respect each other as equals and love each other as father and son. He was very proud of both his sons and we were of him. At times when I was young he'd seemed a stern father but now I saw him in his true colours. Most important of all I was able to overcome, with his help, the feelings of guilt I'd had about going to Beirut and putting the family through all that pain. He never once criticized or blamed me.

Although it was wonderful to have developed that closeness, I am conscious of a certain irony in that my relationship with him now seems more comfortable than that with my darling mother, with whom I'd always felt more intimate. Although logically I can tell myself that had she lived we'd have found the same closeness, the emotional reality is that we are marooned in a kind of limbo land.

When I'd taken up the picture of my mother and me beside the Ogham stone, I knew I shouldn't put it away again. Now it was time to have a good look at it, to think about her and hopefully to feel able once more to 'talk' to her. Far below me in the hold of the ship, I've got the photos and folder of letters packed in the car. I'm ready to take this journey to all the places I want it to take me.

By taking myself off to Ireland to think all this through I know I might be setting myself up for a lonely and painful time. But I feel I must do it and be alone to do it. I know there are still these hangovers from my earlier life that I need to settle.

*

Boxed up with my mother's letters is a bundle of material to do with the family history. While I was away in Lebanon, Terence, a keen genealogist, and my father had put a lot of this together, continuing the research that had started back in the 1930s when my grandparents had gone to Ireland on a family holiday, and we had taken it up in 1980. Much of the information came from a book, *The MacCarthys of Munster* by one Samuel Trant MacCarthy. Published in 1920, the book was based on a series of articles Samuel had written for the *Kerry Archaeological Journal*. He claimed to have been the MacCarthy Mór. Mór was the ancient Gaelic title assumed by the head of the clan, and there have been surprisingly vicious battles over the right to carry it even in recent times. Other material came from Terence's own researches in archive offices in London and Dublin.

Beyond having an Irish name, we had never really thought of ourselves as being Irish at all but once Terence had discovered a great deal of McCarthy family history we decided to see the place our forefathers came from. That holiday in Ireland in 1980 was the first time we had been to the country.

We rented a cottage on the outskirts of Dublin for our first week. Exploring the city and the surrounding countryside we found that the laid-back attitude of the Irish fitted well with the ease and enjoyment we found in each other's company.

Terence spent the best part of two days in the archives of Trinity College and the Genealogical Office at Dublin Castle, tracking down ancestral details that had previously been unavailable to him. My mother and I were less involved in the research, probably less interested in the details; we enjoyed soaking up the atmosphere of Dublin, visiting the pubs where James Joyce drank and having afternoon tea at the Shelbourne Hotel, watching the bustle of Dublin's social life going on around us.

'Isn't that Stig?' she asked excitedly as a blond man walked past.

'Yes. Well, no, I mean, he's really called Sting,' I replied, pretending to be unimpressed.

'Isn't he tall?'

I think we all liked to feel that Terence's researches into our old family connections were bringing us closer to this country and its people whom we were finding so welcoming. Whenever we met someone, they'd ask how we were and where we were from. On one occasion a man, who was extremely drunk, touched one of us for money for a pint. Although plastered, he still asked where home was and on being told it was in north Essex, exclaimed, 'I built the Great Dunmow bypass!'

From Dublin we headed west to County Kerry in search of a small area called Ardcanacht where our ancestors had lived between the fifteenth and nineteenth centuries. My father had bought a large-scale Ordnance Survey map of the area and while it looked as though there were no present-day homes in the vicinity, something described as an Ogham stone was indicated. In fact when we got to Ardcanacht, on the eastern end of the Dingle peninsula, not only did we find the stone but also some farmhouses that dated from the early 1900s. Nothing, though, that spoke of an ancient residence. We were a bit disappointed, thinking that there might at least have been a bit of a ruin, but we had to make do with the old, carved Ogham stone against which my mother and I posed for the photograph. Terence's research had, however, confirmed what he'd read in Samuel Trant's book: we were descended from an ancient and royal Irish line.

Looking through all this again as we went through the cardboard boxes, I felt I'd missed a trick by not paying more attention to the family history Terence had been uncovering with my father. Now I realized that this all sounded very grand indeed and I found that I was rather impressed with myself. Perhaps the affinity I've always felt with Ireland and the Irish reflected some deep genetic link.

On that first trip in 1980 I felt very at home in Ireland and all my subsequent visits have reinforced that feeling. But these trips have always been brief and I know that my reactions are at least partly informed by the romantic notions that are easily picked up by the tourist. Now I want to get to know Ireland better, to dig deeper and see whether a prolonged stay will change my views of the Irish and their country. Rather than hitting the road and trying to see the whole country or concentrating on the increasingly cosmopolitan cities like Dublin, I want to explore Ireland from a small rural community.

If you say you're going to Ireland, the response is almost universally a smile, a wink and 'Don't drink too much Guinness!' And that's just from people who have never touched a drop of Guinness in their life. Pubs, jolly music, humour – the *craic* – are the first things people think of when Ireland is mentioned. It isn't only foreigners who talk of Ireland in this way; many expatriate Irishmen go all misty-eyed at the thought of the homeland. And of course it's true, the *craic* is great and the welcome genuine, but what else is going on there? As an outsider one hears so much about the sadness and fear that has blighted life in the north of Ireland that perhaps the south has been presented as an eternally happy place where the sun shines even through the rain. And maybe the Irish are content to go along with that, but what is the reality beyond the rosy world of popular imagination and the much perpetuated tourist-guide version?

Images of Guinness and leprechauns seem to underpin a more serious aspect of the Irish, a people of unbroken spirit and unity in the face of centuries of British oppression. The celebration of the heroes of rebellions through the ages, the songs and laments for independence lost, the literature about the tragedy of famine and war all appear to endorse the idea of a nation that has experienced every adversity and triumphed over it, scattering the effects in its wake.

Apart from this impression of political and cultural integrity, there is too an air of holiness, of spiritual and moral vitality. Alongside the *craic* is the Church. Priests form a key group in Ireland's history – what other country pays so much attention to its patron saint as Ireland does to St Patrick? Most Irish conversations are liberally peppered with phrases like 'Thanks be to God!' and 'God have mercy on his soul!' It is part of the very fabric of Irish life. But every now and then recently we've been hearing revelations about abuse of children by priests. How can this have happened? This sits with neither the spiritual nor the caring, family-centred society I've believed Ireland to be, but clearly it is a part of the nation I want to understand.

There is another puzzle I want to explore. Ireland has always had close links with Europe and in recent times has benefited from its membership of the European Union. EU grants helped establish the infrastructure that set Irish business booming, heralding the period in which Ireland has had the fastest growing economy in the world and earned the title 'Celtic Tiger'. Yet over the past couple of years the Irish have started to have doubts about the validity of all this and seem to be turning their backs on others who want to join up.

And while the heroes of the past are celebrated, there are a number of investigations going on into recent corruption among today's leaders. I've often felt that there is a strong element of forgiving in the Irish temperament and assumed this was due to an inbuilt acceptance of the fact that, as human beings, we are all subject to weakness. But perhaps it goes further than this and there is a real difficulty in facing up to the problems within Irish society.

There seem to be many questions and paradoxes. Are the Irish an artistic, caring and devout people who survived oppression to burst forth as a force for good in the world? Or has their spirit and sense of identity actually been so shattered over the centuries that they have lost sight of who they are and taken refuge in the romantic 'theme park Ireland' that the rest of the world buys into and which brings in business and allows major issues to be dodged? By wearing their faith rather than their heart on their sleeve, have the Irish blindly handed over moral responsibility to the Church? And now that the Church's moral integrity is under question, how united in their faith are the Irish proving to be? After running their own affairs for eighty years, how liberal with each other are the people who waited so long for their freedom from an external power? When Irish eyes aren't smiling, how well do they cope?

The lighthouse at Roches Point flashes continuously as *The City of Cork* comes through the sound for the final leg of its passage. The night has been calm, the occasional roll barely disturbing my sleep. Dawn light fills my cabin as we pass between the red and green buoys marking the channel through Cork harbour. Towns and villages show themselves as if in a shy sort of welcome.

Breakfast is a little disappointing but I imagine that the crew are mentally already off watch, excited that they'll soon be on their way home to see their families. The old Polish lady at the till says, 'Ninety pence sterling,' with that east European glottal roll on the 'rl' and a nice smile and then tells me that a lengthy journey by bus across Ireland, then a ferry, then another bus across England and another ferry to Holland then a long, long bus ride on through Germany and across Poland to Warsaw will eventually bring her to her family home. When I suggest she might have a tough trip ahead, she just shrugs. 'That's what we do.' As the ship turns to port, heading directly west for the last run towards the shore, it seems appropriate that this is the last sailing of the season. Though hardly burning my boats, it adds to the sense of committing myself to a long stay. For a long time I've wanted this chance, and I'm determined not to waste it.

A drive of two or so hours lies ahead of me but there is no time pressure now. The wind carries a light rain in from the west and across the ferry's decks. The first day in my temporary homeland is starting grey, but not cold; what the Irish would call a 'soft' day, I imagine. Strolling round the deck I pass small groups of crew and passengers looking towards the shore. Like me, a good few are alone. Perhaps again like me, some look uncertain as they watch the shoreline approach through the drizzle. Are they coming home or going away? I wonder. Are they pursuing dreams or fleeing nightmares?

As I watch the shore come ever closer I try to imagine what someone on an emigrant ship, having been forced to leave their home, for good probably, in search of a better life, would be thinking as they approached a new land. It puts my concerns about leaving my home and my wife Anna, to whom I can return at any time, in perspective.

Outside Cork there is a rush-hour jam, not that the delay bothers me, my time is my own. Flicking through the channels on the car radio I suddenly find myself tuned in to an interview with an English woman who had written a book, for women, on sex. As far as I can tell the author is sitting in a studio booth somewhere in England talking to a faceless interviewer in Dublin who is clearly warming to his subject. The guy quizzes her in graphic detail about good oral sex techniques. Am I dreaming? Is this usual for morning chat shows on the radio in Catholic Ireland?

Once round the outskirts of Cork city I travel along the wide valleys to the town of Macroom, after which the landscape changes to rugged moorland of orange and ochre hues dotted with the white and grey of rock outcrops. The road sweeps up through the Derrynasaggart mountains where a statue of a horse rears up above the roadside as I cross the county line into Kerry. The countryside opens up again to reveal valleys and distant mountains. Giving up on sex advice, I tune in to an Irish-language radio station and let its strange words and cadences wash over me.

Having bypassed Killarney I feel the excitement building in me as I near my new home. At Castlemaine I leave the main road on the last stretch. On my left are the flat pastures of the Maine Valley and hidden away behind trees and high hedges is Ardcanacht where I hope to rediscover the Ogham stone in the photograph of my mother and me. To my right the land is driven upward to the rocky outcrops that run along the top of the Slieve Mish mountains. After a few miles the road swings to the waters of the estuary. It is high tide and rather than a river it looks like a shining inland sea. Unexpected tears well up as I approach Inch and see my house sitting serenely halfway up the hillside. Although the physical journey here has been easy enough, it represents a major emotional step. Arriving at my cottage I feel as though I've at last reached base camp and a sense of happy anticipation, safety even, sweeps over me. All the preparation is complete and the conditions are good. A great opportunity lies ahead in which I aim to explore and scale the peaks on my horizon.

# CHAPTER TWO

A COUPLE OF BRIEF RECONNAISSANCE TRIPS TO KERRY IN THE summer had resulted in my finding what I was sure would be the perfect cottage, a little secluded, but with the most fantastic views.

Ardcanacht had been the first place I'd looked at but, hemmed in as the area is by trees and hedges, it had seemed a little on the gloomy side. I was looking for space, the wide outlooks over water and mountains that I remembered, which would set the mind free, not close it in. While there I did have a cursory hunt for the Ogham stone but with most of the tracks closed due to the foot and mouth epidemic, I didn't make much progress; lowing cattle seemed to be warning the Englishman to stay away in case he might inadvertently be carrying the infection.

When I'd gazed down on the area of Ardcanacht from the far side of the valley, it had looked tiny. Once I'd driven off the main road, however, down a narrow track lined with high hedges which made the rest of the world disappear, it expanded. It felt otherworldly. Dark clouds appeared to squat on the fabulously named MacGillycuddy's Reeks mountains to the south across the river valley. I'd felt a shiver run across my back as I thought, this is the place where my branch of the McCarthys began and I've been here before with my family. But I know nothing about it. I wanted to explore my family past but felt that this place would be too claustrophobic and inward-looking, which might detract from my desire to get a broader view of Ireland as a whole.

A few miles on down the road lies Inch, another place I'd visited on the family holiday. I had a recollection of houses dotted on the hillsides looking out over the river valley and the sea and thought I might find some inspirational cottage to live in there, so I'd pushed on. The great sweep of Dingle Bay opened up in front of me and I parked down by the beach which stretched, flat and wide, into the distance. It all came back to me in a flash as I turned round to look at the buildings on the promontory above the road. There was the Strand Hotel. It looked just as it had when we'd stopped by in 1980. Bloody ugly.

We'd gone in there in search of a drink and a very, very distant cousin, James MacCarthy. We got the drink but it turned out we were five years too late for James; he had died in 1975. My father had hurried back from the bar, his eyes shining with excitement. 'Did you hear what that man said?' he asked, speaking in a low tone as he passed the drinks to my mother, Terence, and me. 'I asked him if he knew anything of a James MacCarthy and he just stared at me and said to the others: "Begod, he's come out of the woodwork!" '

The bar had fallen silent as we'd trooped in. The barman and the three men sipping at their pints had watched us all as we picked a table, and then fixed their eyes on my father as he approached the bar. There had been a sharp intake of communal breath when he'd asked if they knew anything of this James MacCarthy.

Six generations back, around the middle of the eighteenth century, the two men shared a forefather who had lived just a few miles away. If it wasn't the strength of the Guinness encouraging the men in the bar to see a resemblance, then the MacCarthy genes must be pretty strong. Apparently James had died intestate and, in what was later to be revealed as time-honoured tradition, MacCarthy was fighting MacCarthy over his estate which included some land and buildings on the hill around the hotel and the peninsula.

Twenty years on and there was now a busy shop and café on the beach below the hotel. I made enquiries there about any cottages that might be available for a long rent over the winter. The man behind the counter had holiday chalets just above the beach but if I wanted something a bit more remote he said he could ask around. When I explained my reason for coming to the area, he told me he'd bought the shop and the land for the chalets after James's estate had been settled. He also told me that his mother came from a village called Boolteens, just a mile or so from Ardcanacht. I had to listen carefully as he spoke, my ears unused to the strong Kerry accent. It took two efforts to get his name right: Mahmoud.

I stayed a night or two at Inch to carry on my search for a temporary home and since the Strand Hotel was now only a bar, an adjustment made plain by a piece of wood inscribed 'Bar' tacked over the word Hotel, I headed for Foley's Pub a mile back down the road. My guidebook told me B&B was available there.

As soon as I walked through the door at Foley's I had a feeling that everything was going to work out all right. The bar was entirely empty so I had a chance to look around. The room wasn't all that deep but it was wide and the bar stretched its entire breadth. On the back wall there were shelves stocked with all manner and shape of bottles. There were signs giving news of the latest winners in a local lottery and snapshots of people grinning, drinking and playing music in the bar. Shelves ranged high up around the other walls were crammed with a curious mix of items – old sewing machines and lamps, vases, books and old radios. Below the shelves were various framed photographs and old tin trays, the promotional gear of earlier days. High stools lined the bar and a couple of tables with stools around them were positioned beneath the windows. The floors were plain wood. At one end a door led into a smaller room which contained a pool table. At the other end was an open fire and another door into a larger room where there were more tables and chairs. I thought of the great many Irish themed pubs that had sprung up all over England in the past few years. They all feel the same, and that is anything but authentic. This was the real thing. Turning slowly as I looked around, I smiled to myself. The perfect local, I thought.

A door behind the bar swung open and a tall man, who I guessed to be a few years younger than me, came in.

'Ah, hello!' he said. As he poured me a pint of Guinness we introduced ourselves. He was John Foley, and the pub had been in his family for a few generations. For a big man, and for one who worked in such a public place, I was struck by John's shyness. He seemed a very diffident and gentle character. When I reached for some money for my drink, he laughed lightly, saying, 'No, I'll get you this as a welcome to Foley's.'

As he tidied and wiped the bar I told him about my plans. He nodded and said he thought there were plenty of places about and that he'd go and see what his wife thought.

Fidelus Foley, her high cheekbones lifting penetrating dark brown eyes beneath black hair, bubbled with energy and enthusiasm. And while I guessed she'd be adept at pub banter, ready to tease and be teased, she immediately came across as sensitive to others. After a mere few minutes chatting with the two of them I felt as if I was already a regular.

As I explained my connection to the area, Fidelus came round from the bar to show me one of the old photographs on the wall.

'That's James MacCarthy's old house. It's gone now, burnt down a long time ago.'

'Yes, I remember hearing that when we were here back in nineteen eighty.'

It was a dark old black and white image but it gave me a hint of a family home.

Fidelus and John had a room spare so I could base myself there for a few days and explore the area. Estate agents in the nearby towns told me that the best way to find somewhere was to carry on asking the locals. So having made my introductions at the local shops and at the pub I reckoned I could just wait until something cropped up.

Fidelus sent me off to look at an old cottage that belonged to a family called Greaney. It was a little west of Inch and off the beaten track but eventually I found my way to the area. However, I couldn't find the cottage in question. I ended up down on the shores of Dingle Bay beside the ruins of Minard Castle. A man appeared walking his dog and I asked if he knew where the Greaneys' house was. He looked very perplexed.

'Greeney?' he said, echoing my pronunciation. 'Greeney? Well, I've lived here all my life and never heard that name!'

I repeated it a couple of times more but he was still baffled. Then when I showed him the piece of paper Fidelus had given me with the name written on it his face lit up.

'Oh, Grayney!' says he, looking at me as if I'd been talking Chinese. 'Well, if you'd only said that!' He shook his head and went on, 'It's just back up that road you drove down, a mile or so, an old-fashioned little place on the right-hand side.'

I thanked him but part of me wanted to hit him. Was he winding me up? I knew that the whole of the Dingle peninsula from a mile or two to the west of where we were talking was a *Gaeltacht*, Irish-speaking area, but I hadn't expected to meet with such confusion speaking English. Especially as, unlike one or two people I'd met whose words I'd found hard to follow, I understood this man perfectly. Nor did he seem to have any problem with the rest of my accent. Just 'Greaney'.

He wasn't winding me up with the directions and I found the cottage easily. It wasn't quite right, very old and very tiny and while it overlooked mountains, it faced away from the sea. More importantly it was one hell of a walk from Foley's Bar.

Denis Greaney laughed when I told him the problems his name had given me. He was in the pub for a pint on his way home. A small man, he had a conspiratorial sense of humour. He told me to have a look at a couple of the photographs on the wall in a dark corner of the bar. Laughing as I squinted in amazement at the pictures, Denis said, 'It is who you think, John and Fidelus Foley with Dolly Parton!' Looking around the pub as if to make sure he wouldn't be overheard, Denis leaned close to me and said in a stage whisper, 'A changed man he was after! John Foley had the shock of his life that day, I'd say!'

He dissolved into laughter when Fidelus told him, 'Thank you very much, Denis Greaney, that's quite enough from you on that subject!'

Denis was a builder and he started telling me in his quiet way about the hotel he was working on in Killarney and the large amounts of money people would have to pay for the rooms there. 'Some of them have the Jacuzzis and special coloured lights; the people staying there would be a bit kinky, I'd say.'

Coming and going over the next couple of days I began to feel at home with John and Fidelus and their children Katie and Jerry, who of course took no notice whatsoever of yet another visitor to their busy home.

Fidelus introduced me to Bridey Flynn who lives next door to the pub. A small woman with short-cropped grey hair, Bridey fixed me with her bright eyes and said, 'Oh, I knew James

MacCarthy! He was a very nice man. I worked for him for years. So did my husband.'

The view from my room in Foley's, across the fields towards a wide expanse of water, was magnetic. Studying the Ordnance Survey map I learned that this bit of the Maine estuary, where it opens out into the expanse of water, is called Castlemaine Harbour. The evening sun shone through, like a beacon illuminating the houses on the far shore. One or two people had said that they were so used to the beauty around them that they hardly noticed it. This seemed incredible; admittedly I'd been there for just a couple of days but to me it was soul stirring. Perhaps people weren't aware of it all the time but subconsciously it might be having an effect. Some of the women, I'd noticed, had a way of taking a sharp breath, part confirmation, part punctuation. They'd say a kind of 'Ah, hah' as they breathed in and nodded. There was something more to it in my view than simple affirmation and I wondered if it could be a hangover of first witnessing the power and beauty of the landscape around them.

Leafing through some of my father's papers that I'd brought with me, I found a press cutting that I hadn't looked at closely before. It was a column from *The Cork Examiner*, the Ryan Report, dated 24 May 1991. It talked about the campaign for the hostages in Beirut and referred to my Irish cousins' activities for us. The way it opened hadn't struck me previously. Now it did.

The sheltered sea meadow known as Inch faces south into the harbour of Castlemaine with the Iveragh Peninsula opposite and Dingle Bay beyond. It is one of the natural treasures of Kerry with magnificent views and a firm strand backed by sandhills and traces of Iron Age dwellers. People flock to it when the sun shines like it did this week, and yet it retains a sense of relative peace and quiet. It is, therefore, the type of place a person would head towards in order to unwind from the hassle and stress of daily living. And it is a world apart from the strife-ravaged streets of Beirut along which a grandson of Inch travelled on April 17, 1986.

I looked from the photocopied article to 'the sheltered sea meadow' it described, right outside the window, and heard another, 'Ah, hah' and sharp intake of breath, this time from me. Maybe I hadn't read the piece before; surely the reference to Inch would have leapt out at me as it did now. But that decided it; no doubts could possibly remain after this uncanny moment. Inch was the place.

On my last afternoon on that recce to Inch I went for another walk on the strand. When I arrived back at the pub, Fidelus told me she thought she'd found the place I was looking for. Grinning broadly she said, 'It's a bit old-fashioned, used to be a farmhouse, but it's not too big, and it's away back from the road with fine views of the water and the mountains!' My list of requirements exactly. I realized I must have sounded somewhat pedantic telling people *precisely* what I wanted. I knew she was teasing me a little and was pleased about that and very grateful for the effort she'd made on my behalf.

The cottage she had found was only two miles from the pub but set back from the road and high enough above it to give me a real sense of detachment. On a dark winter's night I imagined it might feel isolated but friends down the road would be sufficient to overcome that worry. My landlady-to-be Phil Courtney seemed a very gentle, sympathetic person too. There was an air of sadness or wistfulness about her also – but it might just have been shyness. She was concerned that the cottage might be too plain and simple for me. As we went around the few rooms she pointed out things, the fire, the fridge, the boiler and so on but I wasn't really taking in the details. I was captivated by the atmosphere of the house; it almost felt as if it wanted me to live there. Looking around, I was vaguely aware of furniture and pictures on the walls, but my eyes kept going back to the windows and the view beyond. Back at the front door I stopped and looked across the harbour to the mountains. Away to my right I could see the Inch peninsula and catch a glimpse of 'the sheltered sea meadow'.

'It's perfect, Phil. I'd like to take it please.'

'Oh, are you sure? Well, that's fine!' she said, smiling back at me. 'You just let me know when you're sorted out back in England and want to come over.'

I was so relieved that my hopes for a place of solitude and sanctuary had been fulfilled that I would have liked to move in immediately but I knew I couldn't for a couple of months.

'I'm thinking of it as home already,' I said. 'What's it called?'

'The house doesn't have a name, but the little area is called Caherpierce.'

When I knock on Phil Courtney's door to pick up my key she invites me in, makes a cup of tea and gives me a piece of home-made apple pie. She is just as sweet and shy as when we met those few months ago. As we drive up to my house she tells me about a sacred well further up the valley that runs beside the house. The well is associated with St Brendan and is believed to have curative powers. Phil warns me against going up the valley for a couple of weeks until her son Stephen's cows have been moved down to their winter quarters. 'One of them is a bit contrary,' she advises. 'It's best to keep away for the time being.'

I certainly will, in my somewhat fragile state; confrontation with an irate cow is the last thing I need.

Although it isn't cold, Phil lights the fire in the front room. The sharp smell of burning peat accompanies us as she shows me around the house again. Upstairs there are three bedrooms, all in a row, the one leading into the other. When Phil and her husband Mike first lived here they shared the house with older relatives.

'I should think you'd feel hemmed in, living like that,' I say.

Nodding, she replies, 'It was a relief when we could build our own home down by the road.'

The front room downstairs has a warm, friendly feel to it. The fireplace is on the side wall. On the back wall under the stairs is a cupboard, or press as Phil calls it, and beside it the door through to the kitchen and bathroom. A window and the front door line the wall looking towards the water and the fourth wall is taken up by a door to the sitting room, a dresser and another press. There is plenty of honey-coloured varnished wood which makes the place feel snug.

The sitting room has another fireplace and a suite of brown chairs and sofa. There's a television in the corner and the wooden mantelpiece holds some small vases and a crucifix. Pictures of rural scenes dot the walls. Although this room has the more comfortable furniture, compared to the front room it feels anonymous and lacks the air of welcome.

When we go outside again so that I can run her home, Phil pauses before getting into the car to point out some of the nearby houses. There is a hesitancy in the way Phil speaks, a characteristic that I discover is common among the people in Kerry. It seems to stem from a desire to be helpful but not to intrude.

Raising her hand in the general direction of a large new place higher up and across the little valley to the east of my cottage, she explains, 'That's Anthony Farrelly's house. He's Fidelus's brother. Now the house below him, the big one near the road, that used to belong to Mrs Flynn.'

'Ah, now I think I've met her, is her first name Bridey?'

'That's right, she lives next to the pub now. The house has

been empty for a long time. I think some English people own it but it'll need a lot of work to get it right again. Then you've got the Griffins down there beside the road.'

We get in the car and head down the winding unmade track to the road.

'You have to be careful coming out of here – it's hard to see if anything is coming.'

As if to prove Phil right, a car races past just as I start pulling out.

'I don't drive,' says Phil, 'but Mike says you just have to go for it!'

I do.

Once we're safely on the road, Phil continues the guided tour.

'The Kennedys, Mike and Eileen, live there,' she says as we pass a large house on the right of the road with a sign saying 'Waterside Bed and Breakfast'.

As I drop her off at her house she says, 'Let me know if you need anything and call by any evening if you're feeling lonely,' then waves me on my way.

Back at the cottage I walk around the rooms, taking stock of my new dwelling. Feeling an immediate need to impose something of myself on the place, I begin to move pictures and ornaments about. Clearly I'm going be spending most time in the cosy front room so I rearrange the furniture there to suit me. A couple of surplus dining chairs are quickly squirrelled away up to a spare bedroom so that the table can go right in front of the window. Now, whether I'm eating or reading, I'll be able to revel in the views. Sitting at the table for a moment, I can't quite believe my luck. Even though the light is beginning to fade, I can see that the tide is well out. Where there had previously been an inland sea, there is now a vast expanse of mudflat and a narrow band of river on the far side of Castlemaine Harbour. Given that most of it is obviously too shallow to offer much by way of a safe anchorage, 'Harbour' sounds a rather grand appellation. When the tide is in, it is an impressive expanse of water. The outline of the mountains of MacGillycuddy's Reeks is still clear and I can see their peaks stretching away to the east. To the west, more mountains lead my eye off down the far side of Dingle Bay. A last ray of sunshine suddenly picks out another, more distant range of hills, directly to the south of me, as if the whole panorama across the water is showing itself in welcome. To say I feel blessed is an understatement.

I build up the fire and feel I should toast my successful arrival but in the absence of anything more stimulating, I make do with some of St Brendan's water. As I raise my glass, rain starts sleeting in from the west. Whatever else might happen, I think, there's no fear of that well running dry. Toasting myself makes me conscious of my solitude and for a moment I feel lonely, missing Anna. So I start going through my bags and boxes looking for some photographs to put on the mantelpiece and find two of her and one of Terence that are already in frames. Some of my parents and the one of my mother and me at Ardcanacht are loose. Tomorrow I'll go into Tralee, the county town, to buy frames so that they, too, can keep me company.

With the light fading behind the curtain of rain, the far side of the estuary becomes less distinct and my horizon creeps ever nearer until all is black. In what must be Inch's equivalent of a rush hour, cars pass every few minutes, their headlights marking out the path of the road a few hundred yards below. Strange to think that as many as six hundred years ago my ancestors must have travelled on this road. Less than thirty years ago a cousin lived just a couple of miles away by Inch Strand. Although I know from some of my father's letters that I have relatives living over in County Cork, it is entirely possible, given that McCarthy is such a common name in Kerry, that I might discover other relatives living closer.

While I was away in Lebanon my father had been in touch with some very distant cousins in Ireland though quite how the connection had been made wasn't clear. Going through his old files we'd found a short letter which opened 'Dear Pat', and closed 'your cousin, Jean MacCarthy'. Written from Rathcoole House, Mallow, County Cork, in September 1991, it wished us all well after my return from Beirut, saying that 'all the Irish cousins and friends are delighted and relieved that the ordeal is over'. Jean said she was looking forward to seeing us and having 'a pint of the best' at the local. She mentioned that she had got his address from a Mary Lynch.

As we went through the muddled box of old files and papers, Terence began to recollect that in the summer of 1991, a month or two before my release, my father had told him that Mary Lynch had been in touch to say that there was to be a clan gathering, the first in four hundred years, and that they would be highlighting my plight in Lebanon at the event.

Deeper into the files we found a letter from Mary to our father written in December 1992, which included a booklet, *From Cashel to Carbery, Gleanings from MacCarthy History* by Patrick O'Sullivan. It contained some of the MacCarthy clan history and press cuttings about another clan gathering which had been held that September at Kanturk Castle. One of the cuttings had a picture of Cousin Jean looking rather mysterious and magnificent, standing next to another Terence MacCarthy who was described as the present MacCarthy Mór, the chief of the clan.

These letters from Jean and Mary suggested a familiarity with my father that I couldn't judge. Although their names had cropped up in 1992, that was a long time ago now and much had happened since. My father's death meant that only his correspondents would be able to tell me more. The affectionate tone of the letters and the casual way they talked of us as family also made me want to know all about these cousins. As my plans for staying in Ireland firmed up, I wrote to Jean, the start of a busy correspondence between us.

In her first letter she explained that she'd never met my father and that in fact they'd had only one telephone conversation. But it had been a long one in which they discussed what the Irish relatives could do to help the campaign for the hostages. Jean enclosed a booklet that she had produced in 1996 for the four hundredth anniversary of the death of the last King of Desmond, Donal IX MacCarthy Mór. In her letter Jean says, 'If you read the chapter "The Descent of the Crown of Desmond" you will see that you are descended from many royal ancestors, i.e. Kings of Munster and Desmond. These were real kings and were anointed as such. You are also directly descended from King Cormac III MacCarthy (1123–1138). He built Cormac's Chapel on the Rock of Cashel. This is a matter of record.'

I like that phrase, 'a matter of record'. It has a ring to it, solid and authoritative and just a bit old-fashioned. I have a feeling that meeting Jean will be fun.

Before meeting up with the modern branches of the family and exploring the community of Inch and Ireland today it seems like a good idea to acquaint myself with a bit of history. According to Patrick O'Sullivan's booklet the name McCarthy, or MacCarthy as it is often spelled, has its origins with one Carthagh who was described as a King of the Eóganacht at Cashel. Cashel I'd heard of as a place famous for its ancient tower and chapel but the word Eóganacht was new to me. When I try to say it I sound as though I'm clearing my throat. Then I discover that the Eóganacht were a large family group who traced themselves back to a fellow called Eóghan, or Owen as it would be in English. Now more confident that I can at least pronounce the name, I learn that, as part of a loose federation of other, minor kingdoms, they controlled Munster between the fifth and tenth centuries. With a feeling of sadness and frustration I find that these forebears were not able to recognize what a good thing they had going for them. Rivalries between the various groups left them weak and vulnerable to raiding Vikings and rival factions from neighbouring regions. By Carthagh's time the Eóganacht were in a serious state of decline and there wasn't much job security as a king. The most note-worthy event in Carthagh's life seems to have been its gruesome ending when he was burned alive in his own home with a number of his nobles in 1045. But at least one male child must have survived Carthagh's deathly conflagration since Mac means 'son of'. Strictly speaking then, my traceable family history began sometime early in the eleventh century.

My head starts swimming as I look through the papers Terence and my father had gathered together. I have to admire their skill and determination; without their lead I think I'd have thrown in the ancestral towel. Before and after Carthagh there seem to have been a whole host of kings in myriad kingdoms. As well as Eóganacht Cashel there are kings of Munster, Desmond, South Munster, the Two Munsters, and Cork.

Trying to get a better grasp on this ancient history, I dip into a couple of books I've brought with me. It doesn't become appreciably easier. Various groups held sway at different times and even with a grand-sounding title you might still be a subject of another, slightly grander king. Gradually there was a move towards having a high king of all Ireland but the Irish, even from the earliest times, proved adept at changing sides, breaking agreements and fighting alongside a former enemy. Unity was not a strong point among these old Irish alliances.

The rival O'Brien clan dominated Munster until early in the twelfth century when they found themselves weakened by their struggle with the O'Neills of Connacht for the high kingship of Ireland. While these two were fighting it out, Eóganacht fortunes revived sufficiently for them to gain control of one half of Munster. The MacCarthys ruled the southern half, the Kingdom of Desmond, while the O'Briens had dominion over the northern half, the Kingdom of Thomond.

Understanding the alliances and rivalries is beyond me; the whole thing is terribly confusing. One fact that I glean comes as no real surprise, even after this brief acquaintance with the subject: it was a thwarted candidate for the high kingship of Ireland, Dermot MacMurrough, who invited the involvement of an English (or more properly Anglo-Norman) king, Henry II, in 1166, thus inaugurating nearly a thousand years of meddling. Henry II let Dermot raise troops in Wales, and these were, as it transpired, the vanguard of a long process of conquest which eventually saw Ireland subject to England.

Needless to say the MacCarthys, who by now formed a clan consisting of various family branches, continued squabbling amongst themselves and doing deals with the invading force (which had inevitably developed ambitions beyond those envisaged by MacMurrough), allowing the English to make incursions into their lands in Munster. But now and then they fought back and Cormac MacCarthy Mór, Prince of Desmond, who reigned from 1325 until 1359, was particularly successful at getting land and titles from the English crown while maintaining a strong army. He and his wife Honora had at least five sons, according to the family pedigree. The fourth was called Donal Laidhir McCarthy, described as the First Chieftain of the McCarthys of Ardcanaghty, and was recorded as living in 1347.

This branch seems to have lived on their farmlands here and roundabout happily enough for the next couple of hundred years. Then they appear to have backed the wrong horse in one of the many rebellions and had some land confiscated. My reading revealed this to be an alarmingly common McCarthy trait. In the second half of the seventeenth century they fell foul of the English again and lost more, and perhaps all, of their remaining lands. They continued farming there, either as owners or as tenants, right up to the early 1800s.

Looking at the family tree I see that my direct ancestor Daniel MacCarthy was one of the last of the clan to have been born at the old family seat. Perhaps he saw the writing on the wall as he seems to have left Ardcanacht and moved to Tralee where his second son, James, was born in December 1789. James appears to have been something of a rover, moving to Dublin and then on to Paris, where he worked in the wine trade, before settling in London. My great-great-grandfather John Justin was born there in 1827.

Spinning through some seven hundred years of family history in one evening leaves me in need of some rest. As I collapse into bed, a sound like a burst of machinegun fire turns out to be another heavy squall and as the rain pounds on the roof and the wind howls down the chimney and round the window like a banshee, I start hunting for some earplugs. And I thought this place might be too quiet.

# CHAPTER THREE

THE WIND IS STILL HOWLING ROUND THE HOUSE WHEN I WAKE. It takes a moment or two to remember where I am. In spite of the massed bands of pipers and drummers going at it hammer and tongs outside all night, I did sleep. Although I feel rested there's a certain nervousness mixed in with my excitement at the prospect of living here. After their initial welcome with last evening's panoramic light show, the forces of nature now seem intent on deterring me with their relentless battering of my new home. I sit in bed looking at the closed curtains for a minute or two, gathering my thoughts and preparing myself for a scene of rain and bleak cold outside. When I do open the curtains, I have to turn my head away sharply from the window; not in horror, but because the light is blinding. The tide is filling Castlemaine Harbour to form a mirror that extends for hundreds of acres and seems to reflect every particle of the sun's power directly into my eyes.

Screwing them up, I look again, trying to take in the view. There is movement everywhere, waves on the water, clouds racing across the sky and trees straining from their roots. Only one or two cars pass along the road below, their progress looking slow and feeble compared with the movement powered by the wind.

Even though the wind threatens to lift me bodily and throw me into the narrow valley beside the cottage when I take a turn outside, the temperature is surprisingly mild. Nevertheless the electricity warming the blessings of St Brendan's well is still much appreciated when I have a shower later in the day.

Although the suite of furniture in the sitting room is undoubtedly more comfortable, I sit in the old-fashioned wood-framed armchair in the front room while I have a cup of tea and scrutinize the map for the best way to get to Tralee to stock up on food and other provisions.

The view keeps distracting me; it's so wide, so dramatic and active that the window acts like the world's largest and most seductive television screen. When a squall of rain obliterates the view for a while, I drag my eyes from it and look at the picture on the wall between the window and the door. Vaguely conscious of it since arriving, I haven't really studied it before. It is a picture of Christ and his Sacred Bleeding Heart. My initial reaction is to take it down – I've always found such icons rather gruesome, somehow too rich for my thin Church of England blood. But as I look closer at the fair-haired, blue-eyed representation of the first-century Jew with his heart revealed, wrapped around with thorns but emanating light, I decide to keep it where it is. Such an image has probably always graced the walls of this house and its occupants will have counted on the promises printed on it that 'I will give peace in their families' and 'I will bless the house in which my sacred heart is exposed and honoured'.

As I leave the house for Tralee, the rain has eased again so I go for a quick tour around my new home. A very neat balustrade wall surrounds the small patch of lawn outside the front door. In a landscape where everything is so wild, this is both charming and incongruous. A little way from the house are some old, drystone sheds which look as though they're still used for cattle at times. A track leads straight up the mountain which rises more than a thousand feet behind the house but remembering Phil's warning about the 'contrary' cow, I decide to leave the gate to that track closed until another day. Another track leads into a field with a sign saying that it's for sale as a building site. From the middle of the field I find the view is even more stunning than from my window. There is obviously some madness prevalent in St Brendan's water; I've barely been here a day and I'm thinking of building a home here.

But this little fantasy is abruptly curtailed when the temperature suddenly drops and the rain starts coming down again so I head for the car and Tralee. Even with the windows open so that I can hear any approaching cars, getting out onto the main road is a heart-stopping exercise. Despite my nervous concentration on the road, something significant but unspecified catches my eye, so I pull in at the next track and look back. The field across the road, running down to the shore, is ringed with palm trees. And there is a small pink building at the bottom of it. The rain quickly blurs this unexpected image and I drive on.

Passing Ardcanacht I get to Castlemaine where I turn north to Tralee. A mile or so on and the road surface deteriorates into an alarming battlefield of potholes. I must have missed a sign advertising roadworks, probably a diversion, but no, another car is behind me and I can see vehicles approaching from the other direction. The surface is truly appalling and with all the rain some of the potholes are hidden. The best strategy is to stick to the less catastrophic middle of the road until I'm almost on top of the oncoming traffic and then pull over and slow down as I bounce over the holes. A Sacred Bleeding Heart for motor vehicles is added to the shopping list.

After a few frightening turns the road starts climbing uphill and suddenly becomes good again, just as the sun appears. It's confusing; a bright blue sky, sunshine and the vivid greens of grass and trees in every direction – to all appearances, a summer's day – in spite of the temperature.

Kennerhey's hardware store is one of those wonderful emporia that seem to stock everything you could possibly need to fix up a home. And quite a few things that you would never use but that look very handy at the time. Unable to find an extension cable, I enlist the help of the man behind the counter. He is tiny and very amusing, openly admitting as he shows me around, 'I'll take you the long way, and then you'll see more and buy it!'

He's right of course. Just as I'm leaving with a bulging bag I remember I want some spare light bulbs. He puts two in my bag. 'As a gift now! You'll come and see us again!'

Tralee's main shopping and business area, tightly focused on a knot of narrow streets, buzzes with pedestrians and traffic. Many of the buildings are elegant Georgian or Georgian-style edifices, yet several are brightly painted like something from a sunnier climate, the Mediterranean or Caribbean perhaps. Not what you'd expect in Bath or Bristol, that's for sure.

My last direct ancestor to have lived in Ireland, James, the wandering wine merchant who ended up settling in London, was born in Tralee. When we'd gone through the boxes of family papers we'd come across a copy of a deposition by one Mary Supple. This was sworn before a Thomas Quill, Justice of the Peace, at Tralee in May 1818 and states:

Mary Supple otherwise McCarthy of Tralee in the County of Kerry in Ireland maketh oath and saith that James MacCarthy her Brother late of the city of Dublin but now as the Deponent believes in some part of France, [was] Born in or about the 20th December 1789 in the Town of Tralee.

It goes on to say that he was baptized in the parish but a foot-note of the same date says that the parish register did not contain any reference to James but that because the JP knew Mrs Supple well, he considers the affidavit to be true. Clearly brother and sister were not in regular contact while the 29-year-old James was somewhere in France. And there's the added mystery of his non-appearance in the parish register. I'm not sure what all this means but have a vague concern that my family tree, and therefore its roots in Ardcanacht, are all based on nothing more than a nudge and a wink from a local worthy giving an acquaintance the benefit of the doubt. Moreover, James isn't recorded in Samuel Trant MacCarthy's book *The MacCarthys of Munster*.

I muse over a whole pile of books on Kerry in Eason's book-shop. An awful lot of volumes have been written about the county. By ignoring tomes on Kerry cookery, places to stay, walking and cycling tours, surfing and geology, I narrow the choice down substantially and settle on one volume, a general history of Kerry which looks very detailed indeed. Adding an Irish-English dictionary and an armful of local and national newspapers seems ample to be going on with. As I'm about to leave a strong, fruity voice asks, 'Mr McCarthy! Is your friend Mr Keenan with you visiting Kerry?'

I turn to the smiling face that goes with the voice. 'No,' I laugh, 'Brian's over in Dublin, thank God!'

The man, perhaps around forty years old with grey hair and the air of a bon viveur, puts out his hand. 'Forgive the intrusion but I was sure it was you and wanted to say hello. We share the same first name, though mine is rendered in the Irish – as Sean.'

We chat and I learn that he's doing odd jobs, saving up money before going to college as a mature student the following year. Larger than life and happily full of it, Sean, talking nineteen to the dozen, tells me he's a Kerryman born and bred and knows

Inch well, having relatives in the area. We wish each other well and off he goes.

Back at home I lay the fire, enjoying handling the rough peat sods. I've only seen the highly compressed, store-bought briquettes before, but the stuff piled in the shed across my front lawn is straight from the bog. To be honest it looks like crumbly lumps of earth with tendrils of tiny roots threading through it, something you'd break up and spread over a flower bed rather than put on the fire. Someone had gathered the smaller fragments in the shed and put them in a plastic bag. Phil had called this stuff *bruskar* and said it was good to put on the fire if you were going out, 'To keep the heat in,' she said. She also said a bit of coal helped get things going. Dubious that I'll really be able to get this stuff burning, I fill the grate with all manner of incendiary material: paper, kindling, firelighters and coal then perch a couple of clods of peat on top. Happily, after an initial roaring and crackling, the peat takes and smoulders away, giving out a good heat.

As I put the shopping away and make a cup of tea I realize that I'm beginning to feel very at home. I settle into the armchair by the fire and start looking at my new book. The monumental *Discovering Kerry* by T. J. Barrington appears an absolute goldmine and given the apparent thoroughness of the book I'm intrigued that it appears to be the work of an amateur enthusiast. The word amateur might sound derogatory but I use it because it is how the author describes himself in his preface. The book reflects fourteen years of dedicated research to cover every aspect of the county's life, from ancient folklore and archaeology up to modern politics. Barrington's achievement is all the more impressive as he must have been working on this huge project throughout his busy career, based in Dublin, as a high-ranking civil servant and Director of the Institute of Public Administration.

His opening words immediately strike a chord with me: 'Any group of us is, I suppose, partly the product of shared history, heritage and environment. Some places have more of these than others, and Kerry has a good deal. To understand these forces helps us to know a bit better the kind of people we are.'

Sadly there is no photograph of the author in the book but as I travel around the county, reading his account of a particular place or facet of Kerry life, I've already a picture of him in my mind's eye. In my imagination this tour guide wears a neat grey suit, is constantly taking meticulous notes and photographs and though a very thorough man, has a sense of humour and the sensibility to convey the mystery and majesty he sees in Kerry. Not only do his chapters cover the history of the area, they also include incredibly detailed routes for the visitor to explore. All in all I think he'll prove an entertaining companion and help me get to know the history and landscape that moulded my forebears.

But what of present-day Ireland? Tom Barrington completed his studies twenty-five years ago. In order to feel the pulse of the country I am living in today I turn to the newspapers. They are preoccupied with a debate about whether the economic boom in Ireland is over, whether the Celtic Tiger has roared its last. From the mid-1990s Ireland's economy certainly wasn't pussy-footing around but outpacing all the other big cats of the world economy with growth rates of around 8 per cent of GDP. Foreign investors, particularly pharmaceutical and IT companies, weren't backward about coming forward to lap up tax breaks and other incentives. Government spending on education in the seventies and eighties meant there were plenty of qualified people to go to work in a jobs market that grew by 40 per cent during the 1990s. And on top of all that, inflation stayed low so good times were had by all.

But the economy is now levelling out and the commentators

are stating what seems, even with my limited understanding of economics, blindingly obvious: if the Irish want public services to improve, they'll have to start paying more taxes. The Fianna Fáil government led by Bertie Ahern has been consistently reducing personal taxes over the past few years and there haven't been too many complaints from the electorate. But now large holes are beginning to appear in the health services, in education and the general infrastructure. Holes in the infrastructure? Holes in the damn roads, you mean! They certainly need to invest in some tarmac between here and Tralee. A view I find echoed on the letters page of the local paper *The Kerryman*.

This paper comes out in a number of editions covering the various areas of Kerry, north, south and one for Tralee. Rightly and properly it brings matters of national concern down to the local, and more practical, level. Councillors argue over roads and health spending. One headline particularly catches my fancy: 'Election to focus minds on Kilcummin sewerage crux'. There are features on towns around the county, and reports from nearly every district, with news of the local whist drives and jumble sales. Clearly Kerry people have a passion for Gaelic football, as there are pages on the subject, but there is, too, substantial coverage of the arts. In amongst advertisements for hairdressers, decking, car sales and restaurants there are little snippets of news, largely on the outcome of court appearances by people who'd been acting in an 'antisocial' manner, i.e. drunk. It's a shock to see how many stories there are like this and how many involve women.

There are a great many photos of people standing in a line, grinning broadly, as they are presented with awards for their studies or good works. Surprisingly, government ministers make regular appearances, grinning like hungry maniacs as they have a cup of tea with old ladies who've just moved into a new public housing scheme, or oozing care at a patient in a new hospital wing.

One outcome of the Celtic Tiger phenomenon and the increase in the job market is that Ireland has changed from being a country of emigration to one of immigration. In the century following the Great Famine of 1845–47, any natural increase in population was undercut by people going overseas to build a new life. But economic improvements in the 1950s and 1960s, further encouraged by membership of the EC in the 1970s, created more jobs and saw more Irish people staying at home or returning from abroad. After a slump in the 1980s when emigration became the norm again for a while, the Celtic Tiger padded onto the stage and more and more people started coming home to share in the boom. And it isn't just the Irish or people with Irish parents, foreign workers have also been coming to take up the jobs.

Tuning in to the radio I catch an item about Irish people who'd gone overseas, mostly to England, the USA and Australia, to work and are now wanting to come home but can't. Charities and government agencies are looking at ways of helping them with accommodation and so on and also warning them of the great changes that have come to Ireland during the twenty, thirty or forty years they've been away. The couples in Paddy Murphy's Bar on the ferry had looked so contented, mortgages paid, pensions secure and grandchildren to dote on. Now I'm hearing about the people at the other end of the homecoming spectrum, those who have been less successful, who have hit an unlucky patch, or the bottle perhaps. Given that so many people have had to leave their homeland to seek a better life, it's a good thing that the nation is looking to care for those who didn't find one.

The fire is burning low so I add a bit more coal and some more peat and sprinkle a little of Phil's *bruskar* on top. Looking the word up in my new dictionary, I discover that it means rubbish, junk or litter, which seems to sum up the odds and ends of peat sod perfectly.

\*

The wind and the rain have kept up for days but the temperature is still mild. Whenever there's a break in the cloud and the sun comes through even for a moment, I head off for a walk. The beach, or strand, on the western side of the Inch peninsula has become my favourite spot. To be honest it is not an arduous form of exercise as it's flat for miles and the sand is usually firm. There are rarely more than a couple of other walkers down there, someone walking a dog probably and often one or two women power-walking, a form of exercise that does look distinctly arduous. As does the style of fishing enjoyed here. None of that sitting beside a tranquil stream on a stool under a vast umbrella for the fishermen of Inch; in the hope of catching bass they stand way out in the surf, covered in waterproof clothing from head to foot. They must get frozen.

After ten minutes I turn and the hotel and houses on the bluff above the beach have become little more than white dots. When you look from the road, the peninsula appears large enough but it's not until you are out on it that you realize its true size. It goes on for miles – about four, I've heard – and at low tide the beach is very wide. Getting to the water's edge can be a good stroll. And the sea is always changing, depending on the wind; sometimes flat calm, sometimes pushing up on the shore in great breakers. Often my walk doesn't take me far along the beach because I stop time and again to look at the sea or the mountains in the distance. And there are birds, large flocks of them, all shapes and sizes, some massed at the water's edge pecking about for food, others huddled at the back of the beach, hunkered down in the sand drifts having a nap. Once or twice I've wandered into the dunes and found them to be mysterious and peaceful, but so far my greatest pleasure is to potter along the shore, leaving a meandering trail as I go beachcombing from piece to piece of flotsam and jetsam.

The scale of the place and the feelings of awe and serenity it brings remind me of deserts in the Middle East and South America that I've seen. But this stretch of wilderness is just a couple of miles from my front door. Even a twenty-minute blow clears my head and reveals the world in a crisper, cleaner light. Looking out across Dingle Bay, especially when I can see the sun setting behind the far horizon, lighting the clouds on the mountains to the north and south, sometimes makes me laugh with sheer pleasure.

On the way home I often stop at Foley's Pub for a glass or pint of Guinness – usually the pint – and have a chat with John or Fidelus. Today the pub appears to be closed up and I'm just about to get back in the car when John comes round the corner of the building. He's been over to see Bridey Flynn next door. I've been thinking about how kind everyone has been and ask if he thinks they mind me pestering them with questions. John puts my mind at rest.

'If they don't want to talk, they won't. But talking about ourselves,' he says, 'is like us talking about the weather. It's a national pastime, I'd say.'

The phrase 'I'd say' peppers my neighbours' sentences as much as 'you know' and 'like' litters other people's conversation in Ireland as in England. Written down it looks firmer than it sounds; it is used as a soft reminder that what is being offered is no more than an opinion.

Often there are other people in the pub stopping by for a pint on the way home from work. One evening I'm sitting having a half as two old boys chat at the other end of the bar. Trying not to stare at them, I eavesdrop, fascinated. They are talking Irish and the speech and laughter tumble between them like water running down a mountain stream in spring. Every now and then they speak to Fidelus and she says something back in a low voice or pours them another drink. After a while the old boys go home and I talk a while with Fidelus and ask her if she is fluent in Irish. No, she's not, she says; like everyone, she'd been taught it at school but has since lost much of it.

'You seemed to be managing all right with the old fellows,' I say.

'Yes,' she replies, looking a bit confused.

'So do they live in the Gaelic-speaking area, the *Gaeltacht*, west of here?'

'No, they live above on the hill.'

'Do a lot of people round here speak Irish like that?'

'No . . . well, yes, um, John . . .'

'Yes?'

'The lads were speaking English.'

'Ah! Right. It's going to take me a while to get used to the Kerry accent, I think.'

'Sure you'll be fine.'

One afternoon John tells me they'll be having a band in on the Saturday night. Come Saturday it's windy but there's no rain so I decide to walk. Two miles seems like twenty as I lurch through the blackness along the uneven road. I've brought a torch so cars will see me but use it more often to check whether I'm about to trip over a pothole. It's a little after eight o'clock but the world seems to have gone very quiet and I have the strange sensation of having moved into another time frame. A dog snarling by a gate has me jumping a few feet in the air. At least there is a farmhouse and a light to walk past. Except that I don't recognize the place at all and am definitely feeling a little spooked. Seeing the lights around the pub at last is a great relief.

The place is deserted. I check my watch. Eight forty-five on a Saturday night, and the pub is deserted. The fire is going and there's music coming from the radio behind the bar but no sign of living humans. I *have* walked into another dimension, I think, or maybe the population has been abducted by aliens, maybe a natural disaster is imminent and everyone's been evacuated except me, standing there in the bar as the world's largest tidal wave roars up Dingle Bay. There's a whooshing sound and I let out a yelp. It's just the door at the back of the bar swinging open to admit John.

'Oh, hello!' he says looking almost as surprised as me.

'Hello,' I say. 'Um, where is everyone, what's happening?'

'Oh, you're here early.'

'Early?' So much for the hard-drinking Irish, I think. 'What time do people come then?'

'Oh, ten, it'll be busy by ten thirty, I'd say.'

I nurse a pint while he restocks some of the shelves and then goes back into the house – it's his night off. Fidelus comes through, laughing at my puzzlement over the emptiness of the place.

'Don't worry, it'll be packed in a while. We're open till at least one at the weekends.'

She turns off the radio, puts a CD on and the pub fills with the heavy bass of dub reggae. I tell her I'd been expecting more traditional sounds in a pub like hers.

'Oh, there'll be Irish music later; the musicianers will be playing in the lounge. Why don't you take a seat in there so you won't miss them. Reggae is my music, it keeps me going.'

The street door opens and another woman enters. Like Fidelus, she's all made up and looking glamorous.

'Fidelus Foley, that's the last time I take a drink with you, the fecking head on me today!'

'Martina, this is John. John, Martina.'

Martina gives me a steady look and a smile as we shake hands. Then she turns back to Fidelus.

'I thought I was dying!' she says firmly.

By ten thirty Fidelus and Martina are pouring drinks and pulling pints like they're going out of style. It's almost impossible to move and I'm happy to be perched on a bar stool talking to an English couple, Ann and Barry, who moved to Kerry a few months earlier from Hemel Hempstead. They'd always loved the area so when Barry had to take early retirement they upped sticks and moved over. When I tell them about my confusion over the late pub hours, they say they had the same experience but now they're getting the hang of things though still often feel complete 'blow-ins', as newcomers are called.

With all the chatter in the pub it's hard to maintain a proper conversation but I learn that the woman sitting on the other side of me is called Bridget Fitzgerald, and that she lives nearby and works at the community centre at Annascaul, a village a couple of miles inland from Inch. Around eleven o'clock the music starts and we give up on trying to talk and content ourselves with the occasional nod at each other as we sip our pints.

Two men with grey hair, a large one with a beard and a smaller one with a waistcoat, start singing traditional Irish songs, accompanying themselves on guitars. Intrigued by their voices, I lean over to my new friend Bridget.

'Are they from the *Gaeltacht*?'

She shakes her head and says something which needs clarification.

'That's funny, I thought you said they were from Holland.'

'I did, they're both Dutchmen. One has been here for twenty years.'

I sip my pint, nodding at Bridget, Barry and Ann, thinking how odd it is to be sitting in this perfect Irish pub which only starts getting busy when most bars in England would be calling last orders, listening to 'The Fields of Athenry' sung in guttural Dutch voices. It is an odd, even eccentric, variation on the *craic* but it is of course absolutely genuine. As is the laughter as friends and neighbours pack themselves ever tighter around the bar, across which glasses pass in an unending stream.

Shortly after midnight Inch's latest blow-in admits defeat and heads for home. Before leaving I have a few words with Bridey Flynn who is sitting with her sister Mary in the main bar. They say I can pop round for a chat any time. The wind's still blowing and it's colder now but the Guinness, and perhaps the music, have given me Dutch courage and I stride home without incident. Stars in the clear sky mirror the twinkling lights of the village of Cromane on the far shore of Castlemaine Harbour as I take a last look from my front door before turning in.

'We had the site on the two fields on the shore side. I had the Caravan Club of Great Britain there three months in nineteen seventy-seven. That was very nice.'

I'm having tea with Bridey Flynn and her sister Mary and am learning about the palm trees and the pink building across the road from my house. It had been Bridey's campsite. She and her husband Jimmy used to have the farm across the stream from me at Caherpierce, the one that is now unoccupied and somewhat rundown.

'We became very good friends. We write, oh, now let me see, one lives in, oh, it's near London. Oh, I can't remember the names now I'm getting too old! But we send Christmas cards still. Very nice time it was.'

The council's rules and regulations on running a campsite weren't so nice. I'd have thought there would be practically no restrictions for a simple site in such a quiet backwater all those years ago. Bridey tuts and looks heavenwards remembering how the dead hand of bureaucracy poked into every detail. It doesn't sound like an Irish way of proceeding at all.

'There had to be just so much space for each caravan, the grass had to be just so, and the water had to be just so. The pink build-ing was the bathroom block. There was only cold water – it came from the same well as yours. There's none better!'

Bridey tells me that she is seventy-six years old and that she lived at Caherpierce until her Jimmy died – 'He was a good husband' – eleven years before. She sold the farm and moved into one of the pair of whitewashed bungalows the Foleys had built next door to the pub. Bridey speaks fondly of all the Foleys.

'I watched them grow up. John and Fidelus are very good to me.'

The two old ladies make me very welcome in their home with its old plates and pictures decorating the walls and ornaments on the shelves and mantelpiece.

They both speak quietly and like to laugh; they strike me as being good friends as well as sisters. At one point Bridey is struggling to remember something and asks Mary for help. They look at each other with expectant half-smiles as they search their long memories, but neither can find the detail. They sigh and joke about getting too old. Mary goes into the kitchen to refill the teapot only to appear in the doorway a few moments later, beaming as she presents her sister with the suddenly recalled piece of history.

'So, Bridey,' I ask, 'how have things changed at Inch over the years?'

Her reply makes me laugh. 'Oh, I don't know so much, I've only lived here for fifty years. I'm still just a blow-in!'

She goes on to say that many of the residents are effectively incomers; mostly from other Irish counties certainly, but also from Holland, Germany, France and England. Many of the houses are shut up for winter and it's much quieter then.

Even if she has lived here for 'only' fifty years, my distant cousin James MacCarthy must have been alive for about half of that time.

'How did you get to know him, what was he like?'

'I'd never have come to Inch but for James,' Bridey reveals. 'He was the matchmaker for me and Jimmy, oh yes!'

Having grown up a few miles from Limerick city, Bridey had gone to work for a farming family with whom James had dealings in his cattle business. As well as having his own farm, Jimmy Flynn worked with James, looking after animals on the island, as Bridey calls the peninsula.

'James was a clever businessman; he leased land in, well, various places, I'd say. He bought animals to fatten on it then sold them on. Anyway, he'd met me and then spoke to us both to see if we might like to get together. On his next trip over James brought Jimmy with him. Three months later we were married! That was in nineteen fifty-one. James came to our wedding and played the squeeze-box. He played very well. Oh Lord, he was very nice to me!'

Bridey spent two summers working at James's café on the beach. Those were clearly busy times for the tourist business at Inch, with two bustling caravan parks – James had one as well as Bridey – a café and the hotel.

'I also worked at the hotel with two of James's sisters, Joan and Chris,' Bridey tells me, looking into the middle distance and nodding a little as she remembers those days.

'I hadn't realized that the MacCarthys were up to so much,' I say. 'I thought it was just James, farming the peninsula.'

'Oh yes, they were very busy people. Of course that was back in the fifties, before Inch House burned down. It was lovely; they had seven bedrooms, a large kitchen at the back and a beautiful dining room.' For emphasis Bridey lengthens the word 'beautiful' until it becomes 'beeyootiful'. The house burned down in the night and James and one of his sisters had to escape by ladder from a first-floor window.

When I'd come with my family in 1980 we'd heard that there had been a battle over James's estate between his estranged wife and son and a brother and nephew. Bridey confirms this, saying that it had been a long-drawn-out wrangle.

'There was James's son. He'd come back from America or Australia where he'd been with his mother. He was a nice lad, I think. But I don't know so much about it. You must go and see my friend Maureen Fitzgerald. She was with James for years. She can tell you everything.'

James would sometimes run Bridey back up to Limerick to see her folks. Life for her parents' generation was much harder than it is now, she thinks. 'And with such big families, people had to go away. Many of the girls Mary and I grew up with went to England, America or Australia and never came back at all!'

The sisters' nostalgia is very charming and sweet but I'm impressed that they haven't pulled up the drawbridge and put on the rosy spectacles when looking back. These two old ladies remember the bad as well as the good times.

They share the concerns I've been reading in the papers about whether the community at large is doing enough for the youth of today.

'When we hear of the trouble young people get into, we wish they'd give them a little job or something to keep them on the straight and narrow.'

This is not a worry for one of their nieces in England. 'She drives trucks!' they say almost as one and with a mixture of awe, admiration and shock.

Although there are many blow-ins and many houses that are used only in the summer, I get the feeling from talking to Bridey and Mary that the sense of community around Inch is still strong. Once a fortnight they gather with others of their generation at the old Killeenagh schoolhouse, the community centre, for lunch. And every two weeks there is an outing, also organized by the community centre, to Dingle. 'Then on Sundays there's bingo over at Killorglin.'

There is one thing that the two sisters are certain has got worse over the years.

'The weather was much better fifty years ago,' says Bridey, looking through the window as the drizzle starts again. She sighs. 'We used to have lovely summers then, oh yes.'

# CHAPTER FOUR

THE WESTERLY WIND HAS BEEN BLOWING SO CONSTANTLY FROM the Atlantic that when I wake one morning and it has stopped, I shake my head thinking my ears must have become blocked. I open the curtains. Everything is still and bright, with the sun just appearing beyond the far horizon to the east. A black and white wagtail flits about along the balustrade, its head down as much to balance the weight of its long tail as to hunt food.

Outside, although it is cool I'm warm enough without a coat and walk around the house enjoying the utter stillness of the morning air. The peace of dawn seems to be offering the hope that there is much to look forward to after all. It is as if the world is a patient emerging from a long illness and period of convalescence to think, 'Ah! I am well again.'

Yet it isn't silent at all. As my ears adjust to the relative peace they regain their fine tuning and I can hear the cries of birds coming from near and far. And there's something else, a continual background hum. Pied Piper-like it leads me out of the back gate and down the track. Close up the stream sounds mighty and powerful in the still morning, but I can see nothing of its hectic motion as it runs through a deep ravine which is further shrouded by thickets of wiry and impenetrable vegetation. How strange to have a place right outside my back door where no one may have walked, or even looked, for years and years.

In front of me, totally visible for the first time since I've been here, are the mountains of MacGillycuddy's Reeks. T. J. Barrington, or Tom as I think of him, says that the top of the range is Carrauntoohil, at 3,414 feet the highest mountain in Ireland. I've been wondering if this was just a tall story, but now for the first time I can see it clearly. Given that it is so often shrouded in cloud and that the winds, fierce enough here, must be atrocious near its summit, I take heed of Tom B's caution that 'this is a mountain with which no liberties should be taken'. Turning to the west I can see across Inch Point to Dingle Bay, blending into the Atlantic Ocean in the furthest distance.

Behind me is the mountain called Beenduff or Bhinn Dubh, which with the help of my Irish dictionary I interpret as Black Mountain. Covered with pale grass, stones and bracken it doesn't look particularly black to me but perhaps there is a dark side to its character. At any rate, the Courtneys have moved the contrary cow and their other cattle from this high pasture so, taking advantage of the break in the weather, I set off up the steep mountainside to explore my backyard a little.

Beenduff is one of the peaks that form the Slieve Mish mountains. As I trudge up the first couple of hundred feet along a well-marked path I go through what I've been learning from Tom Barrington about these hills. He tells me that the geology of this area around Inch and up into the Slieve Mish has some of the oldest layers of rock in Ireland, Ordovician, dating back 500 million years. Some are even older, going back at least another 100 million years to the pre-Cambrian era.

Barrington recounts the pre-history of the mountains and the legends of battles fought between the invading Milesians and

the resident Tuatha de Danaan people, the People of the
Goddess Danu. The old sagas have it that the Milesians took
their name from their leader, Milesius or Míl, and that they came
from Egypt by way of Spain. Milesius didn't actually make it to
Ireland but his widow Scotia came with various sons. According
to the old tales, the Milesians arrived between 1500 and 1200 BC
– just the sort of time Joshua was supposedly conquering
Canaan. The invading forces didn't have it all their own way
and lost many warriors and two queens, Scotia and Fás, but they
did win the battles in these mountains and went on to subdue the
Tuatha de Danaan. From then on there were two realms, one
above and another, *otherworld*, below ground. The Tuatha de
Danaan were reduced to running the basement.

I come to a stone wall that forms a barrier between fenced
fields and the open land above and climb gingerly onto it to take
in the full sweep of the ancient landscape. Those legendary
fighters might have come this way, or even had a skirmish here;
there are certainly plenty of rocks to hurl at one another.

As I clamber on up the hillside, the moss and wiry grass
sodden with rain, clouds drift across the distant sky, blotting out
my view of the Reeks little by little. A large fishing boat
suddenly appears on the far side of the harbour, turning this way
and that as it trawls, drawing an intricate and mysterious
pattern. Then, in seconds, everything goes dark and a fierce
breeze so ripples the water that it looks as though it is being
pulled away fast to the Cromane shore under a dark cloud now
issuing stair rods of rain. Anything might happen out there, and
I fear for the trawler crew. Their boat could be sucked down into
a terrible maelstrom or up in some fearful, unending spout, such
is the drama of the moment. To the west along the Slieve Mish
where I'm standing, those same clouds are racing towards me
and I hurry downhill to get home before the rain catches me.
When I look up again, the boat has gone; in fact the whole world

across the water has gone. As I scramble back over the stone wall, the rain begins hammering down around me like the devil's nails.

Slipping on the treacherous ground I fall on one knee, covering the trouser leg in mud. I swear, earlier feelings of returning good spirits evaporating into a cloud of irritation. It's almost as if the weather patterns reflect the shifts within me: fine and fresh one minute, then howling fit to flatten everything the next. This has happened once or twice since coming to Ireland and usually with no obvious or immediate cause. Powerful waves of sadness wash over me, knocking me sideways like a broached yacht. These squalls keep me heeled over queasily for a while before I right myself and get back on course. But while the moments last, I seem to lose all energy. Feeling useless and worthless I want to give up and go home. But that only makes it worse because I know deep inside that if I did pack my bags I'd be letting myself down. After all, compared to many, many people, I have an easy and uncomplicated life.

I seem to be caught in the cleft stick of having a personality that is at once relentlessly optimistic and punishingly self-critical, so that while I can see the sunny horizon I doubt that I'm able or worthy enough to reach it. While I do believe there is a value in being positive I know that this has to be balanced with an acceptance of the negative. The trouble is that I have faced up to this obvious insight only rather late in life. Perhaps the feelings of worthlessness, which are far from constant, are a stepping stone towards greater understanding and acceptance; they might even be part of an ostrich-like avoidance of thinking too deeply. Very likely this is why I've been getting anxious about being on my own. With no immediate responsibilities it's hard to pretend that displacement activity is anything but that. But this is really why I am here, that's why the solitude is important; I want to deny myself the chance to hide.

Basic psychology tells me that my personality comes from nurture as well as nature, so as part of this process of self-examination I need to reconnect with the place I came from, my family.

Back at the house I close the front door on the wild elements and catch my breath.

The picture frames I bought in Tralee are sitting on the table so I steel myself to sort out which photographs I want to put in them. The one of my mother and me by the Ogham stone at Ardcanacht comes first, then another, my father and Terence sitting on the terrace at our old home, and then another of my mother, sitting indoors on a sofa. Placing them on the mantelpiece alongside the photos of Anna and Terence I realize that this is the first time I've put out a picture of my mother since I came home from Lebanon. That's more than ten years. I shake my head, laughing a little, incredulous: why has it taken this long?

Looking at the pictures, their 1980 fuzziness echoing the sense that she is still just beyond my reach, I regret all the conversations that we were denied. Although we were very close, it would have been so good to have talked, as I did with my father before his death, and to know that we really understood each other. They are old but I have the letters she wrote to me when I was at school and university. I get the box out.

As I'm about to take out the pink folder holding them, I see a thin black volume. It's the bound copy of the Service of Thanksgiving for her life. The service was held at St Bride's Church on Fleet Street and was attended by the then Archbishop of Canterbury, Lord Runcie, and the Foreign Secretary John Major. My mind races away from the intimacy of conversation and personal letters to this extraordinary public event at the end of her life, of which I was completely ignorant at the time. We'd been a normal, private family. My kidnap had altered all our lives for ever. Not only had she been battling cancer and aching for the return of a missing son, she'd spent those awful years to some extent on public view. It was so alien to the private, intimate person she was. That even her death should have become a political football is enough to make me angry at myself. My heart aches. What must it have been like for her and for my father and Terence trying to deal with such stress and sorrow?

Obviously I had no pressing desire to get kidnapped and I know I'm not responsible for the actions of other men but I worry that I had departed too casually to a dangerous place. Even prior to that trip, I am aware that I hadn't done enough to support the family. They had done so much for me as a child and a young man. What had I given back?

Such bleak thoughts deter me from carrying on with the letters now so I leave the folder in the box. It's all so perplexing; part of me says climb aboard this emotional roller coaster, while another inner voice calls for caution: there's plenty of time and no need to rush anything. The urge to prevaricate succeeds. Looking out of the window I see that the rain has eased and the sun is forcing a way through the dense low cloud. The little wagtail has just appeared again and his eccentric movements along the balustrade make me smile. It's OK to stop worrying for a while.

'We don't notice it,' Phil admits. 'Perhaps we should, but we don't.'

It's been another typical Kerry day, with the weather showing off and making mockery of any detailed weather forecasting. But now the view across the harbour is beautiful in the early evening light. Though it's cool, the hues of blue, grey and a little gold lingering from the sunset are as calming as a good massage. Phil rubs her arms, shivering slightly, and speaks wistfully of the warmth of Australia and the Holy Land.

'We went to Australia one November,' she remembers. 'The hot sun came in through the windows at six in the morning. I don't like the long cold days.'

With the amount of grim weather we get here it's a wonder she has remained so long in Ireland.

Phil and her husband, Mike, have often said I could drop by if I felt like some company and I do now want to be away from myself. I also want to know more about my house and the area.

'I spent most of my childhood in your house,' Mike tells me. 'It belonged to my Uncle Dick.'

Mike's family lived up the road at Keel, a couple of miles away, and one day when Mike was about four and a half years old, Uncle Dick had arrived in his pony and trap.

Apparently the little boy hopped in the trap and went to live with his uncle and aunt who had no children of their own. This surprises me but Mike explains that it was common for relatives, particularly if they had no children, to take in nieces and nephews. The extended family worked well and he still saw his parents and siblings.

He reckons that my house was built in the 1930s. 'You know those two old, drystone barns near the house? Well, they were houses once. Over the years, when they could, the family built bigger and better homes and used the old places for the animals.'

Right up until the 1960s most families ran small farms, growing and rearing all their food.

'There was hardly any money to spare,' Mike says, 'but most people didn't suffer as they had what they needed.'

In those days the pub was a far more occasional venue than now but there were one or two houses in the parish where men would gather once or twice a week to play cards. Such a place was called a 'rambling house'. My house up the hill was one such.

'There was no horde of kids, just me like,' says Mike, 'so the house would have suited it. Eight people used to sit playing cards around a large table in your front room. Others would be on chairs around the walls.'

'Would the stakes have been high?' I ask.

'Oh no, they only played for pennies or sometimes a chicken.'

At Christmas time he remembers a goose was often up for grabs, but with such a big prize it might take a few nights' play to decide the winner.

In those days there was no press or cupboard under the stairs, just a bench and a large flour bin.

'On that bin was a list of all the family members and what they had done and where they'd gone. My uncle liked to keep track of everyone.'

Many had gone to the States. Indeed the aunt and uncle with whom Mike went to live in Caherpierce had been living in the States and only came back when Dick's brother's wife died and he needed help, and, Mike reckons, company, to run the farm.

Mike himself was away in England for some twelve years and it was in London that he and Phil met. Phil was a Limerick girl. They came back when the aunt and uncle were getting old. Remembering what Phil had told me about living with the old couple, I ask what it was like coming back from one of the world's great cities to a quiet backwater like Inch.

'We loved it in London,' says Phil. 'I didn't feel happy here at first. The windows in your house weren't as big then and the old people had this huge TV on the windowsill in the front room, blocking out that lovely view and the light.' She shakes her head then goes on, 'Then after, oh, three years or so, I just felt fine and now I wouldn't want to move again.'

Many of those who went away never came back, Phil tells me, and I recount what I'd heard on the radio about the difficulties some people were having now in coming back.

Mike nods. 'One uncle came home from America when he was very old but wasn't able to recognize the old place, he'd been away that long. He was so upset, his son had to take him back to the States again.'

How devastating that must have been for the old man, I muse. What a cruel twist of fate to live all those years thinking of some-where as his real home, no doubt nourishing fond memories of people and places, only to find that he'd been living with a mirage that vanished for good when he tried to touch it. I feel a shiver run through me. It's almost as though, like the old man in Mike's story, I'm living in a kind of exile, not from a physical home but certainly an emotional one. In the back of my mind a fear still lurks that if I look too closely for the old home life, the place I know and cherish won't be there.

This isn't the moment to be dwelling on my immediate family background; distant cousins seem to offer a more palatable reality so I ask Mike what he made of James MacCarthy.

'Reading between the lines I get the feeling that James was a bit of a wheeler-dealer,' I say. 'Was that part of his appeal?'

'Oh yes, yes, I'd say so,' he replies. 'But I liked him, I think he was a good man, he had the natural touch, you know. He wasn't stuck-up like. His dad didn't like people going down to take sand, for building or to put on the fields, from the beach. But James just used to wave you on.'

One time when Mike had gone down with a trailer for some sand, James had flagged him down as he got to the beach and inveigled Mike into doing him a little favour first. The track into James's caravan park was looking a bit tatty so he asked Mike to go to the great pile of old sea shells which lay about halfway up the island. Mike duly obliged and a mass of shells was spread over the track. By the time Mike had been down to the beach and filled the trailer with a load of sand, half an hour later, the holidaymakers had come out of their caravans and scooped up all the fine shells to take home as souvenirs. The track was as tatty as ever.

'What did James say to that?'

'He just shrugged and laughed.'

The next morning I learn from Tom Barrington that aside from any aesthetic value, the shells so casually acquired by the souvenir-hungry tourists might have had some real historical significance. I've got the radio giving me background entertainment with some middle of the road music while Mr B educates me about middens, or shell dumps. There are two of them on the peninsula and likely they date back thousands of years. Man first came to Ireland around 6000 BC, settling on the coasts, hunting and gathering food. The beach had continued to be used for collecting and cooking shellfish down through the ages, right up until early in the last century, but some of the dumps must effectively be the backyards of the very earliest occupants of the land. The idea of continuity of human life from early times is reassuring; it offers a sense of community. By a chance of family tree, I have landed in a place where people have been dealing with the issues of living, birth, death and all the woes and joys in between, for many thousands of years. And not only is this a place where we can trace our physical, archaeological reality, but it is also home to many myths and sagas that try to explain where we came from in a metaphysical way.

Something catches my eye and I look up, but there's nothing on the track – it must have been a bird flitting past the window. Then, halfway between me and the road, a green van appears round a bend in the track.

Ah, hah, I think. That must be the postman.

I go out to meet him.

'Mackartay here?' he asks.

I nod.

'Nice day,' he says, handing me an envelope.

'It is.'

He jumps back into his van and drives off.

It is an income tax return form from the Inland Revenue at home – more midden than metaphysical. I can't believe my ears when a voice on the radio starts talking about rubbish dumps and taxes. A man earnestly implores citizens to pay their household waste charges. 'Don't dump on the rest of us!' This call to civic duty is sweetened with the added information, 'They're tax deductible!'

There are many more public service announcements on Irish radio than I've ever noticed at home.

The local station, Radio Kerry, has a greater intimacy and very definitely a more bucolic atmosphere than any local station I've come across in the UK. You don't have to listen for long to appreciate how important agriculture is to the region. Regular updates on crop news and the prices for cattle at local markets are interspersed with advertisements for animal feeds, fertilizers and treatments for horrible sounding afflictions like liver fluke. Well, I assume that's to do with animals.

As well as the focus on the mainstay of the local economy there are programmes on cultural issues, and reports on social events, sports and job opportunities. One thing that has taken me by surprise is the amount of air time given over to death. County Kerry has a population of around 130,000 people spread over a wide area so why should there be much of an audience for the morbid and very local fare that's contained in the extensive and detailed announcements about recent deaths? The presenter intones the name of the deceased, then advises that he or she is 'now reposing at such and such a funeral parlour and there will be a rosary tonight'. The date is then given for the removal to the church and details of the Requiem Mass and the burial afterwards.

But I've begun to realize that while people might be spread out over the county, indeed over the country, there is a very strong connection among neighbours and family. While these lists seem dull and morbid to me, to most people such a string of announcements would likely contain information about someone they knew or at least knew of. And deaths, as is brought home to me at Foley's later that evening, aren't marked just with the funeral service, but with the wake.

Driving down to the pub I pass rows of parked cars at a brightly lit house. The road is unusually busy and a good few of the cars are pulling in at the place.

As I order a pint I observe to Fidelus, 'Looks like someone is having a big party down the road tonight.'

'Oh no,' she informs me, 'that's a funeral, people are stopping in to pay their respects. The old man was in his eighties, but it was still a shock. He was in here last week. Some nights he was the life and soul of this place, he was a great singer. I'll miss him.'

Soon the bar is busy with folk coming in from the wake.

'He was after going quietly in his sleep like,' Bridget Fitzgerald confides in me. 'A nice way to go, I'd say.'

'There'll be a few folk who won't be riding in my Ark, that's for sure!'

My words die away and I find myself looking into the face of a man standing on the far side of my desk. He is looking at me with a quizzical expression on his face.

'Were you speaking to me?' he asks.

'Um, no, no, I must have been talking to, um, myself.' I laugh nervously, turning red.

Ancient Irish history is proving to be a minefield. The day began with minor confusion when I drove to Tralee and got lost trying to find the library. A young woman, pretty, palely pink and plump, at a little store-cum-post office had helped me

out and blushingly told me the way. Since I got to the library
the written guides I've consulted have been significantly less
lucid.

What is clear enough is the archaeological history that
identifies general periods of ancient occupation: the Stone Ages
– in Ireland from around 6000 to 2000 BC; the Metal
Ages, Copper then Bronze, from 2000 to 800 BC, and then the
Iron Age from 800 BC to AD 400.

What is far from clear is who actually did the occupying. The
books I'm looking at keep leading me along confusing paths.
Whenever I feel I'm getting a grasp on this list of people, the
writer explains that some of the information is based on a work,
compiled probably in the eleventh century AD, called the *Lebor
Gabála, The Book of Invasions*.

Eventually it dawns on me that, as with most history, this was
spun or made to fit the views of the people in charge at the time.
Various myths, legends and folk tales had existed and been
retold over centuries and in *The Book of Invasions* these have
been collated and edited to provide an approximate chronological history back to the beginning of time.

The book identifies six invasions.

The first invader, a woman called Cessair, takes us all the
way back to the Ark builder. In some stories she was a daughter
of Noah, in others her father was Bith, a son of Noah who
was barred from the Ark. Whatever her parentage, she set
off for Ireland with a couple of boats and blokes and loads
of women. The journey took them seven years. Their
conquest was not altogether successful in the long run. Only
three men survived the long sea passage and two then died.
The last man couldn't cope and fled. Cessair died of a broken
heart.

Three hundred years passed before Parthalon tipped up on a
beach, in what is now southern Kerry, on 14 May 2680 BC (nice

bit of detail there, but was it morning or afternoon?), with a party of one hundred from Greece. They struggled with the demon Fomorians for thirty years and then all succumbed to a plague in a week. Or maybe not. Another version has it that they were the Fomorians in the first place. Then again there is always the possibility that they might have been Canaanites expelled by the ancient Israelites. Why hasn't anyone looked into the possibility that they were alien invaders from the planet Fomor? I ask myself. Wouldn't that be simpler?

By now I'm beginning to feel as at home with the *Lebor Gabála* as I am with the income tax return form that arrived a few days ago.

Next on deck was Nemed in 2350 BC, but he and his followers had a rough time of it at the hands of the Fomorians. The day and month of their arrival is not recorded.

Then came the Fir Bolg. The name translates as Men of Bags. Bags of what? I ask myself. Were they ancient luggage makers, the Louis Vuittons of the second millennium BC? No one is sure but they were rumoured to have had a nice little business taking bags of earth from Ireland to Greece to keep the snakes at bay! Now these characters seem to begin to fit in with more widely accepted history and were probably the Belgae, Celtic invaders from Gaul who went to Kerry and Cork. Legend has it that the Men of Bags arrived nearly two thousand years BC but modern historians say it was more likely 400 BC and that they were the builders of some of the great stone fortresses in the area. The fact that they didn't win out in the end meant that they got a less than flattering press and were often referred to as small, dark and boorish.

The Firbolgs were in charge in the south-west for only a few decades before the next wave of invaders swooped in. The Tuatha de Danaan, People of the Goddess Anu or Ana or Danu, were artistic and magical. They came either from a cloud of mist or from Denmark, which seems to be going from one extreme to another. I think it's wonderful that the two stories could live side by side and imagine the ancient historians discussing the Tuatha's origin.

'I reckon they came from Denmark.'

'Could be, could be. But it's more likely they came out of a cloud of mist, I'd say.'

'Fair point, just as probable, isn't it?'

Barely had they materialized than the kith and kin of Míl (the Milesians) arrived, supposedly from Spain. However, they were probably the Gaels from Gaul. They gradually took control of the whole country under various kings and it was their poets, the *fili*, who wrote the genealogies that traced everything back, making myth blend with history as they went. By lining themselves up with the story of Míl the Gaels formed a link to the genealogies of the Bible and so to Adam. And thus another alternative time line is evolved.

Donal IX MacCarthy Mór, the last King of Desmond and the Two Munsters, who died in 1596, bought into this project and had himself traced back eighty-six generations to Éber, one of the three sons of Míl. Donal IX's family tree met mine at Cormac VI, 1326–1359, which put me right back there with the Milesians who beat those Tuatha de Danaan boys in the first or second century BC. It is while walking arm in arm down this path with Donal and Cormac that I begin to realize my familial connection to Noah and make my unconscious outburst about the Ark. It is a comforting thought to have such a weight of history behind one, even if it has the ring of fable to it.

No doubt part of the cause of all this historical confusion, and my frustration, was that until the coming of Christianity, with Latin and its alphabet, the Irish had no real form of written language. While the Celtic languages of the peoples of Britain were pushed to the fringes of the Roman conquest, to Cornwall,

Wales and Scotland, and replaced by Latin, Irish Celtic remained resident, and illiterate, from around 300 BC.

The first definite, recorded event in Ireland was the Pope's installation of Palladius as a bishop in AD 431. No wonder the country's history was in such a mess. But then again I don't suppose anybody who counted minded too much. In those days, no doubt, the sword was far mightier than the pen. The stories served for history, passed down through an oral tradition which must have sufficed to give whoever wanted it a sense of place or grandeur in the overall scheme of things. It's only when trying to make sense of it all a couple of thousand years later that such conveniences prove to be an insurmountable barrier.

In fact, just before the arrival of Christianity, a limited system of writing had been developed in Ireland. Ogham, or Ogam (pronounced Oh-am), was carved on stones and possibly bits of wood, its letters formed of five notches which, depending on length and angle, make up twenty-five Roman letters. The script was probably only used to mark gravestones or boundaries. Writing a poem would have been a labour to daunt any artist; even James Joyce might have thrown in the towel when dreaming up *Finnegans Wake* if his publisher had given him a chisel and a lump of rock to write it with. Then again, maybe not.

Given that story-telling and the recording of legal and religious information were always the preserve of the elite, I wonder whether this crude script was a last-ditch attempt by the pagan establishment to outmanoeuvre the incoming literacy of the new faith. The experts answer this in part, saying that Ogham did represent an Irish used by priests, which gave way to the more common colloquial language as Christianity moved into the country. Nevertheless, Ogham was in use between the fourth and seventh centuries AD and some three hundred Ogham stones have been found in Ireland, most of them in Munster.

# CHAPTER FIVE

THE RAIN IS EASING AS I TURN OFF ONTO ONE OF THE SIDE roads down to Ardcanacht. Now that I know a bit more about Ogham I'm off to have another look for the stone. At the back of my mind, though, is the idea that this might be a gentle way of touching base with my mother through my own memory before getting to grips with her voice in her letters. I've framed the photograph and am finding it easier to look properly at her so maybe this will help me move on and close the emotional gap a little more.

Right down at the end of the track is a farmhouse. I knock on the door and a gentle woman immediately welcomes me in, bringing me bread, jam and tea as soon as I start telling her what I'm looking for. There may be questions about modern Ireland's concern for the under-privileged and the country's commitment to care for them but the Irish, at least those I've met in Kerry, are instinctively hospitable to strangers; it's no myth, no sham for the tourists.

The woman says she's not too sure she knows where the stone is. There are more than one in the area, it turns out. She goes into the farmyard to consult with her husband who comes back in with her and says that the Ogham stone I'm after is probably down one of the other tracks off the main road. He recommends I visit Florence O'Sullivan, the blacksmith at the nearby village of Boolteens, who is interested in local history and has talked of some connection with the MacCarthys of Ardcanacht.

I thank them and as I drive away from the farm, the heavens open again. It seems that fate doesn't want me to go rock-hunting today. I'm sure my parents would have liked the idea of my going off to investigate this new lead on family history instead.

At first sight Florence O'Sullivan cuts a wild-looking figure as he moves around the jumbled piles of metal and rust at his forge, wearing ragged work clothes and a frayed baseball cap. When I arrive he is loading a newly shod horse into a trailer so I shelter for a moment in the doorway to the forge, tripping on various weird and wonderful shapes of detritus, vaguely recognizable as parts of tools and machinery. When he's finished he comes back to see what he can do for me. When I tell him I'm interested in MacCarthy history, he explains that one of his brothers has done some research and that sure enough they have a connection, on their mother's side, with the family.

'He found out we're related to that one who was a hostage in the Lebanon,' he says casually.

'Oh, right. Well, that was me.'

Florence's mouth opens slightly and with a hand on my elbow he guides me into the daylight at the doorway. His eyes twinkle and he grins.

'Well, it's very nice to meet you, John.'

The rain comes down again and he says I should come in for a cup of tea.

His house is incredibly neat, a complete contrast to the angular chaos in the forge and yard. With a plain cement floor, stove and a dresser, it has a homely rather than austere feel to it.

On the window shelf at the back of the front room there are crucifixes, rosaries and a Sacred Bleeding Heart picture. High up by the ceiling, a Sheila maid clothes airer looks after some socks and a couple of caps. Nearly every hook and doorknob has some plastic goggles hanging on it; the welder's essential piece of kit, I suppose.

Florence takes me through to the equally neat kitchen where he offers me a whiskey, stating, 'I joined the [Temperance] Association and it seemed to work for me.'

Although I've certainly taken no pledge, it is a little early for hard liquor so we settle for tea and biscuits. Being a teetotaller might well account for the bright blue eyes and sharp brain of this man who looks closer to sixty than the seventy years he's about to reach.

As I tell him more about my time in Kerry and where I'm living, Florence nods. 'Oh yes, the Courtney place. So away from your missus, you're a bachelor like me!'

Not having a wife or children has given him no regrets; he has plenty of nieces and nephews. One brother living in the village, who used to work as a smith with him, has one child away in the States working in IT, another is an architect in London, while others still are studying or working in Dublin.

'I expect I'll leave one of them this place,' says Florence, 'and then they can do what they want, sell it, knock it, I don't know!'

As we talk, it occurs to me that I'm following his speech much more easily than I would have done just a few weeks ago. My ear has obviously become attuned to the Kerry accent, but I still have to speak slowly and clearly so they can understand me. Florence is the first person I've noticed using the phrase 'she gave' for 'she spent'. He says that one of his nieces 'gave five years to study in Trinity College'. I suppose it's another way of saying 'she dedicated five years'. At first I'm confused when he starts talk-ing about the 'leaving', then realize he means the 'leaving certificate' you receive when you finish school.

Outside, the rain has dried up and afternoon sunlight filters in through one of the windows at the back of the house, warming up the pale walls and yellow oilcloth table cover. It also lights up Florence's hair which although greatly thinned on top still has a strong red tint to it.

Across the plain front room from the kitchen, there's a more formal sitting room where papers and books are stacked on the table and chairs. He shows me pictures of his family, the two sisters who live in Dublin and another brother who also works in the capital. This brother has been in the civil service for years, working his way up through the Taoiseach's office, and has served there during the administrations of, among others, Jack Lynch and Charlie Haughey. He is now with the Attorney General's department. The third brother is a priest in the United States, a monsignor in Tallahassee, Florida, and it was he who had done the family research and to whom I owed thanks for discovering this new relation. Florence says he can't remember all that his brother found out but knows there are some McCarthys buried at Keel churchyard a couple of miles from Boolteens towards Inch, and that at some point a MacCarthy had been priest at Kiltallagh, another nearby parish.

'Ah yes,' I say, 'I've seen him on the family tree. He was the priest there in the early eighteen hundreds. I think his brother, Justin, seems to have been the last one who lived at Ardcanacht.'

'You know your crowd at Ardcanacht were called the Slught Fineen Duff?'

I nod, that was also on the family tree. Not a particularly attractive sounding name, I'd always thought.

'Well, Florence is the English for Fineen or Fingin.'

'Ah, and *duff* means black, doesn't it?'

'It does, and *slught* means tribe.'

'The Tribe of Black Florence! Blimey, they sound a scary bunch, don't they?'

The family tree shows that the name Florence, along with Justin, had been very popular with the MacCarthys. So too with the O'Sullivans, Florence tells me.

Seeing as he's nearing his seventieth birthday, wasn't he thinking of retiring?

'No, no plans for that.' But it's a relief to him that there's not so much call for the tiring work of horse-shoeing these days. In the old days that was a major part of his business as few people had cars but everyone had a pony or donkey and cart.

There's a documentary series, *The Years of Change*, on RTE (Radio Telefís Éireann), re-running some of the first Irish television programmes, black and white newsreels about the country. I've been fascinated but also surprised by how archaic the country looked in the fifties and sixties. Florence is shocked by the newsreels. 'To think we were like that such a little time ago!'

When electricity first became available some forty years back he and his brother had been keen to install it so they could stop welding in the forge's fire and use electrical gear instead. But they needed to convince enough neighbours to sign up to it too before the electric company would agree to put the village on the mains. A few years went by before the rest of the village came round to the idea. They weren't sure of the technology, and they weren't sure about having to pay regular bills in cash either. Until then few things were paid for on the spot, and much was paid for in kind. Most of Florence's customers would settle up at Christmas – 'But they'd bring a bag of spuds or a goose as well. We used to be self-contained here, a bakery just across the road, a cooper, a butcher. The pub over the road sold clothes and groceries.'

I learn that the old pub owners, the Rae family, used to have a lot of credit out to the farmers. I'd met David, the only Rae still in the village, when I'd come over looking for a place to stay. He's an estate agent, commissioner of oaths and auctioneer as well as sometime publican. According to Florence he had also been important in developing tourism and I remembered him telling me that he used to have a lot of business from Germany and Switzerland, with people looking for getaway and retirement homes. Since the fall of the Berlin Wall, David reckoned people had lost their fear of the east and so didn't feel such an urge to scarper to the western edge of Europe. He's now almost fully retired and I'd had a pleasant half-hour with him in what had served as his office/antique shop/tearoom, surrounded by odds and ends that never made it past his gavel: busts of Kennedy and effigies of Christ in torment, garden benches, gramophones, lamp stands, picture frames and some old garden tools.

Florence continues, 'There was the great dream to be self-sufficient, but we couldn't just rely on the agriculture. Most of the trade was with Britain.'

With the advent of the labour-saving tractor and the realization that Ireland couldn't survive on agriculture alone, many people had left to do seasonal work in England, sending money home: a rural diaspora all too common across Europe. Many of Florence's older relatives left for Canada and the States.

The Sunday papers are spread out on the oilcloth, with headlines about domestic and international stories, IRA arms decommissioning, political corruption, the Middle East and the latest thoughts on the Irish squad that would be going to the World Cup in Japan. Florence is up to date on all the main stories. Chatting with him makes me feel good; I like the way he views the world and that he is conscious of and amazed at, but basically accepting of, the way the world has changed in his lifetime. He seems the epitome of many strands of Irish life that I've been observing.

With a population of less than four million people, close to that of Greater Manchester and Lancashire combined, Ireland is a small nation and there's a sense of intimacy across the country, with people tending to know someone who knows/works with/ has met someone in the papers. It's a country where the Prime Minister is almost universally referred to simply as Bertie and where most people have at some point dated someone who used to go to parties with U2. It's a country where a smith in a tiny village on the Dingle peninsula has a brother in the higher echelons of the country's civil service and relations all around the world. And a country where you can turn up and be offered tea and cake, time and hospitality by people who don't know you from Adam.

Having spent an afternoon with this humble, concerned, gentle man, it comes as no surprise that everyone I meet sub- sequently who also knows Florence speaks very highly of him.

Apart from revealing how much Ireland's economy had changed in the past forty years, RTE's series *The Years of Change* also shows how, by the 1950–60s when these programmes were actually filmed, there was a realization that the Ireland the nation's founding fathers had hoped to create after independ- ence, a Gaelic-speaking, rural-based, self-sufficient and devoutly Catholic society, hadn't developed.

The endless coverage they'd shown then of ceremonies marking the events, some seemingly of no real historical merit, of the War of Independence concealed the fact that ideals espoused at that time had not been achieved. It wasn't the language that had taken off but the people, who'd left in droves to seek a better life elsewhere. And of course the great national achievement of defeating the British oppressors was immediately followed by the nightmare of civil war. The old newsreels seem to have covered far less of the uncomfortable and divisive ceremonies, parades and Masses marking events from that period.

Whatever the political hangovers from the Civil War, the authority of the Catholic faith continued unabated at that time and Ireland was a country which took its religious activities to great and sometimes hilarious levels. The national airline Aer Lingus would endeavour to bring its entire fleet of aeroplanes together at Dublin airport once a year to have them blessed. Cars, too, would be doused with holy water and while their counterparts in London and Brighton would be concentrating on chrome, wing mirrors, parkas and taking on motorcycle gangs with bicycle chains, the motor scooter riders of Dublin and the provinces would meekly line up, in suit and tie, so that the priest could bless their Vespas.

Apparently the railways and roads were also blessed, which might account for the parlous state of the roads today. Down the years this may have instilled an attitude of laissez faire in county planners and engineers. What can they do about the state of the highways if they are, after all, in the hands of the Almighty?

Another beautiful morning and with the wagtail chirping a greeting from the drive I get up, have a quick breakfast, listen to the news (a dispute between farmers and processors over sugar beet prices tops the agenda on Radio Kerry) and am down on Inch Strand by nine o'clock, determined to get right out to the tip of the peninsula. I've been reading about this spit which stretches some four miles out across the bay. Jeremiah King, writing in the first two decades of the last century, was a man in the same mould as Barrington. King wrote a detailed history of Kerry and went on to compile a list of all the parishes and town-lands (parish subdivisions) and all the people who lived in them. I found an interesting snippet in his book *King's History of Kerry*, where he thanks Justin MacCarthy JP, father of James, of Inch

House, for looking up the family records and also the parish book of his great-grand-uncle, the Rev. Charles 'who lived at Ardcanacht when his brother moved from the ancient residence'. So it looks as though my forebears did quit the ancient family seat early on in the nineteenth century. From King I learn the various meanings of the place names. His entry for Inch is 'Inch, inis, inse, incha, island, isthmus, river meadow', which explains why many locals refer to it as 'the island'.

My oldest informant in these matters is a thoroughly arrogant Englishman, Charles Smith, who wrote *The Ancient and Present State of the County of Kerry* in 1756. He kicks off with a grovelling dedication to 'Robert, Lord Viscount Jocelyn, Baron Newport, the Lord Chancellor and one of the Lord Justices of Ireland' in which he says, 'This Kingdom [of Kerry], my lord is a kind of terra incognita to the greater part of Europe' and goes on to point out wherever he can the ignorance and incompetence of the Irish as against the sophistication and success of the English who have settled on their land.

For all his haughtiness, Smith gives a good description of the peninsula:

> . . . one continued range of sand-hills, some of which are 30 or 40 feet high. They are covered with a long kind of sedgy grass that renders them compact, and binds the sand together. When the country people cut and carry away this sedge, as they frequently do for thatch, and other purposes, the sea and wind make great irruptions into the sand-banks . . . Towards the southern point of the island, considerable quantities of white peas grow spontaneously, the seed of which was probably scattered here by some ship wreck. The sand is here very whit, hard, and of a fine grain. The air when I was on this isthmus was very hot and parching, occasioned, by the reflection of the solar beams from the sand-banks: and it was with some labour that I measured a base line,

in order to adjust the distances and bearings of the points and head-lands of the adjoining bay, which hath been for many years infamous for ship-wrecks; and never laid down with the least degree of truth, in any former sea-chart or map.

Tom Barrington gives an alternative, more Irish explanation for the many shipwrecks, which goes beyond mere navigational ignorance. Apparently the locals would tie a lantern to a cow's tail on a stormy night and let the beast wander on the strand. A ship further out would assume the light was on another ship navigating its way over the bar into the inner harbour. Then it would ride itself up onto the beach and the locals would help themselves to the proceeds.

This morning there are no wreckers as far as I can see, only a few other walkers about and one fisherman. The beach stretches out endlessly and the scale of the dunes is awesome. As I go in among them, the atmosphere becomes mysterious. The high banks of sand shield me from the breeze and muffle almost to nothing the sound of waves washing the beach.

Most of the 'island' is owned by a family who live on the other side of the Dingle peninsula. They bought the place once James MacCarthy's estate was settled, hoping to build a golf course on it. Some of the locals back this scheme for the tourists and employment it would bring. But it is also an important sanctuary for wildlife; one neighbour explained to me that it is one of the few habitats of the rare natterjack, or 'chatternack' as she called it, toad. The battle for planning permission has been a long-running saga. As a 'blow-in' I'd keep this special place sacrosanct. I wander through the dunes then back onto the beach, following the spores of some creature, fox or otter perhaps. The trail leads me down from the dunes to the waterline where a hole has been dug: somebody or something after mussels maybe?

Flocks of birds are moving over the wide beach. Not being much of a twitcher I'm only confident in my identification of some oystercatchers. There are smaller birds with white undersides and grey tops and long black beaks which scuttle about amusingly, like crowds of elderly yet sprightly gentlemen playing an eccentric game. I guess they are trying to catch some tasty little creatures in the waves lapping on the shore. They all scamper away when the bigger waves crash in. There's another group of smallish birds hunkered down a little way from me nearer the dunes, like little sentinels among bumps of sand and seaweed.

Walking on, I pick up shells and floats from fishing nets and tug at a length of rope emerging from the sand. Uncannily and immediately I'm back in my childhood on a family holiday, pulling on an endless piece of rope that has buried itself in a shingle beach in Devon. We'd discovered a hidden cove called Shipload Bay. As I'd trotted back to where my mother was laying out our picnic lunch, she was laughing. 'I thought you were going to pull in a whale!'

As we ate our lunch we had plotted how to use the rope and bits of driftwood to build a raft. The finished article looked quite substantial, something Robinson Crusoe would have been impressed with, but sadly when launched its seagoing abilities were never tested because the waves of the incoming tide kept pushing it back up the beach.

Although I feel the usual tug at my heart which accompanies thoughts of my mother, I'm noticing that I can hold on to them for longer and accept them for what they are, simple memories. Since I've put the pictures of her up in the cottage I've been getting used to looking at her, and smiling back. She always looked forward to our holidays so much and made our outings and expeditions into adventures. Although I'm sure she was content in her role of wife and mother I know she was frustrated at times at not having done more with her life. As a schoolgirl she'd loved acting and had hoped for a career on the stage. It never happened but she did leap at the chance of joining in a production put on by the Women's Institutes from all over the UK in the late sixties. *The Brilliant and the Dark* was a massive undertaking, bringing choirs and teams of dancers together to perform a dramatization of the nation's history. My mother absolutely revelled in every stage of the production, through all the local, regional and the national rehearsals up to the crowning moment when she took to the stage of the Royal Albert Hall. Her menfolk had watched proudly, just able to distinguish her among the myriad dancers from where they sat high up above her in the gods.

It was a tragedy that in later years she succumbed to agoraphobia. But even then her spirit remained strong and she struggled to cope with her fears, in her case not inspired by open spaces particularly but more by being away from the familiar places near her home. In fact she was able to go more or less anywhere if she was with one of her family. Thinking of her agoraphobia pricks my guilt again; I should have done more to help her. But I pull myself up. In her way she had been prepared to take risks and rather than allowing myself to wallow in self-recrimination I must celebrate and enjoy the happier memories, and at the same time follow her example and use this time at Inch to take my own risks and find her again. She had fought to be free of the constrictions the phobia placed on her and never sank into a depression where she might have given up on any attempt to overcome it. I remember once she and my father were due to go to London for a formal dinner. She was very anxious about going but was determined to try. In the event, halfway there on the train she just couldn't go on and they had to come back. Although very upset, she wouldn't let herself see it as a final defeat, but more as a setback.

Resuming my walk, I at last reach the far end of the peninsula and see where the Maine River meets Dingle Bay.

Losing touch with family and friends and the difficulty of re-establishing that context is the theme of one of the great stories of the Fenian Cycle. This series of Irish legends recounts the exploits of a band of warriors, the Fianna, who followed the great Fionn mac Cumhaill, or Finn McCool. These men protected the ports of Ireland and went hunting a good deal. One of the tales tells of one such hunting expedition near Killarney when Fionn's son Oisín lost his heart to the beautiful Niamh. The princess arrived on a white horse from Tír na nÓg, the Land of Eternal Youth, which lay somewhere beyond the sea. The two lovers mounted the white horse to fly back to Tír na nÓg together. Many years later Oisín tries to return to his old friends but finds that they, without the benefit of eternal youth, have all long since died. Different accounts give alternative locations for the launch pad for this fantastic trip.

The morning light is bright and as I gaze at the clearly defined mountains across the water, beyond Inch's twin peninsula of Rossbeigh, and enjoy 'the reflection of the solar beams from the sand-banks' which Smith had found discomforting but which for me adds to an otherworldliness about the place, I am very happy to go along with Barrington who sticks by the version of the tale that says the magical wave Tonn Toime, which is supposed to roar between Rossbeigh and Inch, was the starting point for Oisín and Niamh's journey.

An announcement in the *Irish Times* has advised me that Killarney library is the venue for a talk on 'Irish Traditional Spirituality'. Given the importance of the faith throughout the centuries and the role the Church has played in modern Ireland I'm keen to hear this. I arrive far too early and slope off down the High Street for supper. Unlike Tralee which has the air of a real working market town, everything in Killarney appears to be aimed at tourists, with virtually all the buildings housing gift shops, 'traditional' pubs and restaurants. The streets are all but deserted and English and American voices outnumber the Irish.

A few people are already gathered when I return to the library at ten to eight. Most are well into middle age (even older than me) though there are one or two young faces. The event has been organized by the Kerry Archaeological and Historical Society and its president, a Mr Flynn I think, introduces the speaker, Rev. John J óRíordáin, as a 'Missioner' (not a word I've come across but later learn describes priests who go, often in pairs, for brief visits to parishes to reinvigorate the faith and church attendance of the local congregation). The introductions are made in Irish. Then the lecturer begins to speak – in Irish.

I realize I'm going to have to sit here for at least an hour for politeness' sake.

Surreptitiously looking around, I conclude that getting to the door would make too big a disturbance. I quickly make a plan to leave it for five or ten minutes then develop a terrible coughing fit, do the noble thing and scarper. But I'm relieved of any need for evasive action when Father óRíordáin finally turns to my native tongue and begins with a joke.

'I'm six foot seven, sixty-four years old and fourteen stone. If you want to know any more you'll have to look at the Garda files.'

He goes on to argue that Celtic Christian spirituality followed on naturally from the Celts' pagan religion because both faiths emphasized the themes of seeing and feeling God everywhere, of believing in an afterlife and of giving importance to the individual and the community. At heart it was essentially a very warm tradition of a closeness with God, says the priest. Talking about the intimate relationship some people have with the Holy Trinity, the Virgin and the saints, Father óRíordáin recalls how, as a young priest, he went into a house and saw the usual pictures, Sacred Bleeding Heart, Mother Mary, St Patrick, all turned to the wall.

'Oh, are you decorating?' he asked.

'Not talking to them!' came the reply.

Making the point that life has so much more to offer if you see everything as a gift, he describes himself hurrying down a street one night, raincoat pulled tightly round hunched shoulders as the rain lashed down on him. A door opened and a woman stuck her head out.

'A filthy night, Father, thank God!'

The atmosphere in the room seems to echo óRíordáin's themes of warmth and welcome, and his audience, particularly the older members, join in as a rumbling echo when he quotes poetry or prayers in Irish. And while I like what I hear and he makes me laugh and think, I end up wondering whether there isn't a hefty pinch of that romanticization of Ireland's past that has been falling out of fashion recently. Much of the talk is ultimately comfortably reassuring stuff on the antiquity of the faith in Ireland, the special nature of the people and how, despite all the intrusions of the English and their Puritanism or the authority and bureaucracy of Rome, the Spirit has continued. But to what degree does the generosity, the welcome of the Irish, which so far has proved real for me, come from their brand of Roman Catholicism or from their inherent nature?

In a way I suppose this is all part of the Father's 'missioner' work but I wonder whether it would make any impression on a younger audience, whether the emphasis on the natural world, which I can identify with, would make a lot of sense in an urban environment and to what degree it would help counter diminishing congregations. I've always distrusted the confidence and authority which seem to go with a dog collar, and while Father óRíordáin comes across as sincere and caring, I can't altogether quell my concerns at his being 'Father', the man who has, since a young adult age, been treated with automatic respect as one set apart with special powers. However, without talking about falling church attendances or the undermining of the Church's authority through revelations about widespread sexual abuse by priests, he does acknowledge that at times an institution can run out of steam and direction and need to reinvent itself.

A big man with florid face and white hair stands up and rambles a little as he gives a vote of thanks for Father óRíordáin's speech, then adds a personal note to the priest which I'm not expecting:

'I admire and am grateful for your nature and spirit.'

Fidelus and John Foley's generosity never ceases to amaze me. Even when they are frantically busy they'll stop what they are doing and offer me a cup of tea or coffee and will never accept any money when I use their phone line to get on the internet. Often I've half expected them to tell me to wise up and go to an internet café or something. The first time Fidelus replied to my request to use the phone with the phrase, 'Walk away!' I half thought she meant 'Don't be cheeky'. When she saw me looking puzzled she smiled and said, 'That means help yourself.'

When I get down to the pub one afternoon, John's out the back putting the finishing touches to a large wooden box that is going to hold logs in their living room.

'Therapy like, you know, one of those things you just want to do all of a sudden,' he says. 'I'd been in the house all afternoon.'

Trying to keep Katie and Jerry under control and away from the power saw he's using, John is, as always, displaying his gentle nature.

'Now, Katie, don't be bold,' he says when the six-year-old answers him back. She makes a face at him and runs off after a kitten. Her little brother Jerry, two years her junior, complains for a moment and tries to pick up the saw but so blatantly that it is clearly just a game, and then he runs off to play on his tractor.

For all the cheek and reprimands, the atmosphere of love in moments of play like this and the obvious mutual adoration between these children and their parents is touching. There's a universal quality about it; they could be talking any language and you'd know what was going on. Even though I'm looking in from outside this family circle I feel I understand it because I appreciate the father's concern for the kids' safety but can also remember being a little boy and wanting to do 'man's work' with my father and being frustrated at not being allowed to use the saw or chisel. On one occasion I remember breaking the rules and going to the tool drawers in the garden shed and pulling one out. I tugged and tugged with all my strength and suddenly it came flying free, showering the shed and me in hundreds of nails. I ran out across the lawn to find him, tears (as he often remembered in later years) literally spurting from my eyes in sorrow and fear. But rather than reprimanding me, he picked me up gently, carried me back and made a game of collecting and sorting all the nails into their right compartments.

John goes indoors to wash up and get ready for our night out. We are taking part in a fundraising quiz night for the school up at Annascaul. We'll be driven over there by John's elder brother Pat and his wife Máire ní Riain, who is the principal of the school.

The bar room at the side of the Brackluin B&B in Annascaul is heaving, young children, their grandparents and every generation in between are there. Máire is dynamic and, seeing as it's her school that everyone has come to support, is greeting and chatting to people left and right. Pat, tall like his brother, is also a principal but his school is a few miles away. He moves with a deliberation that suggests a rather formal nature – I later learn that the stiffness is purely physical; the one-time county footballer still suffers from back injuries. The quiz teams are made up of fours and Pat, John and I are joined by their sister Ann, another teacher. Although Ann and Pat are quietly spoken like their younger brother, they all share a keen sense of fun.

The quizmaster is the lady of the house, a stern woman called Kitty.

'She used to be a nun,' Ann confides.

Everyone seems terrified of her. Aside from the fact that I'm surrounded by teachers, there is a strong feeling of being back at school, despite the Guinness and hilarity, as the four heads at each table bend together to mull over each question when the po-faced Kitty announces it. Everyone, including representatives of the teaching profession who happen to be in my vicinity, cheats at every opportunity. Contestants eavesdrop on the ponderings of neighbouring teams, play for time – risking the wrath of God and Kitty – by asking to have the questions given once more, and blatantly squint at any written answer that somehow waves itself in front of them. No one really gives a damn and the relaxed atmosphere encourages Kitty to reveal a softer side and begin giving the most crushingly obvious clues to half the questions.

There is a certain amount of confusion between each round as papers are collected and more drinks bought. Team Foley's Pub comes second, winning ten punts each. When I suggest that we might give our winnings to the school fund, Pat shakes his head firmly. 'Not at all!'

Down at the pub one afternoon, I'm checking the emails and having a cup of tea while Fidelus gets the children's tea ready when Bridie Foley comes in. John's mother could be sixty but is in fact just about the same age as the Irish state, eighty years. Having lived in the pub all her married life she moved into a bungalow of her own half a mile from the place sometime after John and Fidelus took over running things.

Bridie has come in to discuss travel plans and outfits for a big family wedding over in Galway. Once the two Mrs Foleys have worked out the arrangements for a trip to Tralee to buy shoes, the conversation turns to Jackie Healy-Rae, a local, independent Teachtaí Dála (member of the Irish parliament, the Dáil) and something of a character, by all accounts. He wears a flat cap above a face that makes me think of a potato. Under the cap is one of the most startling 'comb-over' hairdos you could imagine.

Fidelus tells us that he'd stopped off at the pub on Sunday evening. Having seen him on the local TV news I wish I'd set eyes on him in the flesh.

The Irish have a more immediate relationship with their politicians than I've experienced in the UK. This can lead to problems when coupled with what seems to be a sneaking admiration for what they call 'fine rogues': if you've done well but had to bend the rules a bit, well, 'fair play to you'. However, too many important people started taking more and more liberties with this attitude and the legal system is now straining under a whole series of inquiries and tribunals trying to get to the bottom of various shenanigans in high and public places.

The Moriarty Tribunal, the follow-on from another tribunal which started its investigations in 1997, is still running, exploring alleged bribery and corruption involving the former Taoiseach Charlie Haughey and various others from the 1970s into the 1990s. This tribunal has uncovered wider issues of fraud and corruption involving a broadening number of people using illegal offshore bank accounts to evade paying taxes.

But the tribunal most in the news at the moment is the Flood Tribunal which is investigating allegations that a couple of politicians around Dublin took bribes in exchange for giving planning permission for various property developments. One of the politicians called to give evidence, Liam Lawlor, has been sent for a stint in jail (he's been there once before) for failing to comply with orders of the tribunal and present the information it has requested. What amazes me is that elected representatives are quite happy, and able, to keep wasting the taxpayers', their employers', money by endlessly stringing out the investigations.

At times I get the impression that while people are frustrated by such antics, there is an air of inertia about the matter. It may well be that as other, ordinary people started enjoying the new prosperity of the Celtic Tiger era, tolerance for the 'fine rogues' was reinforced.

Just before three o'clock I head over to the post office at Annascaul to make the final collection. Almost every trip to the post office so far has resulted in something of a wait. Sometimes there's a queue but even when you're the only customer, you are still  kept waiting as the postmistress disentangles herself from what sound like intriguingly complex telephone conversations. Today the wait is extra special as a customer has some very large, wide and flat packages to be weighed. After the weighing – a lengthy affair in itself – is at last completed, negotiations commence over the use of some sort of special credit card to pay for the postage. It is clearly an unusually elaborate conundrum and even when the postmistress's friend is consulted, at length, on the phone, no solution is discovered. It's cold in the building and those of us in the queue are shifting from foot to foot and rubbing our arms. The woman with the parcels eventually elects to come back tomorrow for another attempt to sort it out. The transaction, or rather lack of it, is all low-key, very polite and with many apologies passing between the main players and also offered to their growing audience. A man comes in and exchanges a few words with people he knows in the line. He stands there for a while holding a couple of envelopes and then looks at them, realizes they have stamps on and says a bit sheepishly, 'I might as well put these straight in the box!'

A shame we didn't have a mind like that on our quiz team, I muse.

The post box is curiously positioned. It's at knee height which is fine for small children but inconvenient for taller folk, and for anyone who has any stiffness in the back, positively exasperating. Having got down on one knee, I push my envelopes through the flap and then let out a howl of pain. My fingers are caught in a vice-like grip. Gingerly I use the other hand to push the flap open against its powerful spring and release my stinging digits. A red weal appears between the first and second knuckles but mercifully no blood. I know the post is meant to be secure once in the box but fitting a mantrap is taking things a little too far, I'd say.

# CHAPTER SIX

INCH COMMUNITY CENTRE, FORMERLY THE KILLEENAGH National School, built in 1883 as a plaque on the wall announces, is heaving – clearly the Auction of Work is as popular as I've been told.

'The man with the mike up on stage, that's Mick O'Connor. We call him Micko, he's the auctioneer,' explains Kathleen Daly as I take a seat behind her at the back of the hall. I've met Kathleen and her husband Donal at Foley's Pub a couple of times, and am pleased to feel that I'm not a complete blow-in nowadays.

'Where's himself?' I ask.

Kathleen points out Donal who is also up on the stage and appears to be writing down the results of the bids. 'He's chairman of the centre this year.'

Although it's already around ten thirty at night there are still many young children about. Kathleen's little boy Patrick keeps presenting his mother with trophies he's won at the lucky dip, and then scooting off clutching another coin for a further go.

'More tights!' she groans, laughing as he bounds back again.

'No, Paddy, if you want more money you'll have to ask your daddy.'

With an 'Oh Mam!' Patrick disappears into the throng of adults and older children who are moving around selling books of raffle tickets as Micko, Donal and their aides do the business up on the stage. The place is full of noisy good humour and smiling faces. I catch Bridie Foley's eye across the room and we nod hello. Little Patrick is back, the corners of his mouth so far down it's impossible not to laugh.

'What did your father say?' Kathleen asks, trying to be serious.

'No!' comes the reply, close to tears. His mother's hand takes his and his face lights up as he feels a coin pressed into his palm.

A smiling woman emerges from the throng and introduces herself. 'Hello there, I'm Eileen Kennedy. We live down the hill from you – at the Waterside B&B.'

We chat briefly about the weather and tonight's auction. Eileen then casually gives me an amazing piece of information.

'We think my husband, Mike, may be a relation of yours.'

Eileen is laughing as she tells me this; my expression of surprise must be amusing. Half wondering if she's taking the mickey, I say I'd very much like to meet him.

'Drop round anytime. Mike would love to see you.' Then she's off, gathering up two or three little girls as she goes.

Still absorbing this piece of information, I bump into Phil and Mike Courtney and we go into the kitchen area for a cup of tea and a sandwich. I tell them about Eileen's surprise news.

Mike nods, adding calmly, 'And I think you've other family above at Annascaul.'

We don't pursue this as the parish priest Father Tom Crean arrives and the Courtneys introduce us. Softly spoken, dressed in a black suit, grey shirt open at the neck, with the white dog collar in his breast pocket, Father Crean comes across as very relaxed, saying a word or two to everyone and cracking the odd joke. By now it is getting late and he doesn't stay long. As he was there only briefly and had limited interplay with the many people in the hall, I can't work out how his parishioners view him, whether they are comfortable to be chatting with him or a little embarrassed and wishing he'd move on and be nice to someone else.

What a very odd life a priest must have; what a very strange job, come to think of it. A priest leaves home to be looked after – mothered to some degree – by whatever community he serves, where he is accepted as the moral and social guardian of the community although in all likelihood he has had no sexual experience and knows little of relationships between the sexes and none of the dynamics and responsibilities of parenthood. The old joke about the Italian man commenting on the Vatican's dictates against contraception comes back to me: 'You no playa de game, you no makea de rules!'

It doesn't feel like the moment to share a hackneyed gag.

Although midnight is fast approaching, the auction is still in full swing and all manner of items are going under the hammer: cafetieres, lotions and potions, frankly alarming-looking knick-knacks and a fair amount of booze. Despite the general view that things will continue for another couple of hours and that the bidding might well get wilder when people start to arrive after a night in the pub, I decide to head home to my bed. The previous year they raised two thousand pounds for the fund, which is used to give the old folk a special Christmas dinner and then maintain the fortnightly lunches at the community hall and trips to Dingle that Bridey Flynn and her sister Mary had told me they enjoy with their friends throughout the year.

*

Thinking I've missed the post, I start flashing my headlights when I see the van coming along the road towards me. The postman stops and we wind down our windows. As usual he is wearing his flat cap above his post office uniform. In his fifties I guess, the man has a nice smile and I've come to enjoy our brief meetings. Today, blocking the road as we are, there is no time for our usual exchange about the weather and he gets straight down to business.

'Ah, Mack-Car-Tay,' he says. 'I have something for you.'

He hands over a small packet which I trade for a couple of postcards.

'Would you mind taking these?'

'Not at all. Bye now.'

Dingle, like Tralee, has many brightly coloured buildings but is a smaller town with a more relaxed atmosphere. Unlike the rather inappropriately named Castlemaine Harbour that I look over from the cottage, Dingle has a huge natural harbour. Ringed by hills, the harbour has a narrow entrance between cliffs to protect it from the worst of the storms.

Barrington informs me that Dingle was the principal harbour in Munster from the fourteenth century and that at that time Spanish traders came and settled there on the streets which fan uphill from the port area. There is still a large fishing fleet but the number of restaurants, B&Bs, hotels and shops selling gifts or walking/hiking/surfing/swimming gear tells you that tourism is now Dingle's main business.

On Green Street I browse round a bookshop and buy a collection of Patrick Kavanagh's poetry. Father óRíordáin had quoted him and I'd particularly liked one poem he'd written for his mother.

## In Memory of My Mother

I do not think of you lying in the wet clay
Of a Monaghan graveyard; I see
You walking down a lane among the poplars
On your way to the station, or happily

Going to second Mass on a summer Sunday –
You meet me and you say:
'Don't forget to see about the cattle –'
Among your earthiest words the angels stray.

And I think of you walking along a headland
Of green oats in June,
So full of repose, so rich with life –
And I see us meeting at the end of a town

On a fair day by accident, after
The bargains are all made and we can walk
Together through the shops and stalls and markets
Free in the oriental streets of thought.

O you are not lying in the wet clay,
For it is a harvest evening now and we
Are piling up the ricks against the moonlight
And you smile up at us – eternally.

Although the scenery is not what I had shared with my mother, the simple intimacy and warmth is something I immediately recognize. It echoes the comfort I'd found in the thought that even though my mother had left this world and for a year I did not know it, she'd been a very real presence in my thoughts and in that way could always be with me. Now I'm working on the grieving process and while I'm aware that I have some distance to cover before I can get back to having that sort of easy relationship, things have been moving and it's becoming normal to say hello to her along with Anna, my father and brother when I see their pictures on the mantelpiece each morning. I'm daring to look forward to that state of resolution and eternal smiles that Kavanagh speaks of.

Walking on down Green Street I'm overcome with a sudden feeling of tranquillity. The air is still and cool, yet almost balmy, and though the sky is overcast, there is a soft light. In this peaceful atmosphere a woman cycles steadily uphill (the wrong way on a one-way street), and calls out a greeting to a little gnome of a woman who is walking the other way. The shrill shouts of a couple of young boys in their Kerry football shirts might be the cries of gulls.

'Whatever it really was, it's taking up valuable parking space!' Tim Collins points at the 'Holy Stone' of Dingle as he drives his minibus up Goat Street on the way out of Dingle.

The stone in question is a great hunk of red sandstone which has been lying about since the Ice Age and is now neatly 'parked' by the modern kerb. To what degree it is holy is the subject of debate. Certainly it is holey in that it has pockmarks across its surface, though whether these were used in pagan ritual or for grinding corn is unclear. As ever, the history isn't too exact.

Leaving Dingle we pass the hospital which started life as a workhouse. During the years of the Great Famine, between 1845 and 1849, thousands of people came to this place, and many died here. Ireland was no stranger to famine; over the previous three hundred years the country had endured periods of starvation as severe as the Great Famine, just as mainland Europe had, but this was the last and most clearly remembered in folk memory.

Reading about it and now talking to Tim has made me realize

how complex the history of the famine was. There are some basic facts: three million people were dependent on the potato as their staple diet, thus when the crop failed year on successive year, affected by a virulent blight, the scale of the human disaster was necessarily enormous. The smaller tenant farmers and labourers suffered most and the population of Ireland dropped from 8.2 million by nearly 2.5 million during the period. Around one million people died, the majority through disease rather than starvation. One and a half million people emigrated.

I've always assumed that this tragedy was a defining moment in Irish history, that hatred of the English government and the absentee landlords reached its zenith at this point and that a sudden change to the Irish rural way of life was brought about through death and emigration. The more I learn of this period, the more I realize that all these elements are only true to a degree, they cannot paint a complete picture. Suffice it to say those who have spent years studying the issues are still evolving their theories. What surprises me is that emigration had continued at a growing pace throughout the century before the famine, and the exodus from Ireland persisted thereafter. Indeed, as I'd heard on the radio, it is only in the very recent past that immigrants have started outnumbering emigrants.

As we drive along, Tim, a retired officer in the Garda who now runs historical tours of the Dingle peninsula, points out small ridges left by old cultivation high up the mountainside, abandoned, as far as he knows, when the crop failed during the famine. Some of these high fields were farmed before the famine, showing that the population was growing bigger and bigger and every inch of good and often less good land was needed for crops. There were forty to fifty thousand people living on the peninsula in the nineteenth century; now there are some ten thousand.

According to Barrington, as much as 40 per cent of the

population of the peninsula – from just east of where I live at Inch to the Atlantic – died or left during the decade from 1841. The horror and misery for the population over that ten-year span can barely be imagined from the comfortable and plentiful perspective of the early twenty-first century. After that, people left steadily right up until the final decade or so of the last century.

Mike Courtney has told me that while the population had only dropped a little in his lifetime, there are clusters of old, deserted houses in every townland. Up the next track, or passage as he calls it, from the Courtneys' house, which is in the townland of Caheracruttera, there are now a couple of homes. There used to be ten houses up there; given that they had larger families then, Mike reckons there might have been a community of up to one hundred people living there. As in many other small centres, the events of the nineteenth century ripped their hearts from them.

As Tim steers the minibus along the narrow roads he gives me all manner of information, conveyed in a simple, digestible form befitting a retired police officer. Hedges of fuchsia line most of the roads we are following, their vivid red flowers contrasting with the greens that dominate the views. Tim explains that fuchsia arrived from South America, probably from Chile, along with other subtropical species like the palms at the bottom of my drive, early in the nineteenth century. My direct Irish ancestor James MacCarthy had left Kerry by 1818, according to his sister Mary's deposition in that year, so it occurs to me that these plants, now such an intrinsic part of the landscape, would have been alien to him.

Tim, well turned out in collar, tie and jersey, has a quiet way of speaking. He freely admits that his is an amateur knowledge and that if I need really detailed history of the area I should talk to his son. When I explain that I'd heard an archaeologist talking on the radio and made preliminary efforts to get in touch with him before hearing about Tim from Pat Foley he asks, 'What was the radio man's name?'

'Well, I won't be able to say it properly as it's Irish, but I've got it here in my notebook. I dare say you've heard of him.' I hold out the pad to him.

Tim looks at the name and laughs. 'Oh, I've heard of him. He *is* my son.' He points at the name, Miceál O Coileán. 'O Coileán is Irish for Collins. He likes to use that.'

As we continue on along the peninsula heading away from Dingle, round the Ventry Bay and on along the coast road towards Slea Head, I begin to wonder whether a tour by the archaeologist son would include some of his father's data. One minute Tim will be telling me about the most ancient times: 'The first settlement in the peninsula dates back to 4500 BC.' Then he'll slow the van to point out a wide field perched on dramatic cliffs with the sea behind. The location of a prehistoric settlement perhaps, or the site of an Iron Age battle? 'That's where they filmed some scenes for *Far and Away*, with Tom Cruise and Nicole Kidman.'

Looking at the Ordnance Survey map, I can see that this little area, a narrow strip of rough land between Mount Eagle and the sea, has a huge number of red symbols on it, indicating ancient sites. Tim confirms what I've read in Barrington (I can imagine the two men getting on famously), that this four-mile strip of coastline has a concentration of archaeological remains unsurpassed anywhere in Ireland. And they make movies here too! What more could one want?

His talk of films almost takes us past the Dun Beg promontory fort. Dating from as early as 500 BC, the site is right on the cliff's edge, a real 'backs to the wall' place. A great drystone wall seals off the approaches and there are defensive ditches within this before you get to the living area. Archaeologists have found little debris on the site so they surmise it was used only occasionally, perhaps by intruders setting up a base camp or by locals under threat, as a last retreat. Although its origins go back half a millennium before Christ, it could have been in use until AD 1000.

During its active life it saw the rise of the Firbolg (those Men of Bags), the Celtic tribe whose local branch was called the Corcu Duibne and who probably built the place. These in turn became the subjects of the Gaels, and then were gradually converted to Christianity.

Accounts of the legends and sagas of the invasions of Ireland that have been written for the amateur historian like myself are usually split up into discernible and separate time zones, making them easier to understand. In reality, however, there was a confusing overlap of the people and their powers and their faiths, periods of conquest, periods of more peaceful coexistence and then the eventual disappearance of the weaker group, as with the Corcu Duibne, who seem to have evaporated altogether in the twelfth century.

At Slea Head we pause to take in the spectacular view of the Blasket Islands. The islands were inhabited until 1953 when the very hard life of fishing and subsistence farming ceased to be viable. The islands are mainly unoccupied now except during the summer when the largest island, Great Blasket, is visited by day-trippers and some who stay longer to study the islands' history and the Irish language. Back in the seventeenth century the islands were owned by the Ferriter family. They'd come to Ireland as part of the Anglo-Norman invasion that started in the twelfth century. Four hundred years later they were thoroughly Gaelicized and the head of the family, Pierce, or Piaras, was a leader in the rebellions against the English. He had a castle and hideout on Great Blasket. Looking through the binoculars I can imagine that these bleak outcrops would feel safe as a final refuge, with the thousands of birds that wheel and circle above them acting as your sentinels.

The southernmost island, Inishvickillane, provides something of a hideout for a more recent Irish leader, the former Taoiseach Charles Haughey. The Moriarty Tribunal has been investigating alleged payments made by businessmen to Haughey while in office. Tim has that curious Irish attitude to those who've fallen under suspicion of having had their hands in the till.

'He did a lot for the country,' he says with a sigh.

Looking down from Dunmore Head to Blasket Sound I appreciate another reason why the islanders might finally have chosen to call it a day. Even in calm conditions the tides here are fearsome; we watch as a powerful fishing boat, at times slowed almost to a standstill, pushes round Slea Head and on to the safety of Dingle harbour. On 1 October 1588 the *Santa Maria de la Rosa*, a 945-ton vessel and part of the Spanish Armada, didn't have the power to round the headland and came to its end. One or two other vessels went down in these waters in the stormy conditions. Very few of the great fleet made it back to Spain. Nearly every crewman from an Armada ship that made it to the Irish shore and sought safety is believed to have been killed by the English.

The ruins of the medieval church in Dunquin are in sight of the Blaskets. Tim tells me that on bad days when they couldn't make the crossing to get to Mass, the islanders would stand on one of the island's cliffs so that they could see and be in communion with their church. The image of this remote congregation, probably in pouring rain, looking across the storm-tossed waters of Blasket Sound, saying their prayers in approximate time with their neighbours in the church, speaks movingly of a strong faith and particular character. Looking at the grave of Tomas Ó Criomhthain I cannot doubt the words of the epitaph, taken from his book *The Islander*, one of a number of books written by island folk about their life: 'the likes of us will never again be there'.

Dunquin is disappointing given the spectacular approach to it round Slea Head and there seems to be a great deal of execrable building going on there. Perhaps I have a romantic visitor's eye but I grimace at the ugly bungalows that are replacing or obscuring the older buildings which, to my mind, blend in far more harmoniously with the landscape. Recently, planning laws have become much more stringent so maybe such monstrosities, particularly the lime and puce Southfork style favoured here, will become a thing of the past. Many of the modern buildings aren't even serving local residents but are only used in the holiday season. Tim informs me that at Dunquin the ratio is 2–1 holiday cottages to homes.

Tourism in the area received a real boost after the 1970 release of David Lean's film *Ryan's Daughter*. Most of the film was shot on location around the peninsula in 1969, bringing with it a huge amount of money and the added bonus of showcasing the area's natural beauty with glorious photography. In a way it's ironic that in this film, which concerns the important issues of loyalty and betrayal in an Ireland building a revolution against the British, virtually every major character was played by an American or English star, many of whom could only manage the most approximate Irish accent.

Tim pulls the van onto the verge and points to a lonely, largely derelict building.

'That was the school.'

'A long walk from the village.'

'Oh no, the village was quite near. They knocked it down.'

'After the famine?'

'No, after they'd finished filming.'

The drama of Ireland's real story is represented in all its stages on the Dingle peninsula. There are the shell dumps in the Inch dunes, and forts such as Dun Beg testify to settlement in the Iron Age by the likes of the Firbolgs who were then overtaken by Gaelic culture. Then came the Christians. Tim echoed what I'd been surprised to read in Barrington, that when the Christian missionaries arrived, they weren't moving into a remote, un-inhabited region. On the contrary, it's likely they were attracted by the prospect of spreading the word to an already established society.

But though a local king would bend at the knee to a more powerful neighbour, Ireland had not experienced the rigid organization of the Holy Roman Empire and so lacked any centralized form of government. This frustrated the Christian norm, attempted by St Patrick, of having territorial dioceses with bishops controlling the clergy in their parishes. So mission-aries moved into an area and were well received, their new faith fitting in with the Celtic pagan religion, as I'd heard from Father óRíordáin. And the new faith was not so rigid that it couldn't see the advantage of blending in some existing customs. Communities grew and saw the evolution of independent monasteries. It wasn't until the twelfth century that the diocesan framework began to take hold, after some six centuries of local independence.

Autonomy of a more extreme form flourished before the development of the monasteries. A great many hermits set up their simple homes in the area. Some were solitary while others lived in small groups. Tim takes me to Reask, near Ballyferriter, which was a sixth-century settlement of monks. Five or six monks would have lived here. There are two sections, the temporal and the holy areas, with a small drystone oratory. These monks obviously spent as much time at their devotions and as little time in the kitchen as possible. They built their oven with a flue to catch the prevailing breeze and get the fire going and the supper cooked in a jiffy.

A couple of miles away is the Gallarus Oratory, a remarkable place. This drystone chapel probably dates from the tenth or eleventh century. Larger buildings and mortar came with the Anglo-Normans from early in the thirteenth century onwards.

After centuries of relative peace, the peninsula, like the rest of the country, entered centuries of warfare and suffering. The Irish fought the Irish and then they fought the Anglo-Normans. After they'd been here long enough to have become Gaelicized, the Anglo-Normans took on the English. During the Desmond wars of the late 1500s the Fitzgerald family brought in troops from Europe. At the site of a little fort on a promontory overlooking Smerwick Harbour, Tim shows me a simple yet powerful piece of modern sculpture. A column of granite has a series of faces carved on it commemorating the massacre of six hundred of the foreign troops by the English Lord Deputy, Lord Grey. According to some histories, our gallant Sir Walter Raleigh might have been part of that bloody action.

Fifty years after the Desmond wars a nationwide rebellion against Elizabeth I led by the O'Neills from the north of the country saw another period of great hardship for the population. The Confederate War followed, beginning in 1641 as a battle against the crown and ending in defeat by Cromwell's Parliamentarian forces in 1653. The region was in a state of utter devastation from the constant warfare. Many died through famine caused by the scorched-earth policies of the aggressors.

Piaras Ferriter was a local leader in this rebellion. His hideout on the Blasket Islands proved insufficiently obscure and he was executed at Killarney by English soldiers in 1652. This is one of the few periods when the MacCarthys of Ardcanacht come out of the historical woodwork. In his book *The MacCarthys of Munster*, Samuel Trant MacCarthy says that the family, or sept, had part of its lands granted to Trinity College, Dublin, in 1597.

Why this happened isn't explained, although it suggests that my forebears were losing their grip on things. Half a century later, Samuel records, they were still on a downward slide. 'In 1641 the remaining possessions of the sept, then held by John MacFinin Carthy of Ardcanaght, were confiscated by Cromwellians.'

On the drive back to Dingle we pass a particularly vividly painted house and I ask Tim if it's always been the fashion.

'No,' he says, 'people just started thinking that whitewash was a bit dull and wanted to liven things up a little.'

In these instances, there's a lot to be said for dullness, I'd say.

Although it is only about five o'clock, Foley's is busy when I stop in on the way back from Dingle. From eavesdropping on John Foley's conversation with one of the party, Gabriel, I glean that they've been fishing on the beach. Gabriel has a melodious voice and while I can't share his enthusiasm for lugworms I can imagine clearly the joy he speaks of at spending a day out there in the fresh air, regardless of catching anything.

It turns out that the fishermen are from Boolteens; indeed Gabriel lives next door to Florence O'Sullivan.

'He's a lovely man, a workaholic, mind. And he doesn't take a drink.'

We muse on the wonder of this as we sip our pints. He tells me about his dad's pigs. Two of them were fed the slops from the pub (in those days, when Gabriel was a youth, there were no beers to drink, just the Guinness). The pigs were always lying in the gutter, drunk and happy. When the time came and they were taken off to become bacon, the meat was deemed to be of the finest quality. Gabriel's assertion is that the old advertising campaign was spot on, 'Guinness is good for you!'

The fishing party, who had stopped in for one pint, are clearly settling in for a longer session and the youngest member of the group reluctantly accepts that he will be staying to drive his father and pals home. He ruefully orders another soft drink and texts his girlfriend that he won't be seeing her until later. Taking advantage of his enforced moral high ground, he point-blank refuses to sing when called upon. His friends all tut and Gabriel confides in me, 'It's a shame, he has a fine voice.'

There follows a kind of happy ritual as they banter each other into singing.

'Go on now, give us a song!'

'No, I couldn't be doing that. Oh, all right then!'

The quality of the singing is entirely immaterial; everyone listens quietly during the song and gives a proper round of applause at the end. Fortunately they are all too sensitive to ask me to have a go. But Fidelus, who has taken over from John behind the bar, isn't allowed off the hook and sings something sweetly too.

Being from Boolteens the fishermen know Ardcanacht well. When I tell Gabriel of my connection there he calls on one of his neighbours to give us 'The Rose of Ardcanacht'. This man says that he can only remember a couple of verses and no one is sure how far back the song, about a beautiful girl from Ardcanacht, goes.

Although I feel at home in the bar I wish so much that I knew some songs and had the nerve to sing them. Perhaps one needs to feel a profound sense of belonging, of being entirely at one with a community and culture, to have the ability to stand up and sing in that way. The one time I did sing in a pub was some twenty years before when, very drunk in a London bar, I'd joined with an old man, even more drunk, in a couple of slurred attempts at 'I Belong to Glasgow'. The barman had appeared and said, 'I don't care where you think you belong, it ain't here, clear off!'

When I get back to the cottage, I soon have the fire roaring in the grate. There may be more efficient ways of heating the house and of using the earth's resources but there is something so elemental about fire and the warmth it gives is so personal. You make and tend the fire and it gives you comfort and a place to dream in, forgetting the cruel cold world outside. Although it's been a beautiful day, the clear sky indicates that the night will be cold. A distant flock of birds swoops over the harbour as the last of the day's light melds with that of the rising moon. The Cromane shore looms mysteriously through the dusk. Anything could emerge from those shadows – sea serpents, Vikings carrying blazing torches, or Stephen Courtney on his tractor.

When I step out to get more peat I feel a fine rain, a heavy mist really, on my face. It tingles on my skin and generates an inner excitement too that makes me think again of Father óRíordáin's words about the affinity for nature in the Celtic world. But why this should be a particularly Irish or Celtic thing I'm not sure. Standing in the wet and laughing as the light rain turns heavier might be though. Is this some Irish sensitivity in me, a Celtic bent in my soul coming through, or is it just that I'm still new to Ireland and revelling at being here on this hillside fetching the peat? Am I reacting to the place or engaging with it? Am I becoming part of the landscape or is it becoming part of me? Or have I merely had too much Guinness for one night?

Having had some supper (after a few weeks of enjoying preparing and cooking my food I've rather lapsed into bunging something ready-made and frozen into the oven) I stoke up the fire, enjoying its warmth and the memories of a stimulating day out and the pleasure of the singsong at Foley's. I take up the photograph of my mother and me by the Ogham stone and laugh.

'There you are, the Rose of Ardcanacht!'

And I remember her saying, 'One day you'll find an English rose to marry.'

I have, I think as I look at the picture of Anna. It's such a bloody shame you never knew her.

And then my mind clouds, remembering things I'd been bothered by as a youth and wanted to talk to her about when I got back home from Beirut. Issues that we never got to resolve.

Relationships weren't something we ever spoke about in any detail, and talk about sex was definitely off the agenda. We often used to laugh remembering how as a small boy I'd always groan at the love scenes that inevitably interrupted the action in Westerns. My parents found it funny. It was no doubt the reaction of countless little boys but somehow the re-telling of it was emblematic of a taboo on the discussion of sexual relations. Of course many other parents, especially of that generation brought up between the wars, would have been anxious not to encourage permissiveness in their offspring, but I'm still saddened that there was a formality, a lack of open emotional interchange between us in spite of the openness we had in almost all other areas. I still smart when I remember my mother saying, 'Is she a nice girl?' when I told her of a new girlfriend. In all likelihood, it was the first thing that came into her head. Indeed she probably went on to ask more sensitive questions, ending up with an open invitation for the girl to come and stay. Looking at her picture I think: But it's that first reaction that hurts me now as it did then. It feels like you didn't trust my judgement, didn't respect me, I suppose.

It saddens me and reminds me how much I wished that I'd gone to a local school so that home, school and social life would have been a much tighter mix. Friends would have been around the house more and my parents would have been involved in that world. I think then I'd have known my parents better and they me. Alongside fond memories and a longing for home during the years in Beirut this had gradually developed into a resentment that my parents had sent me away, and a feeling that they somehow didn't approve of me. I could see that I'd ended up moving between two worlds, living and working in London and spending quiet weekends at home.

When feelings and thoughts are not expressed they can evolve on their own and create avenues of experience and memory that bear little reference to one's path in reality. Long ago I resolved all these worries with my father but some of those feelings still remain with regard to my mother; perhaps it's simply because we never had the chance to talk about them as adults. I made the leap with my father from childhood to adulthood but hadn't bridged the gap with my mother. There seems to be a time lag between reaching maturity in the outside world and reaching it with your parents. I read again Kavanagh's poem about his mother but I feel distanced from it now. Luckily I'd bought another collection, of W. B. Yeats's poetry, and find:

### The Two Trees

Beloved, gaze in thine own heart,
The holy tree is growing there;
From joy the holy branches start,
And all the trembling flowers they bear.

Gaze no more in the bitter glass
The demons, with their subtle guile,
Lift up before us when they pass,
Or only gaze a little while;
For there a fatal image grows
That the stormy night receives,
Roots half hidden under snows,
Broken boughs and blackened leaves.
For all things turn to barrenness
In the dim glass the demons hold,

The glass of outer weariness,
Made when God slept in times of old.

Thy tender eyes grow all unkind:
Gaze no more in the bitter glass.

I think to myself, there, I've told you now, and it's all right. It isn't such a big deal, it just needed to be said.

'Nice day,' I say, smiling at the postman, competing to get the greeting in before he can.

He merely raises my bid.

'*Beautiful* day!' he replies forcefully, laughing as he hands me a letter. It is from my cousin Jean over in County Cork and includes a copy of a letter to Jean's grandfather from a Captain Jeffray McCarthy. The letter, written in Durban in May 1934, refers to his grandfather James who was born in Tralee in 1789. His letter endorses the affidavit sworn by Mary Supple (née McCarthy) in Tralee in 1818.

Jean also encloses an article about the Battle of Knocknanuss which took place in County Cork in 1647. This was an action in the long-running Confederate War that started as a revolt by Catholics in 1641. I've already been hearing and reading about it locally with regard to Pierce Ferriter. It began with massacres of Protestants in Ulster but rapidly spread countrywide. Beyond that my understanding of the unfolding of the war has become ever more confused. The rebellion at various stages included Irish and Old English groups, Protestants fighting alongside Catholics, sometimes for an independent Irish government, sometimes for the King in England. Generals led armies for the King then switched to fight for the English Parliament. Essentially, and I'm beginning to accept that if one has the slightest notion of chronology or participants, one is doing quite

well, this long-drawn-out conflict was fought by the Catholic
Confederacy, first against the crown forces of England and then
against the Parliamentary forces. The Catholic cause failed and
left the English with an even stronger grip on the country.
Knocknanuss was one of the major defeats in the south-west.
Jean points out that included on the list of Irish who mustered
for the battle were 'From Ardcanaghty north of the Maine came
Fineen and Eoghan McDaniel McCarthy . . .'

The general commanding the Parliamentarian side was
Murrough O'Brien, first Earl of Inchiquin. Even the most
cursory look at his life gives one an object lesson on the complex-
ities of Irish history, politics and religion. Thus: the O'Briens had
been the ancient Kings of Thomond (in modern County Clare)
and had regularly fought against English expansion. In the sixteenth century the general's namesake had done a deal with the
crown and become Earl of Thomond and Baron Inchiquin.
Murrough, from a junior branch of this family, was born a
Catholic in 1614. He converted in his youth to become one of the
leading Gaelic Protestant Royalists. During the Catholic
Confederate War he was governor of Munster and won various
battles for the English crown, but as the Civil War continued in
England, Murrough, in 1644, shifted his allegiance to the
Parliamentary side. Sometime after his victory for Parliament at
Knocknanuss he returned to the Royalist fold. After Parliament's
victory in the Civil War and Cromwell's destruction of opposition in Ireland, he went into exile with the Stuart court, where he
was made Earl and reconverted to Roman Catholicism.
Following the restoration of Charles II in England, he returned
to Munster and his estates. Thanks to Murrough's abilities and
those of his successors, the O'Briens continued as one of the few
Gaelic families who were still major landowners in the eighteenth century. So there it is, a very Irish story.

*

Admiring the large portrait of John F. Kennedy I ask if he was a family hero.

'He was someone, I'd say, special for me. I bought that painting at the time he died.'

Maureen Fitzgerald's home at Ballinagroun is about halfway between my cottage and Foley's Pub. Bridey Flynn had told me I should drop in and see her as she'd known James MacCarthy of Inch very well.

Maureen steps out of the living room for a moment and comes back with a wooden shield with a cameo bust of Bobby Kennedy on it.

'I have a son in America and he was doing up this house for the Kennedy family's doctor and he gave him the bust,' she tells me. 'It actually did come out of Robert Kennedy's house. Bobby gave it to the doctor and the doctor gave it to Michael and he gave it to me.' Maureen starts laughing. 'The story goes that the doctor absolutely hated them! Even though he was their doctor!'

Maureen goes out to make some tea and I sit down, enjoying the fabulous outlook from the picture window which takes in the eastern shore of Inch Island, Castlemaine Harbour and MacGillycuddy's Reeks. I lay out that part of the McCarthy family tree which has details of James's immediate family.

Maureen comes back with tea and cakes and when we are settled I ask what she had made of James.

'Well, I thought he was a very nice man but some people didn't like him.' She laughs. 'Maybe they were jealous of him. How would you put it? He was what we called one of the "big people" at the time, so naturally some people didn't like him. But in twenty years he never gave out to me, he was perfect to work for.' She pauses for a moment, laughing again. 'Now James wasn't a real crook, but he was a bit of a rogue.'

Maureen's warm laugh is never far from the surface and her

whole manner is of someone younger than her sixty-four years. With a soft yet rich voice, she takes her time to answer my questions.

Her family home was at Aughils, a couple of miles east of my house, and she attended the National School at Killeenagh, now the community centre.

'There were two rooms and two teachers. In the small room there'd be low infants and high infants, first and second classes, and then in the bigger room, there'd be the third, fourth, fifth and sixth classes.'

She went to work for James when she was seventeen.

'I did the housework, I did everything!' she laughs. 'He had a horse and we'd round up the cattle and the sheep down on the peninsula.'

James bought sheep and fattened them for all the big farmers up in County Kildare. As well as the peninsula, he had land behind the old house, going up to Inch Heights and the mountains.

'Where the new houses are, Inch Cottages?' I ask.

'Yeah, and he had two men working as well. Bridey's husband Jimmy Flynn was one of them, as you know.'

The shop on the beach looks fairly new but there is a fading sign on a dilapidated building nearby that has the word 'Stores' on it. I wonder if this had been going when Maureen was working with James.

'The old sign is on what was a cattle house. We used to bottle milk down there. No pasteurizing then, we put it straight from a cooling tank into the bottle. The stores were where they are now but they've been extended. We didn't sell the arts and crafts stuff they have now, but we did teas and suchlike for the coaches. We made scones, apple tarts and things, and stocked groceries. You had a lot of tourists during the summer. On James's caravan and tent site there'd be about eighty families, huge it was. The people who bought it after James died closed it down. A pity really.'

Old Inch House had burned down by the time Maureen went to work with James but she had got to know it as a girl because she had a brother working for James.

'Oh, it was beautiful; now it was beautiful. And there were beautiful antiques there. They only lived in half of it and let the other half. It was a grand house, not like a stately home you know, but big rooms.'

Looking at the family tree, Maureen says she never knew James's parents Justin and Anne but had known some of his younger siblings. There were eleven children altogether. The five girls were all educated in England and one, Julia, became a nun, Mother Christina. Another sister also settled in the UK, marrying an Englishman. Maisie, Maureen explains, stayed at home with James even when he was married. She died before him. The other two sisters owned the Strand Hotel. They sold it sometime back in the fifties and retired to Dublin.

Of James's five brothers Maureen had only known Hilary.

'Oh, he was a lovely man and he was as straight as a die, he was totally. He was a bank manager and he was very good to the farmers. They were telling me that and I'd well believe it.'

But the others she didn't know and can remember nothing about the oldest, Justin. The next one, Florence, she recalls went to America and she reckons died there. The next two, Patrick and John, had gone to England. 'One of them, I think they called him Jack, he was going to join the priesthood. He left and never came back again. I think they were killed during the war, both of them, in the First World War.'

I've been noticing that a lot of people, the older ones anyway, have a particular way of rolling their 'r's and making an 'e' sound like a short 'i'. So Kerry becomes Kirrry. Also 's' often is said as a 'sh'. Maureen agrees that this is a particular feature of the Kerry accent. She's been referring to the various men called

Justin as Jushtin (there are a hell of a lot of them in the McCarthy family, it hash to be said), and I find myself saying the name both ways and asking her which is correct.

'Oh, I suppose it's Justin really, it's just the way we say it.'

She goes on to tell me of yet another Justin McCarthy, this one living, who has a farm at Clash up near Annascaul. While I was in Lebanon there had been talk in the area that we were related to James of Inch and this Justin's sister had researched the family tree. They'd thought that my father might have been a son of one of James's brothers, Patrick or Jack, who went to England.

'So although my dad wasn't connected quite so directly to James, if this Justin is, then he and I could be distant cousins.'

'Oh, you are! And Michael Kennedy, he lives at Waterside, his father and James were second cousins.'

Eileen Kennedy had told me at the auction they thought we were related and here is confirmation. And now I have another cousin, Justin of Clash I decide to call him. My local, unknown family is expanding rapidly. My mind is whirling with these new Justins, Jameses and Johns.

'But none of James's immediate relatives live here now then?' I ask.

'No. He has a nephew, Hilary's son Jackie, living up north in Sligo, but no one else. We don't know what happened to his son.'

When I'd been here in 1980 with my parents and Terence we'd met a young man, a solicitor, in the hotel who had told us that James's estate was still being fought over.

'His name was Peter something, but he wasn't local as far as I can remember,' I tell Maureen.

'That would have been Peter Callaghan. The white house just above the hotel was his mother, Ann Callaghan's. That house was built on land sold by old Justin (James of Inch's father, I quickly remind myself). Mrs Callaghan died a year or so ago and had her ashes spread on the beach. She loved Inch.'

Maureen pauses for a while then tells me about James's marriage.

As I'd heard from Bridey Flynn, as well as having his own land and animals, James was involved in cattle dealing and shipping. He used to go up to Dublin often and it was through this business that he met his wife Gráinne. Her father was something in the shipping business in Dublin docks. When he got married he left his sister Maisie running the house.

'He didn't want bringing down his wife!' says Maureen laughing. 'And they rented a huge mansion in County Kildare.' She stops and shakes her head. 'It was only six weeks or six months and she had cleared out of the house in Kildare and brought a court case against him for cruelty and everything, which none of us could believe. I'd say if she had been a normal person, they'd have come down to Inch.'

Having borne James a son, Sean, Gráinne had disappeared to New Zealand with her father. The boy had come back to see his father when he was in his teens.

'Sean was perfect when he came from New Zealand.' Maureen sighs. 'But I don't know, he met the Moonies, I think, in England and went to America with them. It was a pity really, because he was a very nice boy. When he came back for the father's funeral he had these robes.'

James had made no will and Gráinne and Sean had come back to claim the estate. There was a prolonged and very costly legal battle between them and James's brother Hilary and nephew Jackie. Eventually the courts settled the peninsula on the son, who sold it, and the house and land above the road on Jackie who subsequently sold it and moved away.

'James left me the shop for while I lived. Then when Gráinne came back that stopped, but then when Jackie got his land the solicitors said the shop was mine for good. So I sold it.'

Maureen looks out of the window for a few moments. 'Do you

know Bishop Casey came in one day to James when he was stay-ing here?'

'The Bishop Casey who was disgraced – had an affair? Didn't he have a child as well?'

'Yes. He's in England now and before that he was in South America. He was a good man. What he did wasn't so bad. Anyway, he had a house on the other side of Inch. He was great friends with one of James's cousins up at Annascaul who was worried that James wasn't going to Mass and that he'd die and go to hell.'

'So did the bishop tell James he had to go to Mass?'

'I wouldn't say that, they only had a talk. It wouldn't do him any good, James was going to make up his own mind.'

'Was he stubborn?'

'Oh, he was, he was a very stubborn man! The local priest tried to interfere when James and Gráinne were separated. The priest said it was wrong so James dropped out of the church, but he used to give generously to the parish priest. He was as religious as anyone apart from he wasn't going to Mass.'

It occurs to me that Maureen must know the peninsula better than most people since she rode and walked all over it when she worked for James. I wonder what her thoughts on the proposed golf course are.

'Before my time there was a golf course there, not a proper laid out one though. I think a golf course would be terrific. You wouldn't notice it – it's a thousand acres down there.'

'Was it true they used to have races and games on the beach?'

'Oh yes, but that was before I was born. Down on the peninsula, somewhere in the middle, there was a race course. There were tents and everything down there for the races.'

'Do you still like to go down there?'

'I haven't been down there since it was sold. I used to like to go right up, about a mile or so, in the car and then walk from there. When James had it you could drive the way down, he never stopped anyone a'goin' down. Now they always have the gate to the track locked.' Maureen sighs and nods, saying 'Ah, hah' in that gentle way the women here do. 'When you are down there, there is such peace. There is a peace that you wouldn't get anywhere. Ah, hah. 'Tis lovely down there.'

# CHAPTER SEVEN

PAT FOLEY'S TELEPHONE CALL IS JUST WHAT I NEED. ALTHOUGH it's a warm Sunday morning my mood is like the tide in Castlemaine Harbour, low. A thick haze has reduced the Cromane shore to an indistinct shadow and Inch dunes to a blurred hump.

'Hello, John. If you'd like some lunch we have plenty of food here.' He pauses. Pat usually speaks slowly and deliberately – perhaps his years as a teacher have honed this clarity – and always with a hint of wry amusement. Now he's listening to a voice in the background.

'Máire says we'd love to see you but there's no pressure.'

'I'm on my way!' I say, laughing.

Although I've witnessed fierce weather, howling winds and lashing rain I've only seen snow once while I've been living at Inch. The prevailing southwesterly winds coming in over the Atlantic are warmed by the water of the North Atlantic Drift which gives Ireland a fairly mild climate (at least, its temperature is mild; the roaring gales and bucketing rain that are at times so unrelenting are rarely freezing). This is fortunate for Pat and Máire and their four children, as their spectacular home is at the top of a very steep drive and snow or ice on the ground would mean rather a long walk.

Pat and Máire have become friends and welcome me into their home just as John and Fidelus have. I know I am spoiled with the view from my cottage but whenever I visit the Foleys I still can't help being envious of the 180 degree view afforded by their floor-to-ceiling windows. Sometimes I'm the only guest but more often than not, especially at weekends, there will be other guests, local friends, Máire's sisters and their families, and very often some of the local Foley clan, John and Fidelus (pub hours allowing), sister Ann and mother Bridie.

Pat's told me that his mother, like Fidelus, has a shrewd business sense and took a keener interest in running the pub than his father who'd inherited it but preferred working their farmland that stretched from the road down to the waterside. And Fidelus, who married into the area and life like her mother-in-law, has clearly enjoyed developing the business, extending the pub so that they can take B&B guests and run a full-scale restaurant. Nevertheless they both admit that running such a business is exhausting. Apart from the long hours, living and working in the same building brings its own strains. Fidelus has said that you need to be able to change swiftly from wife and mother to entertaining host as you move from the house to the bar.

Today Bridie is telling me how filming had brought a boom to the business in her day. *The Playboy of the Western World* was being shot on Inch Strand. This was back in 1961 and the stars, extras and production team were flooding around the pub, constantly demanding food and drink and buying up everything in the shop that they ran in the bar in those days. Although she speaks of it as an exciting time it sounds as though she barely had a moment's rest. She was run off her feet doing all the cooking on both an old range and a new electric stove every day of the six-week invasion.

'The smell in the house was terrible,' she says. 'I couldn't eat meat for months afterwards!'

Had the film been made a year earlier, she doubts they'd have coped. 'We had no running water and had to go down to the well by the bridge to fill up enamel jugs each day.'

So what did the canny Bridie make of James MacCarthy?

Her eyes narrow slightly. 'He was a *plámáser*,' she says but then finds it hard to give a precise translation for this Irish word. Chancer, conman, charmer are suggested and all appear to go part of the way.

'Rogue?' I suggest.

'He was a rogue all right!' says Bridie laughing and shaking her head.

Rogue, *plámáser*, I've met people who liked James but was he a bit of a crook too?

'If you sent James a bill for, say, £100 18s 3d, he'd just give you the hundred,' says Bridie, raising an eyebrow. 'So I used to round up the sum before giving it to him!' Squaring her shoulders with the recollection, she continues, 'He was educated and well-dressed and straight up. Those around who worked for him looked up to him, but he wasn't a generous man.'

One day a man had turned up as Bridie was readying the pub for opening. He was very smart in a grey suit.

'A Yank. I thought he wanted a drink, but no, he said he'd lived here as a little boy. He'd worked for James who'd paid him hardly anything, but my husband, Jerry, had treated him to lemonade and sweets. The fellow had come back to say thanks.'

As we are finishing lunch a battered old car struggles up the very steep drive. As Pat opens the front door we hear a voice booming out in a strong Kerry accent. As well as the 'sh' sounds and short 'e's I've already noticed, some Kerry people talk with a pronounced singsong emphasis. I haven't heard anyone do this more dramatically than the local TD (MP). In fact his name works as a good guide for this. If you say it JACKee HEALee RAE you get the idea. I say to Bridie, 'Sounds like Jackie Healy-Rae!'

One of the girls giggles. 'It looks like Jackie Healy-Rae!'

Our laughter turns to open-mouthed amazement since there he is, Jackie Healy-Rae in the flesh, bumbling across the living room, about half the size of a grinning Pat. The politician is on the stump for a general election that hasn't even been announced yet. His attire is a riot all on its own: flat checked cap, tartan checked jacket, dark turquoise shirt and a ghastly seventies blue-patterned shiny tie. Within a minute he's said hello to everyone, handed round his election flyers and is off again in the battered car. Apparently he normally travels in a smart Mercedes, but out to prove his credentials as a man of the people, he's taken to the campaign trail in an old jalopy.

'So, Bridie, would Jackie be a *plámáser* or a rogue?' I ask.

After a moment's reflection she responds, 'Oh, a rogue I'd say!'

Back at the cottage my Irish–English dictionary defines *plámáser* as 'flatterer' which sounds close but it isn't quite right, I can see. It doesn't mean pointless flattery or banter, or flirtation, but the load of flannel you get instead of a straight answer. Whenever the term is used it's tinged with an element of criticism and people, especially women, are irritated by the level of *plámásing* in society. It might seem caring and supportive, but it sidesteps difficult issues, whether on a domestic level or of national concern. Maybe the Irish have been too tolerant of 'rogues' and *plámásers*. A nation so adept at expressing emotions in language and whose history does in many ways reflect a moral struggle is surely well-equipped to deal with its modern challenges in an open and honest way. Of course the ability to tell a tale, even a load of old Blarney, is one of the most appealing characteristics of the Irish and one wouldn't want them to lose it, just to use it to better effect.

Having come to Ireland to explore any darker undercurrents to the happy reality the casual tourist might experience, the more I learn, the more I appreciate the irony of the Irish scene. While the welcome and consideration of the Irish is genuine, in many ways the darker side is not so much an undercurrent as the main stream.

To say the Irish drink a good deal is likely to earn you a laugh – they are famous for it, it's all part of the *craic*. Equally, of course, it's part of the image of the sad Irish drunk lurching around Camden Town or Kilburn in London. But it's shocking to read newspaper reports about how, in the decade to 1999, consumption of alcohol per head of the population had shot up by 41 per cent. Most of their EU neighbours are either decreasing consumption or increasing it only moderately, which suggests that Ireland must be on a binge of avoidance.

At first I'd been amused to read in *The Kerryman* reports of drunken behaviour and arrests but now I've seen so many, in every issue, that any idea of comedy has turned to tragedy. And this is merely the local end of a nationwide increase in drink-related violence. Between 1995 and 1999 there were just over 110,000 public order offences. Yet between autumn of 2000 and the following spring there had been 51,000 such incidents.

While you might expect an increase in revelry to celebrate the successes of the Celtic Tiger and indeed that Ireland would have its share of lager louts, these statistics are sobering.

Commentators also point out that while the rich are getting richer, the poor, as always, are getting poorer and that for the unemployed, unable to share the Tiger's killings, there might be a need to hide in a cloud of booze. In parallel with this issue, there are growing concerns about the number of people, especially young men, who are suffering depression. There is a marked increase in suicides.

It is hard to believe that these statistics apply to this region of Ireland but the local papers confirm that life in the county is far from immune. Since my arrival someone has joked to me that 'Ireland has the biggest carpets in the world; there's so much to sweep under them!' It is some consolation to see that people are trying to bring the problems out in the open and set up programmes to help the victims and educate the abusers.

Almost without noticing, I know the social topography and have found myself feeling a part of the community. Walking down the road to the pub on a Saturday night, a little after ten o'clock now rather than eight, I'll pass houses saying to myself, 'That's where so-and-so lives.'

Taking up what is rapidly becoming my regular stool at the bar with a pint in front of me, chatting occasionally to Fidelus and Martina as they serve the drinks, I'll relax and nod to people as they come in and greet those I know better.

Paddy and Mary O'Brien live about a mile from the pub on the way to the beach. Paddy spent some of his childhood at Inch then lived in London for many years. He's now been back at home for some twenty years yet sounds as though he left London yesterday. He's a stonemason, a skill that has taken him to some of the most beautiful ancient sites in the area. He's currently working on restoring the cathedral at Ardfert, north of Tralee, and he spent many weeks out on the remote and sheer rocks of the island Skellig Michael, restoring the beehive cells where monks used to live. The nature of his work brings him into regular contact with holy places, albeit usually ones that are no longer functioning. Not being tall or desperately slim and with his close-cropped grey hair, I can't help thinking he'd look the part in a monk's habit. But Paddy remains delightfully irreverent. All smiles and eager to chat, his good humour would have been as valuable an asset in a remote and isolated community like Skellig Michael as it is propping up the bar at Foley's. As he talks about working on the island he becomes very enthusiastic, touching my arm and telling me I must get out to see it. 'It's really something else.'

The problem is the weather. Landing is only possible in very calm conditions and even then the Atlantic swell means you have to jump from the boat to grab a ladder.

Tom Barrington echoes Paddy's eagerness. He writes, 'A journey to the Great Skellig is a high point of a visit to Kerry and is not to be missed if a suitable day offers – this is not often.' The place sounds fascinating; you couldn't get anywhere more remote if you fancied a reflective way of life. And it is beautiful. Paddy says the long slog up to the little group of huts is worth it for the sense of wildness and space. Barrington waxes lyrical: 'How beautiful it is here on the fine mild days: how terrifying in the wild Atlantic storms!' Paddy and his colleagues sometimes had to stay a few days on the island because of bad weather. What was it like then?

'*Really* something else!' he says, breaking into his customary rumbling laugh.

On my way out a man touches my elbow and introduces himself.

'Hello, I'm Mike Kennedy.' It takes a moment or two for this to register. Then my eyes widen.

'We're cousins, aren't we?'

'I'd say we were.'

Mike is about my height, though slimmer, and he speaks in a fast, sometimes almost staccato manner, his eyes lighting up behind his glasses. He confirms that Justin of Clash is another cousin and says he'll try to arrange for us all to meet up.

When I mention Florence the blacksmith, Mike's eyes sparkle again and he raises his left hand for emphasis. 'That's the most honest man I have ever met.'

He says he'll be in touch soon and we say goodnight with a solid handshake of new kinship. Although I've known of Mike for a couple of weeks now, until this moment he was a complete stranger to me. Now he is blood. It is very odd to accumulate family on a handshake at pub closing time.

A friend had given me a copy of David Thomson's *Woodbrook* before I left for Ireland and I've been enjoying reading it last thing at night. In among his main story, about tutoring the children of an upper-class Anglo-Irish family in County Sligo during the 1930s and 40s, and the historical anecdotes he weaves around them, he lets out little bits about himself which are honest and touching. One line particularly strikes a chord with me: 'It is my misfortune to remember distinctly only the shameful moments in my life. The long happy periods survive diffused.' I know exactly what he means. Why is it that those moments of regret when you misjudged something, made a mistake or behaved badly or unkindly to someone, never seem to lose their intensity in the recollecting? The feelings of distress or shame, even years and years later, remain as sharp as the day the incident occurred. I remember a chemistry lesson when I was about eleven years old. It was a Friday and it was the weekly test, so hardly an important occasion. For whatever reason – I hadn't done the homework or just couldn't answer a question – I sneaked a look at my friend's exercise book. The teacher, a friendly young man fresh from university who always appeared completely laid-back and bored with his job, suddenly leapt at me and booted me out of the class, scrawling 'cheat' across the page in my book. Whether there were any ramifications to this or if I was really worried about them at the time I cannot recall. But the feeling of shame still lives on, glowing as brightly now as did my face as I was ejected from the classroom. Why should such a minor crime be remembered so distinctly yet other occasions, when I might have come top in a test, never emerge from my subconscious?

While I realize, like Thomson, that constantly re-enacting such dismal episodes can blow them out of proportion, I am finding that by letting uncomfortable feelings about myself linger on the surface I enjoy a sense of liberation. It seems to allow the happy periods of my childhood and youth with my family, which I'm sure were long and common, to survive in a less diffused way. In order to rebuild the connection with my mother and bridge that gap to an adult relationship I think it is important to recall as much detail of early events, even when they are excruciating, as possible.

Living in Ireland, scrutinizing the people, reading the papers, watching the television and, though I miss them, being away from the distractions and responsibilities of home life, I am becoming aware of how others live their lives and this is, under the surface at any rate, allowing me to step back from my own existence and impose a useful perspective on it.

At times I think Ireland's landscape and weather set off the lives of its people more dramatically than anywhere else I've visited, apart perhaps from the synchronicity between the terrain, light and heat of the desert and the Bedouin I met in Sinai. Here, though, I speak the same language, so people's feelings and thoughts, mundane as well as reflective, have a more immediate impact. People's moods seem to be directed by the weather and, like it, can change rapidly and profoundly, just as the hilarity and music of the *craic* is counterpointed by melancholy, the dark thoughts and sad eyes behind the Celtic fringe.

One morning I wake up with a start, listen for a moment before I realize it's the wind again, then slump back to sleep. But the storm was only just beginning. By eight o'clock the weather is raging, the bleakest I've seen it. Maybe there have been other days like this but then the wildness and changeability of the place had been strange and exciting. Weather-watching has threatened to become an obsessive pastime and I keep thinking that I'll stop noticing it, but now I find myself transfixed at the cottage window again.

Shades of grey stretch from the shoreline below me. The clouds, the water and hills at times look almost like a caricature, needing only an enormous Stag at Bay to complete a Victorian interpretation of nature at its most rugged. But this view is alive and real. Another squall rips in over the peninsula, snatches up gallons and gallons of water and hurls it in a tumbling foaming cloud hundreds of yards across the surface of Castlemaine Harbour. Suddenly the sun comes out and the rain eases but the wind blows ever harder, carrying clouds of withered leaves where moments before it held drops of water. It is exhilarating but also terrifying. There are no boats out on the water and people won't be leaving their warm dry homes unless they have to. Even the cars and trucks on the road seem to labour against the forces of nature. It can also be depressing; too much of this gloom would wear you down.

A couple of evenings later I pop round at dusk to the Courtneys' place. Phil had appeared at my front door one afternoon to give me a homemade apple pie. It was delicious, but even more than the taste of the pie I savoured her thoughtfulness. I've been looking forward to thanking her again when I return the pie dish, but there are no lights on so, assuming everyone is out, I'm about to leave the dish on the doorstep when Peter, one of Mike and Phil's three sons, appears and opens the sliding door.

'Won't you come in, John?'

Inside the kitchen Phil is sitting at the dining table. She gets up, as ever immediately offering me a cup of tea and urging me to sit. Peter sits too and we chat about the weather and then they tell me that Stephen has had a good day at market selling some cows. I'm asking about prices and so forth, but really want to say, 'Why are we sitting in the dark?'

A figure appears at the far end of the room. When it speaks I realize it is Stephen.

'I'll just put the light on to find my socks,' he says with a laugh, flicking the switch and getting a pair out of the airing cupboard.

'I hear you had a good day at market.'

'Oh yes. A good price, we can't complain.'

As we speak, Phil moves across the room and switches the light off again. There is now barely any light in the room and I imagine they must be on some urgent power-saving mission. Then Phil hesitantly, shyly, explains.

'I hate the short winter days, they're so depressing. I like to leave the lights off as long as possible, then it's like we're not giving in to the night.'

Though I can't imagine Phil raging against the dying of the light, she is making her stand and I sympathize completely.

'Soon the days will be getting longer. It's so lovely here in the summer, it stays light until eleven or half past,' she declares longingly.

There are stories of people living solitary and strange lives up in the valleys behind Inch. It has occurred to me that if I didn't have my outlook over the water, where the boats are often to be seen, and the road, which always provides a glimpse of humanity, however anonymous, cabin fever would be an affliction likely to take hold at an early stage of living here.

Sometimes I've seen fellows in the pubs, well beyond middle age, cracking jokes you'd expect to hear in the schoolroom rather than the public bar. They know all you could want to know about the business of farming but perhaps their lives, often solitary for most of the week, have denied them enough experience of the world.

Some people develop a fear of the outside world and rarely leave their homes. I've heard of curious-sounding ménages of couples and the odd brother, sister, aunt, cousin, living in remote valleys with houses full of animals and each other's junk. Some have built new homes across the road from their dilapidated old stone houses and then never lived in them. There are stories of family rifts and feuds that are only settled over a deathbed. It sounds like the stuff of fiction but here it is all too real.

Often these stories are told with a mixture of amazement and amusement which acknowledges the tragedy of a situation but also the comedy. A farmer was desperately busy – it was lambing season and he was up all hours of the night attending his animals. A depressive neighbour phoned him one night just after a long and difficult delivery. The neighbour was feeling very low; he could see no reason for living. The farmer listened, trying to say the right things. The neighbour went on and on, saying that he thought he'd come to the end of the line. 'Dave, I think I'm going to top myself!'

The farmer had heard this before and was almost asleep on his feet.

'I'm sorry, Liam,' he said, 'I can't be dealing with it any more now. We'll talk tomorrow.'

He hung up and started up the stairs for bed then stopped. 'Oh Jaysus, I lent him my shotgun!'

Inspired by all these stories of the eccentric and the crazed, I make an expedition to see Gleann na nGealt, the Valley of the Mad. In an area of dramatic landscapes, this is a gentle scoop of a valley. The rugged peaks of the peninsula are hidden behind the rounded lips of the valley sides which slope gently down to neatly fenced fields of lush grass with hardly a rock in sight.

Barrington says there is a well where madmen used to drink and eat the cresses that grow by the stream to calm their disturbed minds. He tells the tale of how Fionn, leader of the heroes of the Fianna, eloped with the King of France's daughter. The enraged King rounded up all his allies (including the King of Spain, the King of the World and about seventeen other kings) and arrived just outside Dingle to seek his revenge. There ensued the Battle of Ventry, which allegedly went on for a year and a day. During one of the clashes in this epic fight the King of France was so frightened that he flew (obviously this whole story is historically true in every detail) to the Valley of the Mad to gather his wits again.

Whatever the minimal truth in that story, the remedial quality of the water and cresses continued to draw people here for the cure until the end of the nineteenth century. The librarian of the local history section of Tralee library had shown me a battered old book, published in Dublin in 1847, entitled *Letters from the Kingdom of Kerry*. One of them reported a visit to this valley. It was a place, the correspondent's 'guide sagely assured us, to which all the mad people in the world would flee if they could get loose . . . we took our leave of fair Glengalt, and assuredly if any aspect of eternal nature could work such a blessed change, the repose, peace and plenty of this charming valley would restore the unsettled brain of a poor unfortunate.'

One hundred and fifty years later I find myself in total agreement. Although the well eludes me, I walk beside the stream which ripples along at a comforting burble and around which cresses do grow thickly. Walking up one of the valley's cared for but unused roads, a neat grass strip right up its middle, I feel at peace; it is indeed a place that could calm frayed nerves.

The librarian hadn't given me *Letters from the Kingdom of Kerry* because of the Valley of the Mad but because the letters appeared to have been written by someone called Eagar

McCarthy. As well as the letters themselves, there were various newspaper articles glued inside the covers of this particularly battered copy and a whole swathe of handwritten notes.

As far as I can tell there is no connection between this man's branch of McCarthys and my own. But I feel a certain kinship to him. He was clearly a man who liked to gather snippets of information and try to order them and he liked to write about the places he visited. Eagar by name and eager by nature.

This reminds me of a school report of my father's that we found years and years ago in which he was described as 'an eager little chap'. My mother had loved this and I was proud that through all the tribulations of his later years and right up until his death in 1994 at the age of seventy-three he didn't lose that appealing eagerness one bit.

A different outward route, via Scotia's Glen, enlivens my weekly shopping trip to Tralee. At Boolteens I head uphill on a side road and go over a pass which gives striking views even on a murky day. Today is one of those 'where every prospect pleases' sort of days. Unfortunately radio masts dominate the crest of the pass and I start thinking that while the ancient inhabitants of this part of Ireland dotted standing stones all over the shop to some mystical purpose, we just put up great antennae so our mobile phones can keep us in touch with ever more immediate prattle. No need or desire any more to gather the community together to move large stones to make a monument to the gods or heroes, JCBs rearrange the landscape to accommodate new homes with such little effort.

Barrington has convinced me to come on this new route with his talk of Scotia's grave. Queen Scotia was the widow of Miletus of Spain and she came to Ireland with her sons to conquer the land and its people. My Ordnance Survey map has no site marked nor can I see the name Glanaskagheen that Barrington mentions, so I'm relying entirely on his driving directions. As my acquaintance with Tom Barrington has developed, so has my mental picture of him. I've decided that he was a small man with neat features, rather like Margery Allingham's detective Albert Campion. I imagine him with round spectacles, sensible walking shoes, gloves and possibly a tidy little moustache. At first I'd hoped to be able to meet my Kerry guide in the flesh but, seeing that his book was first published over twenty-five years ago, after his retirement, I thought it unlikely that he'd still be alive. I phoned his publishers in Cork and found that he had indeed died some years before. Doubtless in reality he was a large man who wore modern boots, thermal clothing and drove a Volvo, but I can't erase the image of my guide in a grey suit driving a Morris Oxford.

The road winds downhill and becomes narrow where it passes a dilapidated old farmhouse with piles of junk laced into the hedge opposite and bales of hay weighed down with car tyres.

A big sign 'Scotia's Grave' and a small parking space come into view. A gate leads me to a clear, if waterlogged, path. Occasionally a bird's cry interrupts the clamour of the river but otherwise the descent into the glen becomes a journey into another realm. Dead or dying trees, many hung with teal-green moss, a light dusting on the greying, withered limbs, crowd in around me. The stream surges over its bed of rocks and I keep looking up, expecting someone or something to be there; there is a somewhat sinister air of being watched.

A curious narrow bridge of steel and concrete, a rigid version of those swinging jungle bridges made from creeper, takes me across the spate. When I come to a second gate, a very neat wrought-iron affair that is crazily out of place in this wild environment, I think I must have wandered into a disused set for *The Avengers*. The gate would look more at home in Hove, set in a privet hedge rather than a valley of dying, stunted trees and marsh. I continue, the feeling of distance from the real world growing. I cross another bridge and reach a round stone with a hole cut in its centre, like a millstone, set vertically at the top of three stone steps. Can this be the grave? Barrington describes it as a 'huge slab carved with innumerable names'. If not, what on earth is it? I go on over another bridge. For the first time I begin to doubt my fastidious guide. I'd thought the grave would be only a couple of hundred yards from the road; surely Tom B would have detailed all these twists and turns, the gates and the bridges. Then, on a flat area of grass ten feet above the stream, I see a ring of stones, some of them flat on the ground, others upright. No carvings but someone has had a fire in the place and there are one or two cut sticks planted upright in the ground; perhaps it is the site of some pagan ceremony.

On I go again. The path narrows and becomes muddier and muddier until I can go no further; the stream is fifteen feet below me on one side and the hillside rises steeply on the other. Ahead of me a fallen tree blocks the way. A furious scrabbling in the bushes sets my heart pounding. I look up to see the face of the devil, a horrible contortion of red and blue with wicked-looking horns. Turning too rapidly to escape and save my soul, I slip and nearly fall into the stream. One wellington boot sinks into a foot of mud and I am stuck. I turn to face my tormentor. The beast has moved. The red and blue are the dye the shepherd has used to identify his animal and Satan's horns are your common or garden ram's antlers, one of which I can now see has broken off halfway through its curl. 'Baaa-stard!' I mutter. I wrench my boot from the mud and retrace my steps past the campfire site and over a large outcrop of rock. I stop to scrape mud off the boot and I notice there are names faintly scratched all over the rock, though most are indecipherable and look fairly modern. This is the gravestone.

I'm annoyed with Barrington; this gravestone is patently just a bloody rock. He seems to have been diverted from his customary balance of history, myth and evidence for the sake of a good yarn. On the other hand, and once I've got over the diabolical confrontation, I have to acknowledge that it is not a bad one. In fact there are two versions of Queen Scotia's demise. One has it that she died in a great battle fought in 1695 BC here on the Slieve Mish mountains. Another, more gruesome tale says she used to leap straight over the glen but then tried it when pregnant and fell to her death. According to Barrington, Scotia was the daughter of the Pharaoh and although there is a mysterious atmosphere to echo any occult world that might have been familiar to a princess of Ancient Egypt, it's hard to imagine anywhere further from the Nile than this glen, so narrow and dreary compared to the majestic Valley of the Queens.

I come back to Inch by my normal route via Castlemaine. As the late afternoon has brightened, I carry on to catch the last of the sun's light over the strand rather than going straight home. The cliffs of the Iveragh peninsula to the south and the still waters of Dingle Bay are various shades of purple and gunmetal blue. Away to the west the horizon is a cauldron of molten lava reds and oranges which take me back to watching the sun go down over the Nile at Luxor.

And they even have palm trees here, I think. Maybe the Pharaoh's daughter would have rested peacefully here after all.

The bar at Foley's is quiet, just a couple and two little girls on their holidays. Once she's served them some drinks and crisps, Fidelus makes a pot of tea and joins me at a table outside. We talk about the dramatic change in the weather and the sunset it has brought. As I'm telling her of my trip to Scotia's grave and how I thought the Inch sunset was fit for Pharaoh's daughter, she scans the whole view from the mountains in the south-east to the red sky in the west before observing how easy it is to take

JOHN McCARTHY

it for granted. We sit there sipping our mugs of tea, enjoying the beauty and tranquillity of the evening. Every now and then a car rushes past, just a few feet from us, shattering the peace. But it returns and rather than being irritating, the disturbance somehow adds to the moment.

'The hills are further away when it's fine,' Fidelus says.

I've never noticed this before but it seems true, as if the fair weather which lifts the spirits also offers an even broader horizon to immerse oneself in.

Fidelus goes on to say that according to the men 'up the hill', the farmers who live dotted across the hills and valleys behind Inch, the fine weather alters the light and atmosphere and that's why the hills look more distant. Certainly when the weather is bad and the wind and rain make you shudder, the hills across the harbour close in and sit there, big and glum.

'Inch seems to be encouraging me to think, to remember things about my life and family. Especially about the loss of my mother.'

Fidelus nods her head. 'I'm sure of it,' she says and goes on to tell me how the death of a young brother, Dennis, in a road accident had left her absolutely devastated. 'I couldn't bear the heartache, didn't think I could keep going without losing my mind. I was worried for my children. But walking, on the beach and up the hills, sort of helped the pain go away.'

'When I sit looking out from the cottage window or walk on the dunes, things come into my mind, some uncomfortable, some comforting. But rather than panicking as I've often done in the past,' I tell her, 'I seem to be able to let them be for longer and longer. I suppose part of it's being alone, but even when the gales are blowing there's often a sense of peace.'

'Yes,' she says, nodding slowly, 'even when the weather's bad and closes in, there's still plenty of space here.'

On evenings like this the mountains and seas of Inch are big enough to take in all the sorrow and give one the room and time to work through the grieving process. Not only do the weather and scenery seem to shadow emotional shifts, they give you room to shout and weep; the ideal place for personal 'soft days'.

Late that night the sky is clear, 'starless and bible black'.

# CHAPTER EIGHT

IT'S DRIZZLING AS I WALK DOWN THE TWISTING TRACK FROM MY house to Mike and Eileen's at Waterside. The evening light is failing now but I can still make out the far shore of Castlemaine Harbour where the lights of Cromane village are already twinkling. In many ways the outing couldn't be more normal, just popping round to one's nearest neighbours. But the strange and wonderful thing is that not only are they neighbours, they're also family. I landed at my cottage at Caherpierce effectively by chance. I'd hoped I might find some distant MacCarthy cousins in the Inch area, aside from those I knew about over in County Cork like Jean and Mary, but to have them here, on the doorstep, makes me feel especially welcome, as if the people and the place are all striving to help me settle in and find myself and whatever else it might be that I'm looking for.

The three Kennedy girls, Fiona, Louise and Keara, greet their newly discovered cousin politely before swiftly disappearing into another room from whence issue occasional snatches of a tune as they practise their tin whistles.

Justin McCarthy arrives from his farm a few miles away over the hills at Clash, near Annascaul, shortly after me and the first thing we do is confirm the family connection by looking at the family tree. I trace myself back to Daniel MacCarthy who was born at Ardcanacht in 1736. Justin and Mike are descended from Daniel's elder brother Florence, commonly called Finghin Ardcanachta. Both of them had a grandparent who was a first cousin of James the *plámáser* of Inch. Not such distant relations, it seems.

In his mid-fifties, I'd say, with short grey hair, Justin has the same light, quick way of talking as Mike. He grew up on the family farm he now owns and demonstrates a remarkable memory for stories told to him a long time ago 'at the fireside'. It feels good to be sitting at another fireside listening to my cousins swap tales.

Talking about life back in the fifties and sixties, Justin remembers his amazement at hearing that before Ireland's milk and butter business really took off, the greatest export to the UK had been rabbits. 'Everyone would be out shooting, or I suppose setting the odd snare or two.'

Mike sits listening carefully, his eyes bright with interest behind his glasses. Every now and then when he *has* to interrupt, his hand shoots out, breaking the other's flow, so that he can offer his bit of information, his piece of the story. He's a very sweet-natured man, thoughtful and with a shy sense of humour.

I feel a bit like a spectator at a relay race as they recount their stories; one telling part of it then handing the baton to another for him to run with the tale for a while. It amazes me that they have so much knowledge to share about their district, but in their estimation people nowadays know only a fraction of what earlier generations could tell of family and local history.

Mike remembers that as well as hunting rabbits they used to shoot duck and that Eileen's grandfather, who lived on this farm, had a punt gun for the purpose. Whatever your views on shooting creatures for leisure or even purely for the table, you have to admit it takes some skill to hit a bird in flight with a shotgun. The punt gun, however, represented more of a 'total war' approach to the pursuit of game. This amazing piece of weaponry had a barrel four inches in diameter, which would be packed with shrapnel. The punt would be floated into position and the 'huntsman' would then blast away, not at one bird, but at a whole flock. In March 1921 the IRA saw the potential of this domesticated cannon and took possession of it, at least temporarily.

'There was a lot of commandeering in those days,' notes Justin. They were planning to ambush a British patrol. The punt gun was fixed on a bogie on the old Tralee to Dingle railway line, where it ran beside a bend in the road at Lispole. As you might imagine, the gun had a massive kick so the bogie was secured by rope. A man from Annascaul, says Justin, 'was the kamikaze who was going to fire it'. I don't know if there were any casualties among the British targets of the assault, but two IRA men died, though whether in a hail of British bullets or a storm of their own nuts and bolts I'm unable to report.

Those involved in the Lispole ambush chose different sides when the British left and the Irish started fighting each other. Justin says that although the hero on the bogie had been fiercely loyal to the IRA, there were suggestions that he later informed on them to their opponents in the Civil War, the Irish police of the Free State period. Modern as well as ancient history can be complex when it comes to Ireland.

As with many chapters of Irish history that I've tried to understand, this confusing and tragic time becomes more blurred the closer you examine it. Reduced to its absolute basics it looks like this. The nation had come out of long years of strife and confusion and revolt against the British Empire. The Anglo-Irish War had run from January 1919 until July 1921 when a truce gave room for the two sides to negotiate the Anglo-Irish Treaty. This allowed for the setting up of the Irish Free State. That must have had such a phenomenal ring to it in the early 1920s, Irish *Free* State, after all those centuries of occupation and oppression. But, of course, it wasn't as simple as that. Under the terms of the treaty, Ireland was still part of the British Commonwealth and so effectively subordinate. Michael Collins, hero of the war against the British, who'd earlier taken part in the Easter Rising in 1916, and his fellow Irish negotiators felt that this was the best they could get and that full independence would be easier to achieve once this first step had been made.

This was rejected by a large proportion of the IRA and Sinn Féin, the political party which since 1917 had become the centre of the nationalist movement. Its president, Eamon de Valera, had been a leader of the Easter Rising too. De Valera (who was to become the leader of the fully independent Ireland) cannily chose not to take part in the negotiations with the British, and so was free to refuse to recognize the treaty. He lost his grip on the party during the height of the Civil War when the military hardliners took the lead.

After the war, in which his one-time comrade and sometime enemy Michael Collins had been conveniently killed, was over, many members of Sinn Féin shared de Valera's belief that the party's abstention from electoral politics in the Free State was pointless and joined him when he formed a new party, Fianna Fáil, in 1926. It first won a general election in 1932 and, under the leadership of Bertie Ahern, is the party in government during my stay in Ireland. The main opposition party, Fine Gael, was formed in 1933 with pro-treaty politicians at its core. The bitter divisions of the Civil War period have cast a long shadow over Irish life.

James MacCarthy's father, Justin, was, like his son, a Justice of the Peace and as we talk, it occurs to me that he held this position under British rule. Does this mean that Justin of Inch would have been a bit of a collaborator?

Justin of Clash shakes his head. 'No-oh. He was quite radical; the Brits would have been trying to keep him sweet as the local squire.'

'So being a JP didn't mean he was a "shilling taker" then?'

'Not at all, but there was a good story about him during the First War. An Annascaul man who couldn't stand Justin shouted "Up Germany!" at the JP to wind him up. Justin got his own back by sending the fellow to jail for a year by charging him under the British Defence of the Realm Act!' Years later the man successfully claimed a state pension because he'd been locked up by the British for acting against them. Not quite an IRA hero perhaps, but he was certainly a man with an eye to the main chance.

'Justin was an awkward cuss,' Justin of Clash continues. 'He was fine if you knew how to smooth his feathers but otherwise he could be a bit of a martinet, playing the squire. If someone crossed him he'd never let bygones be bygones.'

Apparently he had a bell at the top of the house with a rope running down to his bedside so that he could ring it to make sure his staff was up and about early. 'They put a cloth round the clapper so it made hardly any noise at all!'

His son James was a different type; he didn't play the squire and was able to get on with anyone. If he needed someone to be a friend then he would forget his father's likes and dislikes and go his own, *plámásering* way. Justin and Mike confirm James's reputation as a good businessman, stubborn and tough but honest. One piece of information that surprises and impresses me is that James refused to support the parish priest's demands that local unmarried girls who got pregnant should be sent off to the nuns. I've been reading about the horrors faced by many girls who ended up as tragic victims, virtual slaves of the Church-run Magdalen Laundries.

The reference to the parish priest reminds Justin of Clash of a story that demonstrates the entertainment, rather than spiritual, value of hellfire sermons. In the old days these were a feature of the annual visitation by the missioner priests who came to rev up the parish's religious verve, especially that of the backsliders. The sermons put the fear of God in all and sundry. They were also good theatre. The women would sit at the front while the men, as is common enough at other occasions, sat or stood near the back. During the 1960s one of the men who spent most of the time at his farm up in the hills appeared in a pinstripe suit that would not have shamed Al Capone. Other men gathered to hear the priest denounce the lax morals of the time. As the priest became more and more excited and reached the dangerous and inflammatory issue of miniskirts, one of the young men of the village, a nervous type, became visibly agitated. At which the farmer-cum-mobster observed in a rasping rumble, 'Hang on there, lad, he hasn't yet got to the elastic!' The back of the church fell about laughing.

It wasn't just in the old days that the missioners had a role to play. 'Above in Meath,' Fidelus had told me after a recent trip home to see her mother, 'they were having the missioners in.' Many people want to find their way back to the faith and listen to the priests. She told me that there were large groups attending sessions on grief, addiction, all manner of contemporary concerns.

As we pore over the family tree, Justin of Clash points to one of the sisters of his great-grandfather (and of Justin of Inch), a woman called Hanna. She married a man named Flynn and they lived in Castlemaine. Their son Jack 'the Fiddler' Flynn, who was to become a Fianna Fáil Dáil deputy for Kerry South in 1932, was a member of a twenty-strong flying column of

Kerry No.1 Brigade of the IRA which attacked a Royal Irish Constabulary patrol on 1 June 1921, killing five men.

What hits me most as we sit around the Kennedys' fire is how all this family history is conveyed with such a sense of immediacy. Eileen, Mike and Justin speak of these people as if they were of their own generation.

Justin of Clash has further information on James's marriage. James was fifty years old when he married, Gráinne Lynch was only twenty-two. She had come to Inch on holiday with her father – who as I knew from Maureen was involved with James in the cattle-shipping business from Dublin. Aside from the age difference, and whatever else had been said about her, it would have been a difficult adjustment for a young person who'd grown up in Dublin to even think of living in the country. The Inch of the 1940s would have seemed a very quiet backwater indeed.

Mike and Justin reckon that James must have had a good relationship with de Valera's Fianna Fáil government, or the local party at least, as he was granted one of the rare and lucrative licences to export cattle during the so-called Economic War, a six-year dispute with Britain which ranged over constitutional and defence matters as well.

'God, hadn't they all had enough of wars between them?' I ask.

My cousins explain that in effect it was the next stage in the struggle for total independence. De Valera set it in motion in 1932 when he broke the Anglo-Irish Treaty by abolishing the oath of allegiance to the crown and refusing to pay land annuities. The Free State government was supposed to collect and pass on repayments to the British government for loans made to Irish tenants to buy their farms under various Land Acts between 1891 and 1909. The British responded with special duties on Irish imports, especially cattle and dairy produce. This tit-for-tat war went on for six years.

Thirty years later Justin of Clash, like many other farmers, was exporting himself to England in the winter months to work on the sugar beet crop. After experiencing the wider world of England in the swinging sixties, he says it was strange coming back to the confines of rural Kerry. 'In those days Irish people got an education through becoming a teacher or a civil servant. If not that, then the only way was go for the informal education you could get by travelling.'

Sometimes he worked in the building trade, once as part of a group who came in contact with a ghastly little man who treated them all as dirty 'Micks'. Justin thought things were going to turn ugly and was sure the largest worker in the group was about to thump the little man when, in his grotesquely con-descending way, he asked for their names. The big fellow said, 'Well, boss, I'm Jack Lynch!' Lynch was a minister in the Irish government of the time, who later became Taoiseach. Quickly catching on, the next man called himself Neil Blaney, another minister. The next man said his name was James Connolly, one of the leaders of the 1916 Easter Rising, who was wounded, captured and subsequently shot by the British.

'Eventually,' says Justin, 'this little Hitler had as his labouring gang half a government and a few executed leaders from the War of Independence!'

At some point Justin is talking about Cromwell and he says, 'And then Hitl— um, eh, Cromwell . . .'

I pick him up on it. 'Hitler, was he?'

He smiles and says, 'Well, yes.'

And I suppose he was in his way, so brutal and single-minded, though a long time ago.

Historians and history teachers wield a great deal of power and it is interesting to meet people who have grown up with a version of a shared history which informs a natural but entirely different national tradition. The pink bits of the British Empire were so glorious when I was a boy. Mind you, Cromwell was always a bit of a bastard on the English curriculum too; after all, he killed a king. History is simplified to suit the winner or whoever is telling the story.

A few days later I watch a moving television documentary about Irishmen involved with occupying forces in a civil war. But *Brothers in Arms* doesn't deal with conflict in Ireland; it is about brothers killed while serving in UNIFIL, the United Nations peacekeeping force in Lebanon.

After twenty-three years' service that has seen forty-five of its soldiers killed, the Irish contingent has just come home. The programme looks at the deaths of four soldiers, all of whom were apparently deliberately targeted by Lebanese militiamen. Amal militiamen, fighting a guerrilla war against Christian Lebanese enemies and their Israeli allies, were angry at the Irish contingent's success at clearing Amal mines and had accused the Irish of colluding with an Israeli kidnapping of an Amal leader. A young Irish officer was blown up leading a mine-sweeping patrol on roads near an Irish base. The other three were blown up when their truck went over a landmine.

What comes through is the selfless sense of duty of the peacekeepers. The more I think about it, the more clearly I see how impressive the aims and achievements of the countries supporting UNIFIL and the individual soldiers have been. It has been a huge commitment. Although it couldn't really ensure any definite peace, it has provided some vital elements of community infrastructure as well as bringing money to a devastated and impoverished region. Besides showing the value and valour of such peacekeeping units, the programme also explores their limitations and vulnerabilities; they can do nothing, not even fight back when they catch the young officer's killers red-handed. Above all, the programme demonstrates the desperate and continuing hurt of the relatives of the dead. Two of the dead men have brothers who also served in Lebanon. One pair had been encouraged to go and serve overseas by their father, a career soldier. The surviving brother speaks of an unspoken and unresolved grief that has riven his family. As he weeps over his family's tragedy, I too am crying.

The next weekend President Mary MacAleese and military top brass attend a memorial ceremony in Dublin honouring the Irish soldiers who have given their lives for the peace effort in Lebanon. The event is shown live on television and features in news bulletins and newspapers. A number of articles argue that it is only now, after their duties have finished, that these soldiers are being given the attention and credit they deserve. If so, it's a terrible omission, both here in Ireland and internationally, that soldiers who risk their lives for peace, not conquest or victory, are neither properly acknowledged nor honoured.

One day, as I come out of the bank in Tralee, a little old chap in a battered suit and wellington boots comes gambolling along the pavement looking extremely happy. Something, and I don't think it is alcohol, is filling him with glee and I turn to watch him chuckling on his way.

On my way out of town I slow the car as a horse comes running towards me, closely followed by a car. I curse the driver's foolishness in chasing the beast and then realize, as it draws closer, that the horse is pulling a low and lightweight racing cart with a driver on board. The car following is full of beery-looking supporters shouting encouragement, and a few hundred yards behind them is another cart. This looks like some unofficial and highly illegal race, especially as it is rush hour. This drama over, I crawl, frustrated by the terrible roads, in a long convoy of drivers. Tuning into Radio Kerry I catch the road and travel information. The bulletin's mantra goes, 'Traffic news brought to you by AA Road Watch in association with Kerry County Council,' then, with monstrous cheek, continues, 'committed to road safety.' Perhaps Irish drivers share my frustration, which might account for the curious habit they display at night of finding it very hard to dip their lights. Whatever the reason for this irritating trait, people do seem genuinely more laid-back, less stressed, less critical of others. I've already met a couple of locals who have happily told me the old joke about the Irish not having a phrase which conveys the same sense of urgency as the Spanish word *mañana*.

Maybe my Celtic genes have become diluted and I've lost the fatalism that was part of the pagan Gaelic world and that has hung on despite the centuries of secular domination by the Anglo-Saxons and Protestantism and the clerical supremacy of the Church in Rome. One of those elements that Father óRíordáin might see as a special and integral part of the Irish spiritual world and something that the founders of the modern Irish state liked to believe in and wanted to rediscover; a fatalism which pre-dated and has somehow been reinforced by centuries of troubles.

Even if the dream of independent Ireland as a spiritual place hasn't emerged as the state's founding fathers would have wished, the nation today does still bend the collective national knee, even at an institutional level, to the Christian order. It takes me by surprise still when, every day, the early evening news on state television and radio is preceded by the words, 'It's six o'clock and now we'll pause for the Angelus.' Then we have a couple of minutes of a bell tolling over images of people – children, old men, couples, workers, all looking serene as they contemplate the divine, or perhaps what's for tea.

As a more or less lapsed Protestant with confused views on faith and doubts about the institutions of religion, especially the people within them, I find this practice strange and a little worrying. Defining Ireland so clearly as a Catholic state and making this particular part of the nation's day 'pause' and ponder the 'Good News' of Christ's message surely makes it more difficult to then deliver bad news or criticism concerning the Church.

Of course, having been brought up as a Protestant Englishman I'm trained to baulk instinctively at a 'foreign' institution claiming authority in my country. And although not quite crossing my fingers, I sometimes feel out of place visiting a Roman Catholic church, anticipating that they'll be full of gruesome statuary, dripping blood, and incense and bells. When I was growing up, my parents' generation presented the differences between Protestants and Catholics as concrete and important. I'm sure that today's more secularized society is far less conscious of, or concerned about, such distinctions. Whatever baggage of minor sectarian bigotry I may carry, I am well aware that faith and the Church have played a crucial role in Irish history and the development of the Irish psyche. It is something I need to explore.

I head for the far side of Dingle Bay from Inch, to Cahersiveen, a long narrow town focused on one street. Its greatest and dominating feature is the Daniel O'Connell Memorial Church. O'Connell, known as the Liberator, was the first of the great nineteenth-century Irish leaders to sit in the British House of Commons.

The Penal Laws, introduced in various Acts from the end of the seventeenth century, had forbidden Catholics from teaching or running schools, from buying land, or inheriting it from Protestants, from practising law or serving in the armed forces. Catholic political organizations were illegal and Catholics could not hold office in local or national government or sit in parliament. Catholic bishops were banished and no new priests were allowed to enter Ireland. These laws saw Catholic landowners losing their lands over time, but recent studies show that Catholic leaseholders and those involved in business often prospered and that the ban on bishops and priests was rarely enforced rigorously. From 1774 onwards a series of Catholic Relief Acts, reflecting changing attitudes at Westminster and among Irish Protestants, and an increasingly vociferous Catholic opposition in Ireland, gradually dismantled the Penal Laws.

When the Act of Union of August 1800 abolished the Irish parliament, O'Connell argued that the remaining anti-Catholic laws must be repealed if the British parliament was to have any legitimate claim to represent the people of Ireland. In 1823 O'Connell co-founded the Catholic Association, which soon had so many members that the government couldn't contain it. In parliamentary elections in 1826 a number of candidates backed by large landowners were defeated, and then in 1828 O'Connell, as a Catholic ineligible to sit in the House of Commons, was elected as a Member for County Clare. The British government realized it had to make concessions to the Irish Catholics. The Emancipation Act was passed the following year and O'Connell eventually took his seat at Westminster.

As well as being a politician of heroic stature, O'Connell's reputation for liberating his Catholic countrymen has raised him almost to the level of sainthood. It's no surprise that the church named for him is massive. Coming from the bright daylight into the gloomy porch, my eyes have to adjust but I soon make out a rack displaying Catholic newspapers. I fumble about with a handful of change to pay for one, trying to find the money box, only for my fingers to dip into water. Recoiling, I bemoan the Catholic penchant for holy water and just resist crossing my fingers. Feeling a little chilled and uncomfortable I continue the hunt and eventually find the right box. Once inside I relax a little, warmed by a blaze of offertory candles, until I notice a man lurking by a pillar and looking distinctly unstable, staring at me. My unease returns as I sit at the back of the church. I'm mightily relieved when the odd fellow lurches out of the door.

An old woman kneels near me, praying close to a shrine dedicated to the Virgin Mary and Bernadette of Lourdes. A few candles burn here too and I have a sudden urge to light some more for my parents, wife, brother and me. I'm not sure what prompts this act but feel a sense of bringing my family together with me for a moment. Around the walls of the little chapel printed prayers are pinned up. All are about the Virgin Mary, Queen of the World, Queen of Peace, and there is a sheet relating 'The Latest Message', from Lourdes I suppose. This worship of Mary, alien to my Protestant background, seems to sum up the more subtle difficulties of seeking to understand another culture. We share a language, even some genes, but I find it hard to make the leap of imagination to understand, not just individual religious devotion, but how it becomes a key element of national identity. On this cold, late afternoon the grey stone church, dedicated to God and the politics of liberation, does not offer the insight I'd hoped for.

Whereas many nights on British television will see endless re-runs of old comedy classics, Irish TV schedulers go for something a little more instructive, though after watching some of these shows I'm not sure that carpet weaving, pot making or boat building (using twigs and the skin of a dead animal) isn't just as comical. The commentator, who has all the time in the world to give us bits of historical and practical detail, seems determined to patronize the people who are making whatever they are making. 'Mary assesses the quality of the wool. It has to be just right as this carpet may grace the floor of a palace or an embassy. Mary's job is very important.' Mary, who surely doesn't always wear a cocktail dress to work in a factory, looks terrified and mad as the camera pans from her face to her wool-riffling fingers. Meanwhile Susan and Charlene, children of the sixties whose parents must have decided that it wasn't vital to the national interest to give their girls unspellable, unpronounceable Irish names, grin and chat as they operate the loom in their tight-fitting overalls and flick-back hairstyles. Needless to say there is less pan and more zoom from the cameraman in this section.

Losing interest after a moment of relative intensity when it is confirmed that the man on all fours moving his hands in a regular circular motion is indeed 'polishing' something, I turn back to the archive of personal things I have brought with me and start leafing through one of my files: snippets of diaries and school reports. The school reports remind me how often I have thought that I didn't get the mentoring I now feel I needed. Apart from whatever failings my school might have had, I think being away during term-time must have meant that my enthu-siasms, strengths and weaknesses cannot have been clear to my parents. At home in the holidays the atmosphere was so relaxed and self-contained that bringing in the outside world was per-haps an unwanted intrusion. We were too polite and didn't push to know each other and became adept at saying merely enough, offering some support and then changing the subject.

There were, though, a couple of periods in my childhood and adolescence when I lost my way. The first occasion was when I was eleven or twelve years old and was due perhaps to anxiety over my mother's first brush with cancer. She'd been diagnosed with breast cancer and had to have a mastectomy. Years later she talked about how awful this had been, how for a long time she had felt a freak, but I don't remember her talking about her fears at the time. Naturally, because of our ages, our parents wouldn't have shared their deepest concerns with us, but when she went into hospital for the operation, although we tried to be brave, in our ignorance Terence and I were terrified.

Happily she came back home and recovered well but I think that an underlying awareness that the world was not the perfectly safe place I'd believed it to be took root. I went through a period, a term, two terms, a year, I don't know, when the lessons and exams that I'd usually sailed through became difficult and I had this awful feeling sometimes of dislocation, of being out of synch with the rest of the world. There would be things that my classmates seemed to know and be comfortable with that had somehow completely passed me by. Maths I recall was particularly terrifying and I'd sit in the weekly test thinking, what on earth is this all about, surely I'm not the only one who doesn't understand a word of this?

As a consequence I wanted to go to school less and less, which was very confusing since I'd always loved it. My parents were very patient and tried to understand what was bothering me. It never became clear, but after a while I regained the momentum and everything seemed to be fine again. In that typical middle-class British way, we quickly forgot that anything had happened.

When I was around sixteen I seemed to lose any real sense of direction again. Lessons had no interest for me and I found it hard to concentrate. In retrospect I think this was partly due to a failure to see where my education was leading. Also a natural interest in the world was being stunted by the need to learn things almost by rote. It was as if anything I had to read and study became unbearably dull and difficult. If Evelyn Waugh or Charlotte Brontë were on the reading list, I'd struggle to get through them. Paradoxically, if their novels were not on the course I'd finish them in a flash. Perhaps by not applying myself in areas where my intellectual powers would be open to scrutiny I was avoiding potential criticism or failure.

I've been reading John Simpson's *It's a Mad World, My Masters* in which he quotes W. H. Auden's line, 'Look if you like, but you will have to leap.'

Simpson's observation that he nearly always regrets the times when he hasn't made the leap makes me want to curl up. I'd like to see myself as someone who is prepared to leap but all too often I've stopped myself with thoughts that I'll do that – go travelling, try a new job – when I've got myself better prepared. But then I don't prepare myself and do nothing. With greater experience I realize that often I can take on difficult challenges and relish making my way through them. Even if I still have terrible doubts about being able to fulfil whatever my role might be I know that failure en route somewhere doesn't mean you won't eventually make it. You need setbacks to appreciate the progress.

For much of my life I was happy meandering along, taking up challenges that were offered me rather than setting my own. Maybe there were times in my younger years when I should have had better support, stronger guidance but, at long last, over the past five or six years, I've come to accept the fact that this is my life and no one else can live it for me.

At four o'clock the tide is still way out and the sun is coming in under the clouds from the west. Scores of oystercatchers work the damp sand of the glistening beach, calling to each other to warn of my approach. A rush of excitement shoots through me as a wash of wavelets races towards me, daring me to risk soaked shoes by staying put. Two inches deep, almost spent, wave front meets wave front and crosses to create a shimmering starfish, forty feet across. At the beach's outer edge waves tumble and snort in their own foam, stirred by the sharp westerly breeze. Two big birds, hooded crows, with black heads and wings and grey bodies, alight on the strand and open their wings to dry, looking like two elderly city gents spreading the tails of their frock coats in front of the club fire on a winter's evening.

This beauty, or wonder, is a powerful stimulus and it touches me sharply. But what is the import, the substance, in all this natural finery? What does it mean or what might it explain? Perhaps sometimes it is enough just to look up and see a vertical shaft of rainbow, a kaleidoscope of seaside rock standing steady amid roiling clouds, and feel the blinding flash of appreciation and of knowing 'I am here'.

I stop at Foley's after the walk and enter a kitchen piled with shopping bags. Fidelus, looking somewhat alarmed at what she's done, explains, 'I've just been inside to Tralee to get the food for the Stations.'

A Station constitutes part of the parish and is based on the old area of a townland. In the autumn and spring a special Mass is held in one of the houses in the Station. Households take it in turns, a turn coming round every six or seven years. Fidelus has very kindly invited me to take part in this special occasion at her home although strictly speaking, as I live in another Station of the parish, I wouldn't normally be included.

Back from Foley's and full of positive thoughts about the role of the Church in the community, I settle down with a cup of tea, pause for the Angelus and watch the evening news. I too am getting into the rhythm of this other life.

An altogether different type of church community is the subject of one of the main items. An elderly man is giving evidence to a parliamentary committee about his time at St Joseph's Industrial School at Ferryhouse, Tipperary. He speaks so movingly and with such dignity about the abuse he and other children received there. At one point he leans over the desk in front of him, describing being beaten on bare buttocks. His voice is choked as he explains that children like him had to suffer this to give sexual pleasure to the people who were supposed to be caring for him.

What began with a few allegations back in the 1980s has led to a flood of people, thousands by now, coming forward to say they too were abused in institutions as children. Strikingly, many of those who have come forward are giving evidence of their suffering as far back as the 1920s.

The orphanages, residential homes and industrial schools, through which some thirty thousand children passed in the decades up until the 1970s, were supposedly run under state supervision, but tragically this supervision, reflecting what one commentator called the 'kid glove' attitude to religious institutions, lacked any serious scrutiny.

They were run by many orders but the majority, and those with the worst reputations, had been run by the Christian Brothers. The Congregation of the Brothers of the Christian Schools of Ireland, to give the organization its full title, was founded in 1802 by a layman, Edmund Ignatius Rice. Rice established the order to help poor Catholic boys in Ireland who, thanks to the English Penal Laws prohibiting Catholic schools, had had little or no education. The congregation spread to countries around the world.

RTE is broadcasting a two-part documentary which focuses on the plight of children who suffered at the hands of Christian Brothers in Australia and Canada. Revelations about the conditions in institutions in those countries had led to the gradual disclosure of the awful happenings in institutions at home.

Some of the institutions, like the industrial school attended by the old man on the news bulletin, have been described as being, in effect, child labour camps offering all manner of products and services to their local communities. Children and youths worked in agriculture, clothes manufacture, and so on, from which the order benefited financially.

I had been aware of the broad picture, but my reaction to learning the details for the first time is one of disbelief. The scale of the problem makes it impossible to dismiss it as a terrible mistake here and there, which a few former inmates of such homes and some wild-eyed anti-Church campaigners have over-stated. The disastrous outcome of the policy of entrusting unfortunate children to the largely unsupervised care of the Christian Brothers and other religious orders is not being denied. The government has apologized, as has the Christian Brotherhood. The issue now is how to effect justice for the victims. There are arguments about who should pay any compensation and how much. One almost gets the feeling that the Church institutions, having apologized, considered the matter closed, that they could clamber back on their social pedestals. The more traditional opinion seems to be that it is somehow in bad taste to keep scrutinizing these unfor-tunate incidents and below the belt to argue for religious organizations to make any major contribution to compensation payments. One of the key problems in settling these matters is the state's implicit complicity and the continuing fear, as far as I can judge it, of taking on the men in black, the moral arbiters of the country. Like the rest of the Church, the Christian Brothers had been at the core of the nationalist revival and become a fundamental part of independent Ireland, with one journalist arguing that, 'the brothers are more than just another Irish Catholic institution. It requires but a small degree of exag-geration, indeed, to say that they *were* the Irish Catholic institution.'

It is argued that it was due to the order's influence that the education system failed to become non-sectarian and that piety and obedience became paramount in the early years of the newly independent state. Indeed many of the leaders of the struggle for independence, including Eamon de Valera, had been educated by the Brothers. No wonder it took people a long time to take seriously the allegations against them. It is difficult to contem-plate such malignancy at the core of a religious culture one instinctively trusts. I find myself fuming, as any normal person would, at the horrors I read and hear about. This does not sound like the carefree, caring Ireland of family and faith that one comes to expect. It's a relief to know that a government commission is now investigating the victims' claims and will lay ground rules for compensation. The Laffoy Commission to Inquire into Child Abuse was set up in June 2000 under Ms Justice Mary Laffoy and, such is the weight of evidence to be examined, it is expected to run until 2005.

Inevitably the revelations have affected the respect shown to the Church and consequently attendance at its services. Maureen Fitzgerald had told me that while the Church remained important to her (and to most of her generation, I've found), a great many younger people have given up going to Mass altogether. Eighty years on from independence, one of Ireland's key foundation stones is beginning to crumble. This constitutes nothing less than an erosion, albeit gradual, of the power of the Irish state itself.

'Mr McCoorthy!' I turn to see who is rolling out my name in such a dramatic manner. It is Sean, the man I met during my first week in Kerry in Eason's bookshop in Tralee. It's impossible not to return his smile, and I feel cheered at the sight of him.

'Have you had lunch?'

Although it is dull on the street, the gloom inside the little eatery is so total that for a moment I have to stand still to allow my eyes to adjust. A narrow passage skirts a tiny bar area to a couple of small rooms where people are eating sandwiches and soup. From what I can make out in the darkness, it looks like a lunchtime crowd of office people, some shoppers and a couple of camera-laden tourists, probably wondering what they are doing in this cave.

We order some food and drinks, Sean all the while chatting about the pub, about Tralee, about Kerry and the people. 'You should go and see so-and-so, they know all about the history . . .'

When he asks me how I am finding the Irish I tell him some of my news and experiences, about the warm welcome I've had at Inch, about Fidelus's invitation to the Stations, about the growing number of cousins I'm meeting,

'Ah yes, long-distance cousins!' he interjects, slapping his thigh and laughing.

'Given all the warmth, among families and friends,' I go on, 'I've been knocked right over realizing just how bad this child abuse thing is – how much the Church seems to have hidden under the corporate cassock.'

'Yes, yes, you're right and I'm sure there's a lot more to come out.' He pauses for a moment then blurts out, 'You see, John, I went through that.'

Oh my God, I think as he looks at me, uncertain if he should have told me. I nod and try to look back steadily. My head is reeling, my mind working fast; such a jolly man, apparently without a care in the world.

'So how's this past week been, Sean, with so much in the news?'

He starts telling me his story. His nightmare began in an almost mundane way: the father went off, and his mother found it hard to cope with bringing up five or six young kids. She developed a taste for too much drink that relatives didn't notice at first. When they finally did, the mother's pride kept them at a distance and then they lost interest. Eventually, when things deteriorated, the children were taken into different institutions. Sean and his smallest sibling were carted off to an orphanage run by the Sisters of Mercy, or No Mercy, as Sean says with a tired smile.

An hour or two after leaving what had been, not so long

before, a familiar if somewhat troubled family home, the two little children were in a cast-iron tub being scrubbed and scratched
by a toothless harridan, herself a creature of institutionalization.
A fag hung from the corner of her mouth and her claw-like
fingernails scratched their tender skin. When they yelped the
industrial-size block of carbolic soap would clap down on their
terrified heads. Although he was not sexually abused in the
orphanage, Sean was subjected to incessant ridicule and harrass-
ment by some of his 'carers'. He lived in constant fear of
punishment and with no hope of a comforting relationship with
an adult. It was no surprise to learn that, to block out the painful
memories of this miserable childhood, he had for a period
become dependent on alcohol.

Failed by parents, extended family, the state and the Christian
institution where he spent his formative years, Sean has bravely
embarked on the long voyage back to himself. His elder siblings
were abused in other ways and other places – one sister was
raped by a priest. As a result, the family is probably fractured
beyond repair.

Words tumble from Sean. He develops his sentences as if
flicking through the pages of a dictionary, plucking synonyms
and metaphors, holding them to the light before selecting or dis-
carding them. At times he flounders in an unreserved flow but
he usually gets through to clarity. His verbosity is, I suspect, a
consequence of his childhood trauma and his desire to overcome
it. He is expecting to meet the Laffoy Commission in the near
future and wants to tell his story with emotional power but
concisely and without sentimentality.

What a tragedy it is for this middle-aged man to have to
summarize his blighted life and present it to a board of com-
missioners. However sympathetic they might be, I can see that
for Sean it will almost be as if he is the one on trial rather than
those who poisoned his life.

As we sit at our table we must look like any of the other diners chatting and eating around us. They no doubt assume we are talking about business, the World Cup draw, the Celtic Tiger and Chancellor McCreevy's budget, or the latest episode in RTE's soap *Fair City*. But we are talking of the loss of innocence, the loss of respect for a great institution and the horror of isolation. I can't help wondering as we sit there in the lunchtime hubbub how many others are masking similar tragedies behind countenances as cheerful as Sean's.

There's confusion in the press and among people I've talked to as to how to respond to the continuing revelations about the abuse. Some people, while acknowledging that it was awful, appear bored or perhaps numbed by it all. Others, especially in the press, remain very angry and argue that the Church organizations must face the full weight of the law. One editorial in the *Irish Examiner* put it succinctly: 'This is not really about revenge, it is about facing a sordid reality.'

After fourteen months of negotiations, which were originally expected to take three months, it is announced that the Catholic Church has agreed to put 128 million euros into a state-backed fund for children who suffered abuse in residential care. Bishop Eamon Walsh, chairman of the Irish Bishops Conference, says this is 'a particularly generous offer'. There are mixed reactions to this, with most observers disagreeing with Bishop Walsh and saying that with the compensation expected to amount to a total of some 500 million euros, the state is paying way too much for what the institutions did. While people accept that the state was responsible for putting the children in such poorly supervised institutions, they don't accept that the state is as a result 75 per cent responsible for the actions of the individual abusers.

An article in *The Kerryman* illustrates how in the days when the institutions were at full strength the children who ended up in them were viewed as somehow subhuman. One man in his fifties, whose life story was a catalogue of abuse, bad management and subsequent personal disaster, was quoted as saying, 'State and the Catholic Church saw us as corrupt, as sinners and vermin.'

Some journalists are calling for a complete review not just of what went on in those corrupt organizations but also of society's attitude to the clergy, saying it is time the Church and its members are made subject to the same scrutiny as any other group. And there is a particular and awful irony to be addressed. The very organization that has preached such stern and restrictive attitudes to sexuality for the general population has been harbouring people who were perpetrating abhorrent sexual acts against children in their care. People are calling on the Church to look closely at the issue of celibacy. For too many, celibacy has clearly proved to be an impossible regime to follow; men and women with no experience of normal sexual relations and no experience of the normal responsibilities of parenting are unlikely to be able to take on the enormous role of being a true parent just because they've attended a seminary or a convent.

The confusion people face in dealing with this issue I can understand. The criticism and calls for new thinking I applaud. But what confounds me is that there are still those who feel it's unfair to examine the issue in too much depth.

One or two columnists, while acknowledging that what went on was horrible, argue that the innocent Christian Brothers shouldn't be made out to be pariahs, that they have worked very hard and with great success despite very difficult circumstances in many of the institutions. The efforts of some certainly have been commendable, but how it makes the Christian Brothers and other such organizations any more credible I fail to see. They were incompetent, criminally so, in not being able to maintain decent levels and standards. Some commentators have written that there was physical and sexual abuse of younger boys by older boys and that the children in the homes were often difficult and aggressive. The implication that the people in charge of the institutions should be excused because their task was difficult seems unjustifiable. I cannot believe that serious commentators are arguing that because children from broken homes and troubled backgrounds behave oddly and sometimes badly we must accept gross mismanagement of the institutions we place them in. Surely when setting up an institution to care for such individuals every effort would be made to anticipate likely problems and build in strategies to stop them, not use them as an excuse for colleagues to bugger minors.

The bishops seem very disappointed that the world isn't universally clapping them on the back for apologizing and handing over some money. One bishop even complains that the media doesn't seem to appreciate just how traumatic it is to be in his position at a time like this. The Church hierarchy is demonstrating the tendency, common among politicians, of forgetting that they are there to run the place for everyone; they seem to think it is theirs to do with as they will. The notions of civil and moral responsibility are once again replaced with the more immediate needs of self-justification and evasion.

The victims deserve compensation and it should come from the people or organizations that caused their suffering and if those organizations cannot honour such responsibilities they should be wound up like any other discredited enterprise. If moral bankruptcy leads to financial bankruptcy, so be it.

Whatever compensation Sean may receive it will never make up for the cruelty he was put through. Although the money may provide some respite, I'm sure that the importance to Sean of a settlement would be the public acknowledgement of his suffering. Sean is happy to be alive and can see that despite all his sorrow there is a way forward. The spring is in his step but I fear that he is in constant danger of bouncing into depression. He wants to have a home again where he and his brothers and sisters can come together as whole human beings and be a family once more. I hope they get all the help and redress they deserve in order to achieve that.

After three days of constant rain I'm standing at a supermarket checkout.

'How are you?' asks the woman at the till.

'Grand altogether!' answers the customer.

'You'd get sick of all this rain, wouldn't you?'

Yes, you bloody would! I say to myself. It seeps into you until you feel waterlogged and every little movement or thought is an effort. The life leeches out of you like nutrients from the soil.

Wearing jacket and tie for the first time since I've been in Ireland, I go down to the pub just before ten thirty in the morning feeling self-conscious. All the windows are shuttered or curtained. I go to the lounge bar door where I'm greeted by John who shakes my hand and says welcome and then Fidelus comes across and does the same. It's a poignant moment for me; the two of them have always made me so welcome, quite beyond any call as hosts to an old friend, let alone a more recent acquaintance.

The image of the Irish and their pubs may be a cliché, but the bar is an important force in the community, like the community centre, the school and the Church. On this day that importance seems to be acknowledged by the presence in the lounge bar of an altar, a congregation and the priest in his robes. It is a time to celebrate the strengths, and the eccentricities, of Irish life and not to dwell on the darker aspects of the society at large.

Father Crean speaks very lightly and simply, and the occasion doesn't feel mawkish. Indicating the public bar he says, 'I'd say that room's heard a few confessions over the years. If anyone has anything they'd like to share with me I'll be through there for a few minutes.'

An older man goes through, as do a couple of boys.

Something at the back of my mind has had me thinking that I'd be lost in a Catholic service. But reading the service sheet I begin to relax. Perhaps my mixed emotions come from my status as a temporary guest who wants to belong and yet also partly yearns to be with my own community. My mind wanders back to a recent Easter at home in Suffolk. I remember how comfortable I had felt in church, an emotion that had been missing for a long time. That comfort grew out of a visit I had made to a small community in San Salvador where I saw how important collective faith and worship were for the people there. When the Church works well, in just such circum-stances as this, it has the power to bring people together in determined equality that celebrates their humanity, their com-munity and also their weakness and insignificance. It binds people together, and for a time at least reminds us of moral responsibilities in an environment where our responses, literally, are controlled and follow a pattern that is well defined. That definition is part of its strength, as is the common acceptance of the formal liturgy.

I feel self-conscious as I study the service sheet with un-necessary intensity. Friends and neighbours speak in hushed tones. When I look around at last I see a number of familiar faces, including Bridey Flynn, bright-eyed and eagerly looking about as usual, Fidelus's sister Geraldine and Kathleen Daley. Children sit at the front. Jerry and Katie are chattering to their friends, pretending to ignore warning glances from both their

parents. Martina arrives with her boy and girl, closely followed
by Pat, Máire and their four children.

There are flowers everywhere, on the tables, on the window-
sills and on the bar. The altar table looks immaculate with a
simple white tablecloth, a couple of silver candlesticks and the
crucifix. The usual backdrop of stained-glass windows is
replaced here by the bar's coloured liqueur bottles and optics. A
mixture of emotions, happiness tinged with wistfulness, goes
through me as I sit watching John greet new arrivals, and
Fidelus nodding and smiling at people as she hands out service
sheets.

Father Tom begins the service by blessing and sprinkling holy
water and then prays that the water might renew the living
spring of God's life within us and keep us free from sin. He prays
for the blessing of the salt to drive away evil. Diverging from the
service sheet, he then blesses a small candle on the altar, to
remind us of the light of God and also of the light and warmth
that emanate from the Foley and Farrelly families. Having felt
so much of this warmth and friendship, I am close to tears at this
point. The first reading is from St Paul, Romans 12:9–18, and
two lines stand out for me:

> Love each other as brothers should, and have a profound respect
> for each other. If any of the saints are in need you must share
> with them and you should make hospitality your special care.

The Stations is an important event in the community's
calendar. People have been talking about it for weeks, saying
how glad they are that the tradition continues here and how sad
it is that it has died out in many other parts of the country. It is a
special occasion and whatever my own religious views I value
the idea spelled out in St Paul's instruction that you should open
the house to your neighbours and make them welcome. The

Stations is not just for your friends, but also for those neighbours you might not visit from one year's end to the next. Fidelus has put a huge effort into getting everything prepared. As publicans I imagine the Foleys to be well off – certainly they have no problem providing booze – but I've been told repeatedly that while Fidelus and John wanted and are able to provide the thirty or so guests with a fine meal and drink, tea and sandwiches are deemed sufficient. There might be comments, 'It's all very well for them', or 'Poor old thing, that's all he could manage', but I don't think so. I feel this really is a moment of faithful, neighbourly equality.

We sing the hymn 'Holy Mary Full of Grace' and I realize I've never said or sung Ave Maria before. Most of the congregation take Communion and we all shake hands, 'Peace be with you.' The final hymn is 'Bind Us Together Lord'. This, too, is new to me and I struggle with its unfamiliar tune, but it seems an apt note on which to finish the formal part of the morning gathering.

The altar is cleared away, tables are laid and people sit for lunch. Pat Foley introduces me to his Aunt Maureen. Maureen married one of Bridie's brothers who, I get the impression, was something of a black sheep of the clan. It's rumoured that there had been occasional recourse to his brother, a Garda superintendent, to help smooth things over. I can see that Maureen would have been a good match for a 'fine rogue'. She is very funny and has a rasping voice from years of smoking. With a mischievous glint in her eye she waits politely for a while as two women hold and admire a plate of fine looking cake then suddenly barks, 'Give me some of that!' It sounds rude, but it isn't because it's meant to be funny and it is taken that way. It's her mix of deliberate cheek, eccentricity and honesty that makes Maureen so entertaining. Later on, when I still have some cake left on my plate, she says, 'You haven't finished!' and I say something about being too full. Later again she suddenly commands, 'Finish your cake!'

I get the impression that she likes to tease and wouldn't suffer fools, insincerity or hypocrisy gladly.

# CHAPTER NINE

THE SIDE ROAD PETERS OUT INTO LITTLE MORE THAN A TRACK as it crosses a wide area of scrubland such as might be found in the middle of the Patagonian pampas. Below me in the distance are the dark brown trenches of *turbury*, the peat fields. Small farms and cottages are dotted across the barren landscape and I pass sheepdogs sitting chained to their kennels miles apart to guard the extreme entrances of a vast grazing ground. Driving across these turf bogs, which lie to the east of Annascaul, over the ridge of the Slieve Mish mountains behind my cottage, I'm listening to TG 4, the Gaelic radio station, playing laments. I can't understand the words but the songs match the mood of the grey morning sky and soft rain. In many places the turf has been stripped back to reveal the rock beneath and bleached grasses cling to patches of brown earth where streams cut their little ravines down into the valley.

The track enters a dip that has me hemmed in on either side by great hedges of fuchsias, the drooping bells of their flowers like drops of blood. Consulting the Ordnance Survey map confirms that I am on the road to Camp and going through an area called Cool, place names that in their modern usage sound madly and wonderfully inappropriate.

The chill misty air sets me shivering when I park the car at the roadside to go for a walk. The world is drab, olive green, brown and silent. When a male voice shouts, 'Come on, boy, come on!' I spin round, startled, thinking the man must be right behind me. There is no one. I swallow drily as the eerie silence prevails once more. But the sound returns; 'Come round, come round, boy!' A flickering on the distant hillside high above me, just below the cloud line, catches my eye. Sheep are running. There is the black shape of a dog at work and through the binoculars I can make out the stationary figure of a shepherd. The combination of fog and the bowl of the hillside must be creating these strange ventriloquist's acoustics. The atmosphere, clouds shifting, making and hiding hills, is suggestive enough for sagas to be believed. High above me in the mist is Caherconree, believed to be the ancient fortress of Cu Roi Mac Daire, a chieftain of the Fir Bolg people possibly in the first century AD. The fortress consisted of sheer cliffs on two sides and a massive stone wall on the third. Tom Barrington writes a fair bit about this character Mac Daire, who features largely in the Red Branch cycle of legends and seems to have been as much god as man.

Trudging up through the bog – the hillsides around here are unbelievably wet, inconceivably vertical marsh – I can't imagine a better concealed hideout. It is completely hidden in the low clouds. Without roads and maps, how would anyone ever find their way here without a guide? Luckily, of course, I have Mr Barrington to help me. The route I'm following he describes as being 'quite easy' which makes me wonder if he was part goat. Cu Roi was away from the fortress a good deal, it appears, and as I squelch along in my wellingtons I fully agree with the theory put forward by Barrington, whom I envisage moving smartly upwards in galoshes, that this was 'presumably to dry out'.

Cu Roi's reputation was strong among the Ulster champions of the time, Cuchulainn, Laegaire and Conall. So when they argued about who was the most important, they went to Cu Roi to settle the matter. He made them take a night shift each at guarding his fort. Theoretically this was a simple task as the fortress spun all night long at great speed, making the place impregnable. Nevertheless various terrifying demons (actually Cu Roi in disguise) assailed the guardians and threw Laegaire and Conall out over the great wall. Cuchulainn fared better but the issue wasn't entirely resolved, so they had a re-match. Cu Roi now disguised himself as a giant and said the disputants could each take a turn at lopping off his head if they would let him behead them on the following night. All three took their turn but, says Barrington, 'as the giant's head rolled away, he got up and, spouting blood, tucked it, with the rest of his gear, under his arm and went out'. Laegaire and Conall decided things looked so bad that they suddenly remembered urgent business elsewhere. Only Cuchulainn had the nerve to go back and put his head on the block, whereupon Cu Roi told him to get up and declared him the bravest and most honourable.

After twenty-five minutes I near the cloud line. Or is it coming down to meet me? The overall gloom is shot through with light from the west where the sun struggles to break through the cloud around a crag. Luckily the wind picks up and gradually the cloud retreats heavenwards. After an hour and a half of 'quite easy' puffing, panting, slipping and sliding, I climb the two thousand feet to the top. The howling wind threatens to tip me over the edge of the cliff towards Tralee Bay. The grasses in the smooth inner area of the fort are streaming like the coat on a running animal or weeds in a current of water. The wind has no doubt dried out the ground up here a good deal, which must have been a blessing for Cu Roi and his mates but it sucks the breath from you. The wall of Cu Roi's fort, though largely collapsed, is impressive. After the climb you have to admire anyone building the place, anyone living in it and anyone trying to take it. Tim Collins's explanation of the value of promontory forts like this now makes absolute sense. If some interloper came to your manor you'd just take the animals up to the fort and wait until they got bored and cleared off. The views are outstanding even in murky conditions and it's easy to appreciate how the site inspired fantastic tales. Another walk around, not too close to the edge, then I head home to get warm and dry out.

The great man, magician, god and fort builder never made a final descent, at least not alive. Relations with Cuchulainn went sour after Cu Roi played a decisive part in helping Cuchulainn capture a fortress on the Isle of Man. Cu Roi went off with the defeated chief's daughter Blathnaid. Cuchulainn had set his heart on Blathnaid so followed after them. They had a fight which Cu Roi won, and he further humiliated his young opponent by shaving his head. Having licked his wounds (and grown his hair again), Cuchulainn went to Caherconree and with Blathnaid's help (she persuaded Cu Roi to send his fighters off to get some more rocks for a bit of home improvement to the fort) he surprised and killed Cu Roi. If the dead god and chieftain spun in his grave like his castle had done, he wasn't turning for long as his son Lugaid tracked Cuchulainn down and laid him out permanently with a magic spear.

Quiz night again, this time to raise funds for Pat Foley's school at Faha, has me once more on the Foley's Bar team. However this time Ann isn't with us and Pat is in another group so John Foley and I are teamed with Donal Sheehy and Timmy Hannafin. Donal is a retired former head teacher at Annascaul who still retains something of the pedagogue. Automatically he takes charge of our answer sheets and keeps score, beady eyes flashing behind his spectacles. He had his primary education at the Killeenagh School (now Inch Community Centre) before going on, with a scholarship, to a boarding school in Cork. While at college he worked a couple of summers in England where he was automatically called Pat. I cringe every time I hear an Irishman say that. Timmy is a farmer who looks way younger than someone nearing sixty, and in his jeans, sneakers and a blouson jacket he bears no resemblance to most of his flat-capped, tweed-jacketed contemporaries. When not tending to cattle he has spent his life reading and playing a large role in encouraging and training youngsters in the traditional Irish dramatic arts.

All in all we make a pretty good team and are up there with the front-runners throughout the evening. We all have our share of brilliance and idiocy. All four make one disastrous, adamant claim that proves wrong, provoking good-humoured groans.

The huge pub-cum-restaurant is packed, with children forming as many teams as the adults. The excitement mounts as the final rounds approach and Foley's Bar is running neck and neck with, funnily enough, the McCarthy Clan. We play an extra round, no winner, then another round, and finally, to cheers, smiles and handshakes all round, we win. We've worked well as a team, sipping pints and pooling knowledge around the pub table, but the image of enjoying our prize as an ensemble is less tenable. We are presented with vouchers for a fitness centre in Killarney. I just can't see the four of us slogging along on running machines or even lying, one white body next to another, on the sunbeds.

The night is dark, with stars and moon blocked out by heavy clouds. The wind is roaring around the cottage.

'Down behind, over back,' I repeat uncertainly. 'So where's that going again?'

Pat Foley appeared half an hour ago at the doorway looking ghostly white and a little shocked. 'I took the wrong fork on your track,' he announced. 'The rain's washed out most of that steep corner and the car was nearly stuck in the ruts.'

Now we're drinking tea as I try to understand some of the eccentric phrases used to describe people's movements around the area. This is the best so far.

'Down behind, over back.' Pat speaks slowly, emphasizing every word, looking at me as he might one of his pupils who is failing to grasp some very basic idea. 'It's someone coming down the valley behind the pub, then they head west before crossing the road to the beach.' He pauses, his gaze still levelled at me, then deliberately says again, 'Down behind, over back.'

He looks at me and I look at him, and we fall about laughing.

'Over the road, back the road, up behind down! I'll never get the hang of that if I live here for ever.'

'Below the hill, now that's actually on the other side of the Dingle peninsula over at Cloghane, you know?'

'Stop! It makes sense for a minute then it's gone again. I feel like my head is going to explode.'

Pat is an honest and wry observer of the world and he has a knack for yarning. He starts telling me more about village life when he was growing up.

There had been a post office at Inch then as well as the one I use up at Annascaul. In fact it had closed only a few years ago, when the one survivor of the three sisters who ran it had felt unable to keep going on her own. I remember that Maureen Fitzgerald had said she looked after this old lady now.

Pat smiles. 'It was a great place for a chat and the gossip but if a man went in, the sisters would ignore everyone else and serve him first. The man would have had important work to be getting back to, they said. They used to run the telephone exchange from there as well. If you called from the pub – our number was "Inch 7" – you might be told you'd have to wait while they gave so-and-so his pension!'

Mike Courtney had told me that he'd once been trying in vain to call from the phone box up at the garage but there was no reply. Eventually he stomped down and asked did they not hear the phone ringing. 'Oh yes,' they said, 'but we were awful busy in the shop.'

Mike also said that the ladies listened in on all the phone calls through their switchboard.

'Of course they did!' laughs Pat.

There were no direct calls in those days so exchange had to link with exchange until they got a line all the way through to the person you wanted to talk to. Pat tells me you'd hear the conversation between the operators at each exchange as they moved the call onwards. When he was away in Dublin as a student he'd hear the call making its way to Tralee, then the Tralee operator would get on to the ladies at Inch. 'As soon as they heard them say, "We've a call for you from Dublin," they'd say, "Hello, Pat, how are you?"'

Mike, Pat and others I've spoken to all have fond memories of this former village institution and though no doubt the shop and post office are missed as facilities, it is the welcome and the banter which are most hankered after. The ladies were generous to a fault and would always give you a little extra something, a sweet or whatever – 'Carry this with you.'

Pat was in the last class to attend the Inch school at Killeenagh. In 1966, with cars and buses more common, it made economic sense to combine the school with the one in Annascaul some seven miles away over the hill. Even now, many feel that this ripped the heart out of the village.

Pat remembers the history lessons taught by Master Quill, especially those about Hugh O'Neill's rebellion against Elizabethan England, which very nearly brought Ireland under

the control of O'Neill and his confederate Catholic lords in
1598–99. As Pat says, this was as close as the Irish came to running their own affairs for three hundred years.

On Christmas Eve 1601 a Spanish force disembarked at the
port of Kinsale in County Cork and were held in check by
the English. Then O'Neill and his army arrived, sealing the
English in a pincer. Unfortunately O'Neill abandoned his usual
strategy of maintaining a siege and instead attacked. He was
routed. Gradually the allies sued for peace and the ultimate,
ironic result was that, by the time O'Neill submitted in 1603,
England was in complete control of Ireland for the first time
since the Anglo-Norman invasion had begun four hundred
years earlier.

Pat and his classmates, fired up by the history taught them by
Master Quill, would fight again the Battle of Kinsale. Cursing
the cowardly Spanish for their failure to break out, the noble
Irish lords of the Killeenagh playground would reverse Ireland's
fate and win the day against the oppressors from Elizabethan
England.

Maureen Fitzgerald had lent me a copy of the old school
registers. I'd noticed that from 1934 the names were all spelled
the Irish way, so Pat appears as Pàdraig ó Fóghli. The register is
full of names which have become familiar to me over the past
months: Moriarty, Daly, Sheehy, Foley, O'Brien, Fitzgerald and
Kennedy. These names are constant while others suddenly
disappear. Pat tells me that some families were wiped out in
tragic house fires and some moved away. There were even
horrific stories of people going insane and killing the rest of their
family.

My distant cousins, Justin (another one) and John, the elder
brothers of James, started at the school together in August 1899
and left the same day in April of the next year. Maureen had told
me that these boys had then gone by pony and trap to the school

at Annascaul. Why they should do that was a mystery. Maureen thought that John, along with one of his brothers, had died in the trenches of the First World War.

This is confirmed in a letter from Cousin Jean in County Cork. She encloses copies from a web page about the Irish who died in the First World War and further details on some hand-written sheets. Justin Shine MacCarthy, a lance corporal in the First Machine Gun Corps, was killed in action on 20 July 1916. After his primary education in Inch and Annascaul, he'd gone on to win two exhibitions to Black Rock College in Dublin and then won a further scholarship to Trinity College, Dublin. Intriguingly it was reported that he had come back from Venezuela to enlist. His brother John Valentine joined the Canadian forces and was killed in action on 10 April 1917 at Vimy Ridge. Jean writes that her father had thought that the second boy went out to avenge the death of Justin. Many Irishmen died fighting in that war, but because they were fight-ing for Britain when other Irishmen were fighting against England, in the Easter Rising and then the War of Independence, their names had been forgotten. Jean writes that in her opinion the republic swept all these deaths under the carpet.

I now have MacCarthy material from Terence, my father, Cousin Jean and more recent stuff from Justin of Clash and Maureen Fitzgerald. I sort through it in an effort to update the various branches of the family tree, but get muddled as I flick from one source to another. Phrases like 'insurmountable task' keep popping into my mind.

What is worse, as I look from the papers to the old holiday snapshots on the mantelpiece, I am overwhelmed with sadness and end up hunched forward before the cold fire with my head in my hands. I can't even work out a family tree, I think, and worry that I'm letting the family down by not making better progress. If they were here, I'd gloss over this and not admit to such feelings of inadequacy. Their presence would spur me on to at least try.

But if they were here would I really be myself anyway? Well, why not? I was able to be myself with my father and I know I'm finally starting to do it with my mother. It would just be so wonderful to have an hour as it was in the old days. We could all be staying here on holiday, sifting through this information, looking forward to a new outing, meeting some more cousins, having a drink as we prepared supper. On reflection, I say 'we' but my mother did nearly all the cooking, we'd have done the washing up. My father would be puffing his pipe, my mother and Terence probably puffing on small cigars and me on a cigarette. The air must have been thick in our house some nights. My mother took up smoking in her fifties and never quite got the hang of flicking the ash at regular enough intervals. We'd keep an eye out for the moment when it looked to have reached the critical point and warn her, or put an ashtray in position to catch it. She never inhaled. For her, having a smoke with a drink in the evening added a sense of occasion. She managed to imbue even ordinary, everyday things with her sense of fun. I miss that.

The late afternoon light darkens, emphasizing my feeling of isolation. I keep the curtains open so that I can see the lights of cars on the road and of the houses across the harbour at Cromane. Many people live like this around here, I imagine. It's very hard to pin down the character of solitude. It is fickle, friendly and frightening by turns, bringing a sense of loss and good fortune almost in the same moment. Vast spaces, whether physical or emotional, can have you shouting for joy or leave you mute and cowering.

I am grateful that for me the moment usually passes; something turns a corner in your soul and there is again hope and interest. My parents both had that too. At times I've wondered if this came from a desire to avoid difficult emotional issues. But while dramatic outpourings of feeling were not part of our domestic life I think the optimism and determination came from a realization that negativity tended to breed negativity and that there was a good deal of sense in the old-fashioned idea that one 'just had to get on with it'. More than this, though, my mother and father relished life and, even at the most challenging times, discovered much joy in it. Fortunately this attitude has rubbed off on me and at my darkest moments, when I can see no light at the end of the tunnel, has helped me try to look for, or imagine, another way through.

Next morning I'm up early and go back to the family papers with renewed enthusiasm.

'Nice morning!' shouts the postman as we scuttle towards each other through the rain at half past one in the afternoon.

His delivery is another letter from the indefatigable Cousin Jean, enclosing an article she'd written about her grandfather and his five brothers who had left their home in the tiny hamlet of Coolnacalliagh, a few miles from Inch on the banks of the Maine River in County Kerry, to go and build railways and bridges across the Zambezi River in southern Africa. The eldest sons of Jeremiah and Anne MacCarthy had been involved in the late-nineteenth-century agitation, or Moonlighting, which saw tenant farmers fighting for their rights against the agents of the absentee English landowners. Following their involvement in an ambush on a land agent outside the nearby town of Castleisland, Jeremiah reckoned his sons were going to end up in prison or on the end of a rope if they stayed in the country. The eldest boy John Justin (there's another one) headed for Cape Town in 1895. He was

given a contract to clear bush for the new railway that Cecil
Rhodes hoped would link Cape Town with Cairo. Within two
years all six boys, John Justin, Justin (and another!), George,
Garrett, James and Jeremiah, were out working on the railways.
It seemed incredible that they should find themselves so far from
home, living in the unforgiving conditions of the African
interior, drinking a bottle of whiskey a day to stave off malaria
and, rather than the farming life they'd been born to, managing
the laying of a railway through Bechuanaland, Matabeleland
and the then Rhodesia. One brother, James, was later involved in
the construction of the great bridge across the Victoria Falls, and
Jean's grandfather Justin had a stretch of track named after him.
Jean believes it is still called Justin's Railway – but then I don't
suppose it's as common a name in southern Africa as it is among
the MacCarthys of Munster.

In 1901 Justin nearly died of blackwater fever, the usually
fatal form of malaria. His brother George accompanied him on
the long sea voyage home. When he arrived home on a July
morning he went into the house and his mother, not recognizing
him at all, cried, 'Get out, you blackguard!'

Justin bought a farm a few miles away at Rathcoole in County
Cork. Aside from this man's obvious fortitude I'm impressed by
the fact that he, of the many Justins I've come across in the
family, had a nickname. To modern ears, Patsy might sound
somewhat odd for a roughty-toughty railroader and adventurer,
but I bet he felt smug as hell when, at family gatherings, he
didn't have to look up with twenty others every time someone
said 'Justin'.

The Duhallow Park Hotel, a couple of miles from Rathcoole
House where Jean and her brother Donal are now living, is my
venue for meeting them and two more cousins, Mary Lynch (née
Walsh) and Dan Walsh, for lunch.

Jean is on her feet as I enter the hotel, looking as she had in the newspaper photographs Mary had sent my father of the MacCarthy clan gathering back in 1992, thick grey hair swept back from an imposing face with bright penetrating eyes. She is all smiles and introduces me to Mary and Dan. 'My brother is late of course!' she adds with a laugh.

Mary immediately strikes me as someone who loves life and embraces it wholeheartedly. Dan Walsh is a retired Garda detective, a big chap with white hair. Although quietly spoken and gentle in character, there is an air of authority and confidence about him that obviously comes from a professional life spent dealing with people in often difficult situations.

While Dan goes to get us drinks, Donal appears. There are laughter lines all around Donal's eyes and it is immediately obvious that humour would never be far from this thin man in his elegant dark suit. Introductions now complete, we sit down with our drinks and, almost as one, begin bringing out bits of paper and letters we want to share.

I now learn how these long-distance cousins came to be in contact with my father and joined the campaign for the hostages in Lebanon.

'It was Eamonn that put us on to it,' explains Mary – she calls him Yaymon, I notice. 'He was over from Meath on a visit, for a wedding I think, in October 1990. He said he remembered your family visiting Court Hall years before.'

'Yes,' I reply, my mind suddenly filling with images from a day in 1980. 'Of course, Court Hall. I went with my parents and brother. It was owned by Eamonn Walsh. I remember meeting him. So he's a relative of you Walshes?'

'Yes, one of Dan's brothers. He was sure you had been there.'

I remember the visit clearly now. My mother and I felt a little daft as we waited, kicking our heels, at the end of the drive of a Georgian farmhouse in County Meath, a little to the north-east of Dublin. We looked over the large flat fields set in a rather dull landscape which surrounded Court Hall while my father and Terence spoke to the man who'd come to the door. Then there was a shout and the man was waving us up the drive.

Eamonn made us very welcome, ushering us into the hall, whose walls were adorned with a forest of deer antlers, and shouting as he led us across it, 'Children, come down and meet your cousins! We have family visiting.'

The eldest of the MacCarthy railway builders, John Justin, had bought Court Hall in 1903 after returning from Africa. He'd married Kathleen Walsh from the hamlet of Springmount, about a mile across the fields from where he and his brothers grew up at Coolnacalliagh. Keeping things rather tidy, John Justin's sister Mary had married Kathleen's brother Thomas. The couple at Court Hall had had no children so the estate had gone to John Justin's nephew, Mary's oldest boy, Edward, father of Eamonn and Dan. Another brother, Billy, still farms at Springmount.

'Well, after that,' Mary carries on, 'we decided we must do something, so we got in touch with your dad and the campaign in London. I spoke to him a few times and met him when we were over in England. He was a lovely man.'

Mary, Dan and Jean all started working with other friends, writing letters to ministers at home and in the European parliament. They gathered some six thousand signatures for a petition and joined the Yellow Ribbon campaign, with Mary tying ribbons in the trees around Kanturk Castle in July 1991 during a Clan MacCarthy gathering.

'Pat's phone bill must have been enormous,' says Jean. 'We talked for an hour!'

Mary, Dan and Jean all have bits of correspondence and news cuttings with them for me. Looking over them later back at the cottage I realize how much work they, like so many others, had put in on behalf of me and the other hostages. As usual I am bowled over. So many people joined the Friends of John McCarthy campaign and were in touch with Jill Morrell and other friends at the campaign HQ in London. It always makes me proud and humble, and sad, all at once. Here, though, there had been a different link – 'He's one of us! What can we do to help?' My father would have liked that very much. As well as committing himself to the campaign for my release and pursuing every avenue of inquiry for news about me and the hostage situation in general, he would have delighted in the personal contacts he made. There was something special about his outlook on life that allowed him to look for the positive. And now that those bad times are far in the past I can enjoy these long-dormant, invisible family connections which were brought alive because of that experience.

We move into the dining room and order food, putting documents and papers aside while we eat. I learn more about my cousins. Mary is now semi-retired, having worked in the family hardware business. Mind you, as I'd thought on first seeing her, her idea of semi-retirement is what many of us would think of as full-time occupation. She'd recently co-written a book about her great-grand-uncle, O'Sullivan Burk. This hero of nineteenth-century Fenianism had a remarkable life, going from Ireland to the US, then working and fighting in South America, including Chile, fighting on the Union side in the American Civil War, before returning to Ireland and taking part in the Fenian rising and in the escape from Manchester of members of the organization in 1867. Mary and her family also have a passion for racehorses. With Ebony Jane they'd won the Irish National one year and came fourth in the English National the following week.

Jean is one of those Irish people who you might at first imagine has spent all their life living in the quiet countryside where they were born. Then you realize that they have travelled far and wide and done fascinating things. Jean had been a high-powered research scientist and had taken her PhD at a university in Maryland where she was working on a NASA project for growing food in space. She had been a teacher and there was still something of that about her. She is highly know-ledgeable – and incredibly tough, it turns out. She was afflicted by the horrendous Weil's disease a few years previously. This normally fatal illness left her unconscious for a month. By all accounts it was a miracle she survived. Her zest for life and learning was undimmed. I have the feeling that Jean is a passionate person and that while she might giggle quite girlishly sometimes, if challenged on something she holds dear I reckon she could be fierce too. Among her other passions are family and local history.

While she has a scientist's eye for precise details, I get the impression that her brother Donal is keener on a good tale, or 'yarn' as he often says, and that absolute historical veracity is not so important to him. He is a farmer with some six hundred sheep on the lands his grandfather Justin had bought at Rathcoole after his time in southern Africa.

I'd read Jean's extensive article about the brothers' activities on the railways and now find that it is a subject all the cousins are keen to talk about. One thing Jean hadn't written up in detail was the fact that none of those men wanted to stay in Africa despite being entitled to extensive land grants.

'Granddad was very happy to get away from "the terrible place",' she says and goes on to tell me that when they got home, most of their tales of tribesmen and snakes and rhinos attacking trains were dismissed as wild yarns by their Kerry neighbours (who were no doubt used to spinning plenty of their own). So they didn't talk about it much. As children Donal and Jean tried to quiz their grandfather but with little success. Donal says though that towards the end of his life his own father (who he always refers to as the boss, pronounced 'barss') told him more of what he had learned from *his* father. In spite of drinking the aforementioned bottle of whiskey a day each while in Africa to ward off malaria, they'd all suffered from the disease through-out their lives. Donal remembered his grandfather even as a very old man having bouts of the fever. And he never lost the habit of keeping a bottle of whiskey in his bedroom.

Jean recalls going to Dunboyne as a little girl. They would scamper around the house looking at the stuffed heads and lion skins while Grandfather Justin talked to Grand-Uncle John Justin who was very ill and confined to a bed downstairs before a roaring fire even in summer. Despite the hardships of southern Africa, John Justin's life did not become one of safe and peaceful seclusion on his farm. I learn from Jean that during the War of Independence he acted as a banker for the IRA and that his home was a 'safe house' for men on the run. On one occasion, British Army officers called at Dunboyne while some fugitive IRA men slept upstairs. John Justin, obviously a very cool customer, invited the officers to come in and play cards. Which they did, neither armed faction aware of the other's presence in their host's house.

Swapping tales and filling each other in on details of our lives, we are getting on in a very relaxed way, as any group of people meeting for the first time might, especially if they have some shared experiences. But I am sure that the fact that we are kin, albeit distant, makes all the difference. The Irish take the family very seriously, as I've discovered with the Kennedys and Justin of Clash. It gives me real pleasure to discover and explore these remote bonds, to share family stories and look back into the past to see where we have all come from and establish some reassuring communality.

They are interested to see the new section of the family tree that Terence had discovered and which filled in a blank of over two hundred years in other versions of the tree. After Donal, the founder of the McCarthy clan branch, or sept, at Ardcanacht, who was living in 1347, there was nothing until Florence, the eighth chieftain of the sept, who took part in the Earl of Desmond's rebellion against the English in 1579. Terence had bridged the gap with information and help provided by the Chief Herald's staff, and data from the archives at Trinity College, Dublin.

More recent additions to the tree are finally becoming clear to me too. The copy I have at home ends on the Irish side with the generation of the six brothers who went to southern Africa and a little bit of information on their cousins, including James, who had grown up at Inch.

There is a reasonably good list of the following generations in a commentary included in a new edition of Samuel Trant MacCarthy's book *The MacCarthys of Munster*, which had been brought out in 1997 by the other Terence MacCarthy (there are only two Terences, I promise). At that time this Terence styled himself, and was recognized by the Irish Chief Herald's Office, as the MacCarthy Mór, or chief of the clan. Subsequently the Herald's Office withdrew its recognition and a pretender to the title appeared, and Terence MacCarthy abdicated. There is a huge amount of correspondence about all this on the Clan MacCarthy Society website. In its way it is all rather entertaining, with romantic claims of family gatherings at Paris early in the last century at which the clan chief was chosen by the ancient Gaelic practice of *Tanistry*, where, after the death of a chief, all relevant kin vote for the most suitable successor. This quasi-democratic system was originally employed to ensure that a chief's eldest son, who would automatically succeed under the more common system of primogeniture, would not do so if deemed to be insufficient for the task.

After a while the claims and counterclaims became silly and boring, although I quite like the idea of these people adorning themselves with medals and capes and shouting at each other, 'No, I'm the chief!'

Sensibly, the Clan MacCarthy Society, whose president and website are American-based, takes the view that unless someone can give them clear and honest evidence of their claim and not indulge in pointless wordplay, the society will take no further notice of them. The members of the society are interested in the clan's history, the Gaelic world and on building up an association of MacCarthys around the world.

I've also learned that Samuel Trant MacCarthy's claim to the title was less than solid and that he'd even gone to the length of adding Mór to his name by deed poll. Our immediate family tree is irrelevant to these various claims of chieftainship so I can rest assured that there would have been no need to falsify any of it. Given that my interest is to get a feel for my old connections with Ireland and to discover and enjoy current relations, this is good news for me. It is fun to explore a common past but it's much more rewarding to share and understand the present.

Donal smiles when I say that I've become more and more suspicious of the arguments over claims to the MacCarthy Mór title and I'm pleased that when I mention that according to Terence MacCarthy's edition of *The MacCarthys of Munster*, he is the Lord of Ardcanacht, he replies with a snort, 'It means nothing to me!'

Donal, I feel, hates pretence, likes the history well enough, but above all enjoys the 'yarns'.

Jean still has some sympathy for Terence MacCarthy's title claims, which may derive from her not wanting to let go of something she had accepted as true. But it is also certainly bound up with her contempt for the bureaucrats at the Irish Genealogical Office. She told me in one of her letters that the

Irish Chief Herald's Office only gives 'courtesy recognition' to Gaelic titles. Such matters are actually covered by the Irish Constitution. Under Article 40, which deals with personal rights, you cannot accept a title of nobility or an honour without the prior approval of the government. All this sounds reasonable enough on the face of it, but having seen the documents on the MacCarthy Mór case, Jean feels that the professional skills one might expect to find in the Herald's Office have been sadly lacking.

Returning to more local family news I tell them what I have found out about James at Inch and ask if they know anything more of his wife Gráinne and the boy Sean. They recall a front-page story in the *Sunday World* in the mid-1980s about a huge bill they had run up at the Shelbourne Hotel in Dublin, confident that they would win the battle for James's estate. My Cork cousins had always thought that James's brother Hilary and nephew Jackie had got it all so I explain that eventually it had been split between them and the son. I am just telling them that James had apparently set up a second home for his young wife in Kildare and that Gráinne never came to Inch again after the wedding when Jean suddenly tells me very firmly, 'She did go back to live at Inch but James kicked her out. He said she was having an affair.'

'Really? My neighbours at Inch seemed very sure she never—'

'Daddy went to the Inch house and James said she and "the man" were always whispering out at the back.'

One way and another Gráinne must have had an unhappy relationship with County Kerry and it seems that she died there, in Killarney. Jean had learned this from an Eileen Egan in Toronto when she was writing her article about the railway-building brothers. Eileen, who was a daughter of railroader George MacCarthy, also reported that the railwaymen's mother,

Anne Nagle, was born in Ardcanacht. A chilling reminder of the horror of the Irish Civil War comes with the story of Anne's nephew. George Nagle was killed at Glencar across the water from my home by the Free State troops in 1923, during the Civil War. According to T. Ryle Dwyer, in his book *Tans, Terror and Troubles: Kerry's Real Fighting Story 1913–1923*, Nagle was wounded during an attack by the Free State troops. When his IRA comrades retreated and Nagle was captured, he was shot on the ground where he lay.

The horror and intensity of the Civil War – and by all accounts Kerry saw some of the worst of it – shocks me. After so long fighting to be a free nation it still amazes me that they'd turned so readily upon themselves.

Donal laughs. 'First they fought the British, then they fought each other. It would have been very unusual to have done it differently!'

The 'barss' had passed on memories of the War of Independence to Donal. A bridge at Rathcoole had been blown up so the British soldiers took to using a makeshift bridge that took them on a track right through the courtyard at Rathcoole House. The IRA decided that this would be a perfect spot for an ambush. Buildings in Rathcoole had been burned by the British after a previous IRA ambush nearby so Grandfather Justin (Patsy) knew that he'd lose everything if the planned attack went ahead. Rather than try to dissuade the IRA, Justin simply went and 'knocked' the makeshift bridge and the British stopped using the track. End of story.

One day the 'barss' was walking with his father to one of their farms some distance away. By following the railway line they could shorten their journey but they became anxious when they heard a plane overhead. The IRA often blew the railway to prevent supplies getting through to the various Black and Tan barracks, so being spotted on the line was dangerous. Justin told his son, 'Keep your head down and keep walking as if we're railway engineers checking the track.' The plane came round a couple of times. 'Don't look up, act as if you've got a job to do.' The plane went away after a while and they were safe.

Donal shares another piece of family wisdom that he had gleaned from the 'barss': the MacCarthys always made terrible priests. This sets my cousins talking about one young relative who was never really suited to being a man of the cloth and had led a very unhappy life, dominated in the end by alcohol. When I mention that back in the early 1800s one of the family, Charles MacCarthy from Ardcanacht, had been the priest at the neighbouring parish of Keel, Donal's eyes twinkle and he announces that this man had been a wrong 'un and got involved with a young woman. Jean, jumping to defend the family honour, denies this emphatically as ill-informed nonsense. Donal just smiles and shrugs – who cares, it's ancient history, and what's more it's a good yarn.

Good intentions for a healthier lifestyle do not quite take off as hoped. Running twenty times (OK, fifteen; well, all right, ten times) round the circuit of rutted track that goes down from the house then up by the washed-out corner and through the old farmyard, nearly kills me. Waves of nausea sweep over me as I gasp and gasp, bent over with my hands on my knees. This time last year I could run steadily for forty-five minutes. However, when I've recovered my breath and had a shower I feel virtuous and confident that a few weeks' building it up day by day will see me marathon-fit in no time.

In Tralee I stop off at the library to see if they can help me with my latest search: a hunt for another John McCarthy. So far I've found just the one reference to him and that's in the enthusiastic but eccentric, by turns exact and vague, *Ancient History of the Kingdom of Kerry* by Friar O'Sullivan, of Muckross

Abbey. I discovered this on the MacCarthy Clan website where it is reproduced from a series of articles edited and prefaced by one F. Jarlath Prendergast, OFM. According to Jarlath, the history was probably written in the middle of the eighteenth century (realizing that even a historian can be confused about when a history book was written makes me feel much less anxious that I sometimes lose the thread of Irish chronology). The reference to this other John McCarthy comes in a section about the cultural attainments of the people of Kerry:

> The county Kerry and Desmond gentlemen were great proficients in the copious Irish language . . . They were not also strangers to the art of poetry . . . also in the heroic verse, and the composure called Tiriv, of whom was Geffry O'Donoghue of the Glinn, Messrs. Pierce Ferettr, Jno. McCarthy of Ardcanacta, and Daniel Garav O'Sullivan.

As he is linked with Pierce Ferriter who was leading rebellions in the mid-1600s, presumably that was when Jno. McC was penning his verses too. So some three and a half centuries ago there'd been a John McCarthy of Ardcanacht, though not one who has ever appeared on the family tree. Of course Friar O'Sullivan might have been wrong, there may never have been such a poet, or if there was he might have nothing to do with my McCarthy ancestors, but I find myself humming with excitement, the thrill of the chase for this new character mixing with the irrational feeling that my distant links with the place have somehow been brought closer. I hunt through the library's numerous books on Irish literature, finding that there are many more writer McCarthys than I'd ever imagined, but I draw a blank for my Ardcanacht poet.

The librarian takes up the challenge, but sadly he is no more successful.

By way of consolation I buy a collection of Irish myths and sagas. Looking through the bookshelves and magazine racks it strikes me as funny, given that Ireland is so proud to be a republic and that there has always been a strong IRA–Sinn Féin presence in the area, that so much is made of it being the *Kingdom* of Kerry. Newspapers and anyone to do with the tourist industry use the title freely.

I automatically turn to Tom Barrington for an explanation of why a kingdom is so popular in a republic. On this occasion he has a number of theories, which if you look at them quickly sound straightforward enough, but if you read them in detail become peculiarly baffling.

The Ciarraige were one of the ancient peoples of the region who might have been Pictish in origin and may have tipped up around 500 BC. The tale was that Ciar was one of the triplet sons of the Pictish Queen Medb and Fergus Mac Roich. Ciar became a king, or *ri* in Gaelic. Hence we got Ciar-raige, or kingship of (the people of) Ciar, which became Kingdom of Kerry. Whatever the actual date of their arrival in Ireland, they were apparently still there and doing business in the sixth century AD. Barrington goes into a long explanation about how the word Ciarraige might have other meanings to do with vassal relationships with other tribes or groups but I'm afraid I rather lose the thread. So had everyone else, it seemed, happy to stick with the Kingdom idea. Perhaps it is politically correct to use the term in modern Ireland because it refers to an ancient local kingdom, not something imposed from outside.

# CHAPTER TEN

ON THE WAY HOME I HAVE A STRONG URGE TO HAVE ANOTHER look for the Ogham stone at Ardcanacht. Following the suggestion of the couple I met on my last attempt, I try another track off the main road into the area. Pulling into a gateway I consult Barrington. What does he know about Ogham stones at Ardcanacht? He makes it sound easy: 'Follow the national monuments sign for the Ardcanacht stones.' Couldn't be simpler, Tom, but what sign? Any other clues? There is this: 'a walk of a half-mile along a boithrin (lane), through a farmyard and, bearing left, over a stile into a field'. Hold it there, Tom, I think, a frisson of familiarity moving through me. It seems odd that a stile would be memorable after more than twenty years, and I cannot picture it, but a stile definitely means something to me in this context. Consulting the Ordnance Survey map, it does seem that if I am on the track I think I'm on, then this section of my Irish journey might be close to fulfilment.

The lane takes me down past one farmhouse, as per Barrington, and on to a bend where it turns to the right across a field towards more houses. A marshy track goes off to the left. Thinking of Barrington and looking at the map again, this looks like the corner I need. There's an unusually elegant iron gate across the track, some fifty yards away, which does not look familiar. I look again and shrug; it's a handsome old gate but that's all. Then my eye travels to the side, where a sizeable gatepost sticks out from a corner of stone wall. That's why I remember it. Large stones jut out, making a stairway over the wall, a drystone stile, in effect. It is neat and well-built and pleasing to the eye but not immediately obvious and I know I have admired it before. The thrill of recognition is almost tangible.

I squelch down the track and climb the stile. There is the Ogham stone in the middle of the field. No tidal wave of emotion sweeps over me, rather a sensation of pleasure and relief to have found the right spot. In fact the main stone and its small attendant rocks are something of an anti-climax and look rather daft. Well, there you are then, I say to myself and recollect that twenty years ago we'd had a similar reaction, pleased to have found what we were after and then mildly amused at the tameness of the find. We'd all been hoping to find an old house or ruin that might have been the old MacCarthy homestead and had to make do with this broken down old rock. Barrington says that the fragments of rock may not be genuine but that the main piece probably is. He refers to the research carried out by one R. A. S. Macalister in the 1940s who argues that the inscriptions on the stone are of a magical nature, though what they were supposed to conjure remains a mystery.

Though pleased to have found the stone at last, I am much more delighted that there is no overwhelming sense of loss here but rather one of reconnection with my family then and especially my mother. The past, for the first time since I've been in Ireland, seems very real. We'd been here together and posed against this curious stone on a family holiday where we'd been looking into our past, enjoying the time together. Whatever the purpose of the magic inscriptions, to encourage or control good or evil, tracing their outlines now I feel that they have helped me make an important step. Rather than running from memories in case they bring hurt, I realize that by seeking them out they can actually bring comfort.

As we did back in 1980, I carry on to Inch, not to the Strand Hotel but to Foley's. While I chat with John I become conscious that I am being sniped at by Jerry. Jerry is four years old and has suddenly taken to playing with me. Just a little while ago he and his sister would say hello when told to by their parents, but at some point they must have accepted me in some way. Being included in their world, shown their schoolbooks, Jerry's tasks so simple and his explanations of them so sweet, fills me with great affection. Hearing him whisper 'Prepare to die' and discovering that his small figure is creeping up behind me with a devil's trident ('We've got two') left over from Halloween makes me long to have a child of my own.

As I drive back to the cottage it dawns on me that the increasing need to grieve for my mother and then remember and rebuild my relationship with her must be spurred, at least in part, by a desire to have a clear head and heart before starting my own family. When I've thought about having children I've questioned whether I'm ready for it. I suppose I'm what you would call a late developer, given that I'm forty-five years old. Because my mother and I never had the chance to talk again, it's as though I've been marooned in my late twenties when I last saw her. She always provided an emotional mainstay – something that I would like to be certain of again, to carry on with my family. Now by beginning to bring the relationship up to date I want to be free to say to a child, 'This is where I came from.'

Valentia Island is a name that has conjured a romantic and remote location whenever I've heard it on the shipping forecast.

It always sounded European, Spanish perhaps, so I'd been surprised to learn it was located on the western tip of Kerry. Jeremiah King's *County Kerry Past & Present* explains that the name derives from the Irish words *beal inse*, the island mouth or harbour, hence it was Bealinche, nothing remotely Spanish at all, except that *b* is pronounced *v*, as in Spanish.

Even though there were no linguistic connections, there had been strong trading links between the people of the area and Spain for centuries. Friar O'Sullivan wrote about it:

> Their considerable trading with Spain till about 260 years ago, when America was discovered, could hardly be believed now had there not been several proofs and instances for it. They had some trading ships of their own, besides some ships of war, and the Spaniards undoubtedly had several colonies and factuaries in several ports, etc. . . . as in Tralee, Dingle, Valentia, Begganish, Ballycarbry, Ballyskellicks . . . so that said trading was very considerable and of great advantage to the aforesaid inhabitants; one sufficient proof of said great trading, as before mentioned, that O'Sullivan Bear had £1,900 a year port charges, anchorage, and other privileges . . . Nothing then in vogue with the inhabitants . . . but Spanish wine, Spanish clothes, Spanish leather, and Spanish swords, which they called Spanish tucks, and other commodities – iron, liquorish, fruit, etc. The trading with Spain grew so familiar with the inhabitants that they made no difficulty of making voyages to Spain. An instance whereof: as a woman in Ballyskelicks (as it passes for truth), calling to her gossip or neighbour for the loan of a mantle being asked how far she intended to go, answered, unconcerned, 'only to Spain'.

Driving around Valentia Island, which is reached by a bridge, I can see clearly two pinnacles of rocks sticking up a mile or two out at sea. These are Skellig Michael and Little Skellig and look as weird and wonderful as Paddy O'Brien had described them to me. They seem so close and yet the approach is so difficult that I have to accept that however much I want to go out there, fate is unlikely to allow me at this time of year.

The landscape here dips and swoops, under and up again from the sea, to create hills, cliffs and islets. My distant and ancient relation, Donal IX MacCarthy Mór, was made Baron of Valentia and Earl of Clancarr by Elizabeth I on 24 June 1565. Donal had done a deal with the English crown to exchange his title of King of Desmond for something more modest in order to keep his lands. Like many of his Gaelic contemporaries he appears to have had difficulty sticking to any deal and would sometimes back rebellions against the English and at other times behave as a loyal subject once more. He gave the title Viscount Valentia to his son Tadg, who sadly pre-deceased him, which brought the title – and indeed the Kingdom of Desmond – to its end.

Narrow winding roads take me on a circuit of the island. There are few people about and I guess they are all locals. In their old farming clothes or overalls they seem a million miles away from the tourists in their neat cars and smart country casual clothes. In summer these roads must be teeming with cars as tourists make the trip round the island and I wonder whether the people standing by the road or at the farmyard gate still politely raise a hand in greeting then as they almost invariably do to me now.

Barrington, in one of his casual, throwaway asides, tells me of a legendary resident of Valentia Island. The druid Mogh Roith, who was known as the Servant of the Wheel, is said to have been the man who chopped the head off John the Baptist. That's all Mr B is prepared to divulge.

A sign, 'The Grotto', takes me to an old slate quarry. In the great, gaping cave mouth there are statues of Our Lady and

St Bernadette. The slate was quarried, with some breaks, between
1816 and 1911 and was used in some fairly impressive locations:
the Paris Opera House, the Houses of Parliament
in London, and at Waterloo and Blackfriars stations. From
this, the highest point on the island, I am looking north-west
to the Blasket Islands. Below me the waters of the Atlantic
shift and sway as the swell rolls into large breakers that crash
in a lather over the shores of Beginish Island and at the base
of the Fort Point lighthouse below me. Between these two is
the entrance to Valentia harbour, the westernmost anchorage
in Europe and once the haven of pirates and smugglers. Looking
further westward to where the sea's swell is still undisturbed, sug-
gesting the passage of a giant sea serpent beneath the surface, I see
the aerials and buildings of the Valentia Coast Radio Station
whose reports on weather conditions first stirred my imagination.

Valentia was the first landfall made by the American aviator
Charles A. Lindbergh when he made the first nonstop flight
between New York and Paris in 1927. I have an image of that
iconic monoplane *Spirit of St Louis* being buffeted through the
grey clouds as the ecstatic Lindbergh realized that he'd made it
across the Atlantic. There was no radio in the plane but had he
been able to make contact with the duty watch down at Valentia,
I wonder if it could have gone like this:

'Valentia radio, Valentia radio, this is *Spirit of St Louis*, over.'

'Hello, Mrs Lewis is it? How are you?'

'Valentia radio, this is *Spirit of St Louis*. Can you confirm my
course for Paris, over?'

'Well now, if I was going to Paris, I wouldn't be starting from
here . . .'


'Mam, Mam! There are men in the bar with funny straw hats on,
like tables!' Jerry, hotly pursued by Katie, bursts into the Foleys'
dining room.

Fidelus looks at Mary O'Brien and starts laughing.

'It's the Biddy Men!' she announces.

'The what?' I ask.

'The Biddy Men. It's St Brigid's Day, they'll be going round all the pubs.'

I follow Katie and Jerry to see this spectacle. Sure enough, there are men in tall straw hats like upturned tables and they are dancing with each other while one plays an accordion. There's a definite whiff of Morris dancing in the air, but no pig bladders on sticks as far as I can see. Three or four girls, dressed mainly in white like the men but looking far less comfortable, forlornly hold up a sign promoting, for a reason which isn't clear, the Killorglin Cycle Club.

When the dance is over, I join Fidelus and her other dinner guests Paddy and Mary O'Brien. Candles everywhere have given the kitchen a cosy, almost mysterious atmosphere. John is laid up in bed with a badly sprained ankle, injured during an indoor football match.

Brigid, I learn, was an ancient goddess of fertility and poetry and a daughter of the great god Dagda. The pagan festival associated with her fell on 1 February, the first day of spring. The festival is also known as Imbolc, meaning sheep's milk, as this is when the ewes start to come into milk. Christianity transformed the old goddess to St Brigid.

This talk of arcane festivals and strange gods and the subdued lighting inspire Mary to tell us ghost stories, particularly those which relate to Inch Strand and the area around James MacCarthy's old house. She and a friend had been up there on a dark track once when they'd heard the heavy panting of someone running towards them and then past them into the night.

'The panting came so close, we stepped aside, but there was no one to be seen! I was terrified, and I thought I must have imagined it, that it was a gust of wind or something, but my friend had heard it exactly the same as me. Your cousin, James, they say his ghost used to walk the beach with his dog,' Mary says, looking at me.

Perhaps his soul was uneasy because he'd failed to leave a proper will for the settling of his estate, I think.

As we enjoy the meal Fidelus has prepared, the conversation moves back to the here and now. I've been surprised that so many people you meet, who talk as though they've spent their whole lives in the area, will casually tell you that they have lived in England, the States or Australia too. I knew Paddy had been away for a long time and unlike most has kept his English accent. Now it's the turn of his and Mary's son Shane to go off and he's leaving imminently for the States, though his plans are vague. Like all parents they seem slightly concerned that he isn't sure where he'll be living or how he'll support himself, but they want to encourage him at the same time. At least they know there are relatives who can look after him if things go wrong.

Talk of connections with the US has Mary, though somewhat laterally, warming to her ghostly path once more. One night there'd been a terrible wailing at a friend's back door. When she'd gone to open it, there was an old hag there asking to come in. She was sent on her way. The next day news came through that a relative had died in America so the hag must have been a banshee, or *bean sídhe*, a female spirit who folklore holds will appear to warn a family of an imminent death.

Of course this could have been just a tale or coincidence but Fidelus says that other elements of traditional beliefs continue to be held in the community. When she'd first taken over the pub she'd found some rotten eggs on the doorstep one morning.

'I didn't know what it was but Bridey Flynn told me it was a *piseog*, something that was meant to bring me bad luck. Charming!'

Apparently Bridey had had the same thing when she moved to Inch fifty years ago. It was assumed that it was the action of some other woman who'd perhaps had her eye on the man of the house.

St Mary's Roman Catholic Church on Dingle's Green Street, built in 1865, looks very traditional from the outside but the interior has a surprisingly airy, modern feel. Instead of the usual series of roofs over the three aisles, it has one pitched roof lined with plain timber. The church was designed in the neogothic style by a J. J. McCarthy (no relation as far as I know but five will get you ten one of those Js stands for Justin) but the new roof had been put on in the 1960s as part of a major refurbishment.

People are drifting in for the evening Festival Mass for St Brigid's Day which is to include traditional singing and dancing. The church is far from packed and the majority of the congregation are women and children. Most of the men who have come are standing up against the back wall of the church – an old custom apparently. I find myself an empty pew about halfway down by the outer aisle.

Some very young children, members of the local Rince na Mara group, dance to the accompaniment of the visiting Glóir Dé musicians. All in black, the small dancers keep their upper bodies rigidly stiff as their feet tap with great speed on the altar steps. The concentration on their little faces as they dance to the tune of 'The Kerry Pipers' brings tears to my eyes. In the pew in front of me a mother sits with three young girls who are riveted by the performance. The Mass follows, with the priest speaking mainly in English but switching to Irish from time to time. He delivers his sermon, on the theme of people in remote places being denied benefits that others enjoy, in a lilting almost rap style, punctuating his thoughts with a 'Yes, oh yes!' refrain.

As he talks about people living on the fringes of society,

whether geographically or financially, he also notes that women in modern times often feel a sense of exclusion. When he says this, I notice the woman in front dip her head for a moment. Then follows the Eucharist, the blessings and the handshakes. When the woman turns round to shake my hand, I think there are tears in her eyes, though she is smiling at me.

At the end of the service the priest announces that there will be more dancing. In front of me the three girls pull at their mother's arm but she shakes her head and tells them they can go over to get a closer look by themselves. As they scoot off, the woman turns to me.

'Hello. It is John, isn't it?'

'Yes it is, I'm sorry, I, um . . .'

'No, we haven't met before – I was reading your book.'

'OK, thank you. That was a pleasant service. The dancers look so sweet, don't they? Do your girls dance – are they yours?'

'Yes, they are, six, nine and eleven. All mad for the dancing!' Clearly she wants to say something and is looking for the right words. 'As I said, I read your book. I really enjoyed it, if it's all right to say that, given what you went through.'

'Of course, thank you for saying so. It was a long time ago now anyway.'

She still seems to want to say more but looks uncertain.

'How are you?' I ask.

'Oh fine, fine!' she says, looking anything but fine.

Then she nods her head as if deciding to go on. 'My husband has been diagnosed with cancer,' she says and swallows hard before rushing on. 'We don't know yet how serious it is, the doctors are being cautiously optimistic, but making no promises. They're doing tests to see what will be best to do.'

'I'm sorry. How terrible, especially with the children so young. How is he taking it?'

'He's being very brave, trying to laugh it off.'

'Yes, we all deal with things in our own way. How about you?
It must be desperate.'

'Thank you, it is. But no, it's not like that, you see. I mean –
oh, God forgive me!' She lowers her voice. 'God knows, you
don't want to be hearing this. We were so in love when we met
and married. But then after a while things were difficult. The
business took up so much of his time and he was always worried
about it. He started drinking heavily, at first it didn't seem to
matter but then it got harder and harder to talk. I was stupid
sometimes, having a go at him when he was jarred and then a
few times he lashed out at me. The last time he gave me a real
beating.' Her eyes are now full of tears but she gathers herself
and goes on.

'I went home to my mother's for a break. He kept phoning
saying he was so sorry and that it would never happen again. But
somehow something was gone, something had died inside me.'

'Why didn't you leave him?'

'I just couldn't do it. My mother said she knew I was unhappy,
but that now he was sorry and that things would be better. She
kept saying that I'd been married in the eyes of God and that it
would be a sin to leave my marriage. So I went back to him.'

'How was it then?'

'Oh, it was better, but I couldn't love him the way I had.
We thought having children would bring us closer. It worked
in a way and they are lovely kids and I hope to God we have
given them a loving home, I think we have. But really I feel
it's just a working relationship with me and my husband.'

There is nothing I can say of course. Her situation is tragic, a
bright, attractive woman with a man who had thrown away
their happiness.

For years she's cried herself to sleep, she tells me, feeling completely and utterly alone.

'How did you, do you, keep going?'

'When the kids were babies I devoted all my time to the family, then when they started at school I got a job and buried myself in that.'

'Buried yourself?'

'Yes.' She smiles thinly. 'At times it feels like I'm only half alive. And now with his cancer I'm all messed up. I can't help it but think it would be best for me if the worst happened. But I know I can't mean that, he's a lovely father to the girls and he works hard for us all. God forgive me though, but there are times when I just want a new start, have a life again. It's funny, I used to be so angry with the Church. If my mother hadn't had her faith I might have been free years ago.' She pauses and takes a deep sigh as I've heard other women here do, but never more sadly. 'But then I wouldn't have my girls. Now I go to church and pray and pray that everything will come right.'

The three little girls come running through the pews, chattering excitedly. They stop when they are near and look at me shyly, uncertainly.

'Say hello to this man, he's visiting from England but his family used to live in Kerry.'

They all nod at me as their mother stands up and gathers her coat and bag.

'Goodbye then, John, thanks for listening.'

We shake hands, and I try to think of something, anything, to say as the kids look on. I'm about to utter some platitude but before I can, they are gone.

I am only vaguely aware of the music and the tapping of the dancers' feet as I sit for a few minutes. I look down at the service sheet and then around me, half wondering if the conversation had really happened. People have told me their stories out of the blue before; Sean, for example, had suddenly come out with the account of his nightmarish childhood. Sitting there in the church watching families gather their things and the dancers standing in a huddle, no doubt talking about their performance, I am saddened that this scene, which appears to be one of happy families in a safe community, could mask such distress.

I leave the church, threading my way between the few people still loitering at the porch, find my car and drive home over the potholed roads and through the drizzling rain with a heavy heart.

I've become a fan of Radio Kerry. On the weekday morning show *Breakfast in Kerry (in association with Spar)* you get a good mix of local and national news and the music is mainly middle-of-the-road, though with rather too much country and western for my liking. Although they rarely mean much, if anything, to me I enjoy the adverts for local events, stores, animal feeds and treatments. Each week there's a report on available jobs in the county. And not only do they keep me posted on the activities of the living but also on the movements of the dead, from mortuary, to church and to grave.

The woman who usually hosts the morning show reads the star signs for the day, so if you want a change of job, or indeed if you're not feeling too healthy, you can use the astrological data to plan your next move. One night I'm listening in and am thrilled to hear on the news that tonight I will have the only chance for more than twenty years to see, with the naked eye, Saturn pass behind the moon. My excitement is dampened when, immediately after the bulletin, the weather forecast advises that there will be thick cloud cover all night. They give, they take away.

The Saturday morning show, *Saturday Supplement*, is a great cultural magazine show that I catch whenever I can. Today they're talking about the play *Solo Run* by Tony Guerin, a retired Garda, that's about to open at the Siamsa Tíre Theatre in Tralee. The play is based on real events that took place in the town of

Listowel in the 1940s. A young woman died in childbirth and people wanted her buried in the churchyard after a proper funeral but the Church was having none of it because the girl was unmarried.

In keeping with a theatre that was set up to promote the old Irish traditions, Siamsa Tíre's home base has been designed to follow the lines of one of the ancient Celtic ring forts and so the various public spaces are curved. Off the main foyer is an exhibition area. Currently on show is an exhibition called 'Once Is Enough' promoting awareness about domestic abuse. The main exhibit is a long dining table with a chair at either end. One chair, the woman's, has a chain attached to it. Over the table hangs an array of domestic objects and utensils that could be used in a violent attack. As a piece of modern art this is striking enough but terrifying too. In the next room one wall is covered with little shelves with a flower laid on each, a memorial for women who have died as a result of domestic violence in recent years. The exhibition grew out of the work of the Family Resource Centre in Dublin.

Since my conversation with the woman in church, I've been trying to find out whether domestic violence is an issue in Ireland as a whole. The facts are staggering. Reported cases of domestic violence have doubled in recent years. One statistic I read says that four out of every ten women who have had a sexual relationship have experienced domestic violence. Reports and revelations about the horrors acted out in some Irish homes seem to come thick and fast. The nation is beginning to accept the scale of the problem and how much needs to be done. The most terrifying figures, to my mind, come from the *Sexual Abuse and Violence In Ireland* report commissioned for the Dublin Rape Crisis Centre. This study shows that 42 per cent of women and 28 per cent of men have been sexually abused or violated in their lifetimes. More children are sexually abused in Ireland than either the rest of Europe or North America.

I've read these figures with a mixture of revulsion and disbelief. Yes, some men beat up their wives, and some parents abuse their children. In Ireland there is the particularly horrible problem of priests who've abused helpless children. But to learn that the scale of the problems is such that similar issues in Europe or the USA are overshadowed is frightening. Trying to put it into perspective I look up the last census and work out that the report's findings indicate that more than three-quarters of a million women and over half a million men have been victims of some form of sexual abuse. That is more than 1.25 million people out of a population of less than 3.7 million. Why? How has this come about in a land famed for its political, emotional and spiritual sensitivities? Reasons put forward are: alcohol misuse – love for the *craic*; separate sex schooling – Church-inspired terror of sex; social isolation – too many men living without a sexual partner. Whatever monsters might be prowling the city streets, the dangers could just as easily be lurking in schools and quiet rural communities. From both the press and local opinion I get the impression that people know that, with one in three people having suffered abuse, the problem can no longer be swept under the carpet.

The play *Solo Run* centres on an ageing former All Irish footballer Colm Casey. As the local hero he is looked up to as a leader but, although courageous, he lacks the intellect for such a position. And he has a hunchbacked son he is ashamed of. Not a particularly unusual character or situation then really. Only his wife knows, and has to deal with, his doubts and worries. The community looks to him to do battle with the canon over the young girl's funeral. The canon chains the churchyard gates closed and Colm, driven on by the roars of the crowd, breaks the chain. Guerin's play is well-written and alongside the anger and action there are plenty of laughs. Interestingly, during the most powerful scene when, under threat of excommunication and the influence of alcohol, Colm starts to throttle the canon with the chain from the church gate, there are laughs and a few cheers from the audience.

Guerin's play is just right for this moment in Irish history; people are struggling to express their anger with the Church as the last vestiges of infallibility crumble.

The wind and the rain are rattling against the house when I wake, putting me out of sorts immediately; there will be no majestic views beyond the curtains today. At the back of my mind I know the weather could easily change in an hour or so and that the afternoon might bring sunshine and rainbows over the water and mountains. My low spirits really come from the fact that, over the past couple of weeks, the Ireland I half hoped I wouldn't find has materialized.

On top of the sad accounts I've heard first-hand, from Sean and the woman in church, and the reports on abuse I've read and heard in the media, the nation is gearing up for a referendum on abortion. The newspapers and airwaves are humming with the debate, though most people I meet seem little interested. Today the news is full of a story about a fifteen-year-old girl who gave birth in her bedroom. Her baby died. No one had even known the girl was pregnant. Gerry Ryan's show on RTE 2 Radio is often hilarious; the host can be funny and is usually provocative. Today he is in sombre mood, clearly touched by the story. He recalls other incidents when young girls lost their babies, and some who died with them. He and the listeners who call in to the show ask themselves when Ireland is going to wake up and start dealing with such issues properly. The fifteen-year-old's story would be tragic enough at any time but the abortion referendum debate makes it more poignant than ever.

Under the Offences Against the Persons Act of 1861

(inherited from Britain in 1922) abortion has always been illegal in independent Ireland. Attempting to procure one carries a penalty of life imprisonment. This latest referendum aims to give constitutional backing to legislation that would overturn the 'X case' decision which allowed that abortion could take place when a mother's mental health endangered her life. Previously only the mother's physical health was considered.

The 'X case' was that of a fourteen-year-old girl who'd been abused by a family friend and become pregnant. Supported by her parents she was going to England for an abortion. They wanted to prosecute the man responsible so had told the Garda who, rather than setting up an inquiry into the alleged abuser, told the Director of Public Prosecutions who informed the Attorney General who sought and gained an injunction (in February 1992), on the grounds that 'there was real and imminent danger to the life of the unborn'. The family had to come home and the girl was placed under medical supervision. The parents appealed. The court considered the evidence of the girl's suicidal feelings and decided that on the grounds of 'a real and substantial risk to the life, as distinct to the health, of the mother, which can only be avoided by the termination of her pregnancy, such termination is permissible, having regard to the true meaning of Article 40.3.3 of the Constitution'. Bizarrely this is the same Article, concerned with personal rights, which deals with deciding who are the legitimate chiefs of the ancient Gaelic clans.

The daft thing about the debate is that everyone knows that up to seven thousand women cross the Irish Sea every year for abortions in Britain and that they are legally entitled to do so. The whole debate is a meaningless moral bubble which aims to keep the country cocooned from reality. Rather than dealing with the major issues in society, Ireland is wasting time with a concern from which the rest of Europe has moved on. It is currently the only country in Europe where abortion is still illegal.

Apart from once again restricting the circumstances in which abortion would be permitted, the referendum proposes to specify the prison term for anyone convicted of seeking or aiding an abortion. The previous open-ended life sentence will be exactly twelve years.

The tragic consequence if the referendum were to succeed would inevitably be that young girls would continue to be terrified of looking for help if they became pregnant and that rape victims would have to go through the additional distress of going abroad to terminate an unwanted pregnancy.

Aine O'Connor writes a good piece in the *Irish Times* on how all the pro-life rhetoric fades after the birth. 'This country, whether Mother Ireland or Celtic Tiger, is not a good place to be needy.' She points out that the government formerly opted out of caring for the needy and handed responsibility over to the religious orders and then tried to paper over the terrible abuse that ensued. Since the state took back these responsibilities improvement had been slow, with little provision for troubled children or their families, for the families of people who need round-the-clock care, for adults with intellectual disabilities, and for the elderly. 'Ireland is the third richest country in the EU now, and third from the bottom for child poverty.' There are far more pressing matters to be dealt with than a national vote on abortion, but it's hard to identify them with one's head in the sand.

What is really telling and truly pathetic is that after weeks of debate the referendum takes place and, to my mind fortunately, is defeated, only to be followed by an immediate atmosphere of 'So what?' Most people just shrug and seem happy that an issue that was extremely complex and poorly explained in the public debate has gone away. In spite of the media's blanket coverage nearly everyone I spoke to was confused about the issues and what a 'Yes' or 'No' vote would mean. Most shared the view that while abortion was something no one would actively encourage, it was necessary at times. A poll in the *Sunday Independent* shows that a majority are in favour of a woman's right to choose.

So now the politicians have strutted their stuff, the bishops have of course claimed that they must be listened to as they have a role to play in guiding the people – though sadly no particular role, it seems, in guiding their colleagues away from raping and abusing children – and now it's all over until next time.

At seven thirty the dawn is beautiful, a tequila sunrise in the east with a stiff Atlantic breeze coming in from the west. Opening the curtains onto such a morning is a privilege. I find myself half humming, half singing 'When Irish eyes are smiling, sure it's like a morn in spring' but fortunately can't remember the rest. Hearing about all the sorrows of Ireland is helping me put my concerns about my own family into perspective.

The folk song keeps coming back into my mind. I have seen and shared much laughter during my stay, but I have also heard about so much sorrow and pain. Certainly when Irish eyes aren't smiling it is likely to be the bleakest environment imaginable. Perhaps in some way the light and dark sides balance each other out; perhaps the two have to come in equal measure.

All societies are struggling with these concerns and perhaps the Irish have a peculiar genius or passion that prevents them finding a comfortable balance. The old legends talk of two divine races in two *otherworlds*, one a place of happiness and life, the other a region of darkness and death. The Irish are famous for their artistic power, especially in words and music, yet with these real contemporary issues to face, the lament seems to die on the air and the words become mumbled, incoherent.

# CHAPTER ELEVEN

AN ALMIGHTY CRASH WAKES ME IN THE NIGHT. I LISTEN anxiously – it had sounded so much like something large breaking that I think the old tree outside must have finally been ruptured by the violence of the wind. As I tense, half expecting the window to shatter or the ceiling to cave in as flailing branches topple the chimney and bring in the roof, a light flickers outside, followed by another crack of sound. Lightning and thunder of course. The air outside is filled with sharp, staccato noises as if the wind is snapping and shredding every little thing it picks up as it races along.

Once or twice over the previous few days I've felt slightly spooked at night. Probably it's Mary O'Brien's talk of ghosts that has me unable to resist looking over my shoulder into the next room or the back of the car on a strange road. I'll be nodding off to sleep only to force open my eyes in the dark of the bedroom, uneasy that I am being watched. Perhaps the isolation is getting to me. Not believing in ghosts and banshees doesn't make a blind bit of difference in that heart-stopping second before I realize that the curtain is moving because the window is ajar and admitting a draught. The grimness and ferocity of the weather speak of forces beyond human control and lead the mind to think that there could be other forces out there that we cannot fathom.

Certainly I've been hearing much that seems to defy appearances and common sense. Most of us need company and a sense of community, and many argue that current social ills derive from a loss of traditional ideas of family and social responsibility. On the surface Ireland appears to have maintained such customs: people talk to each other, they care about their families, they help their friends, yet hand in glove with this there is a conservatism that leaves much unsaid; failings, or crimes, ignored or even condoned through lethargy. The danger is that society doesn't really move on, it just keeps treading water and one thing is for certain in Kerry, there is no lack of water to tread.

One of the fundamental reasons for my coming to Kerry and renting this quiet cottage is to tackle my perceptions that my family missed opportunities to talk, and to lament that the conversations we should have had at times like our holiday in Ireland never took place. We didn't open up fully to each other, I think now, because we never thought to. We rarely talked about hopes and dreams, or discussed important subjects like love and politics. At times, out walking, or lying in bed waiting for sleep, I ask myself what we did and what we didn't do and if we went wrong somewhere. How was it that we loved each other so much yet now I'm worrying that we never really got to know each other? Such doubts often lead me to thinking about my mother's agoraphobia and regretting how little I did to help her, how easy it had been to enjoy my life away, at university then working in London. In fact she must have talked about the agoraphobia as it was something we all worried about. While she would quite often say, 'Oh, I know it's just me being silly!' we were well aware that it wasn't as simple as being silly and hoped that the doctors she saw would be able to help. If she was

with one of the family she could usually go more or less anywhere, though there were times when she would have a
paralysing panic attack and have to go home. Her real frustration came from not being able to go anywhere alone, except
within a short range of her home. I remember when I was about
nineteen she and I went up to see an exhibition in London and
she said she felt fine while she was with me but that if I hadn't
been there she'd have been terrified. 'And to think I used to go
everywhere on my own,' she said regretfully. I suggested that we
make an experiment, I suppose it was a kind of basic aversion
therapy: I would walk a little way down the pavement from
where we stood, say no more than two lamp posts away, so that
she could see me all the way. If other pedestrians obscured me
once or twice, she'd know I was still there. She agreed and off I
went, a distance of no more than thirty yards and then waved to
her when I thought I'd gone far enough. She came up to me after
a minute or so.

'I did feel frightened,' she said giving me a hug, 'but I knew
that any moment I'd see your face and it would be all right.'

I wish I had done this sort of thing with her more often,
though I know it could hardly have really dealt with her fears,
even if it had given her a technique for believing that wherever
she was, home wasn't going to go away.

She sometimes wondered about how it had started. She had
loved being able to make her way to new places, by car or on the
train, so the agoraphobia did represent a profound change in her
character. She was sure that the mastectomy had really shaken
her up, not just the fear of cancer, but the way that she felt her
body had lost a vital piece of its femininity. What I didn't realize
until much later was that the surgeon had taken it upon himself
to perform a hysterectomy at the same time as the mastectomy.
My mother had been entirely unprepared for this and her
questions about it at the time, she said, were dismissed with a

wave of the hand. It was routine and the doctor knew best. The arrogance of the prognosis and the doctor's reaction is mind-blowing. The patriarchal society was still so strong then, back in the early to mid-sixties. To think that a woman of around forty would be treated in so casual and high-handed a manner seems inconceivable now. Coincidentally, a doctor in Ireland today is under investigation for performing unnecessary hysterectomies. He won't get away with a wave of the hand; he may face criminal charges, quite rightly in my view. How she coped with the trauma of cancer, losing a breast, and coming out of hospital on the far side of the menopause, her reproductive capabilities gone overnight, one can hardly begin to comprehend.

When I'm not beating myself up for having failed to help her enough, I'm aware of great feelings of frustration at having been unable to talk to her after my captivity. Although claustrophobia was more of a concern for me than agoraphobia I can see that there were distinct parallels. I was living through her nightmare of getting stranded away from home. While I longed to roam the world a free man, it was the thought of home that kept me sane and determined to carry on. I'm sure that had we talked about it we'd have been able to help each other to insights about our experiences. What I find difficult to accept is the notion that at our moments of greatest need, we could not come to each other's aid.

I potter along the shoreline below my house late one afternoon. Apart from the occasional noisy intrusion of a passing vehicle, the place has its own sort of serenity, the tranquillity of abandonment. No one comes here. Mike Kennedy's rowing boat is lashed down just above the high water mark but, judging by the amount of debris inside it, he hasn't been out in it much lately. Every few feet I come across modern rubbish – plastic bottles, toys, wellington boots, fishing floats and endless black bin liners, beer cans and heavy plastic bags for farm chemicals. Mangles always seem to feature in modern middens such as this and, sure enough, slap bang in the middle of one of the streams that bubbles across the beach into the harbour there's one rusting to eternity. Further along is a fractured steam iron. Perhaps a local laundry went bust and dumped its gear here. Strangely it doesn't feel as though most of this detritus has been abandoned at the shore but rather that it has blown or floated here to this unvisited spot. Each spring the council clears the rubbish from the beach at Inch but here, I imagine, the junk will be left to drift back and forth for ever.

At times the laissez faire, laid-back attitudes of Ireland frustrate me. Whether it's rubbish on an unvisited beach or the awful state of many of the roads, I can't help thinking that they've bungled some of the opportunities that came with the Celtic Tiger. In conversation, in the papers, on the television and radio, there are constant laments about the weaknesses of the country's infrastructure. Roads, health, education, law and order all need powerful injections of ideas and money yet these commodities, which led and determined the Tiger's track, seem to have dried up in an attitude of political caution where the obvious need for better public management and probably higher personal taxes is forever being finessed rather than financed.

The television programme *Agenda* one Sunday looks at the issue of homelessness, talking to homeless people to find out how best their problems could be helped. The young host David McWilliams points out that the prevalent attitude around the country is that lower taxes are the most important thing to most people, not social programmes. Ireland has become an aspirational society where, if you have enough money, you can make yourself into whatever you want to be. But this ignores the fact that nearly everyone needs some form of community at some point in their lives and so the idea of focusing on a core society should remain fundamental. But who is going to make sure that happens? Too many people seem content to build their Southforks and have no involvement with anything beyond their backyard.

One surprising government action for the general good has come with a new law banning shops from giving away plastic bags – you have to buy one if you need it. The amount of plastic floating around Ireland is alarming; it's not just on the shorelines but drive along any road and the hedgerows will be decorated with flags of carrier bags.

The shopkeeper in Annascaul says that within a couple of days of the law coming into force people brought baskets and bags with them as in earlier times. I think this is a great piece of legislation. It doesn't address any of the greater ills facing society but at least it is one step back from thoughtless consumerism.

Plastic bags aside, preserving Ireland's natural beauty provokes continuous debate with An Taisce, the heritage watch-dog funded by the Department of the Environment which comes in for equal measures of support and opprobrium. While it seems the watchdog hasn't bothered to go sniffing along the shores beneath my house, it has concerned itself with plans to develop Inch peninsula as a golf course. Apparently permission had been granted for the project to go ahead but a high court injunction called for by An Taisce had stopped the plan in its tracks. The argument is that the development will destroy an area of natural beauty and an important wildlife habitat. The counter-argument, one which has often been expressed to me by locals, is that the course would blend in with the dunes very well and that it would be good for the local economy. Other locals argue that once completed, there probably wouldn't be that many new jobs and that the club house and car parks would alter the look of the place dramatically. And even if the course is visually unobtrusive, the fertilizers and other chemicals needed to maintain the greens and fairways up to snuff could poison what is an important bird sanctuary.

The injunction was subsequently overturned but it is by no means assured that the golf course will go ahead. If not, the owners might be due compensation from the heritage and wildlife bodies for not being able to develop it. It all sounds a bit crazy to me. On the one hand of course the peninsula should be left unspoilt but I can also appreciate the frustrations of people wanting to expand business in the area to make a living. The planning system as a whole is not working smoothly. Aside from business developments, locals are finding it harder and harder to have their voices heard. Although everyone expressed delight when the disgraced politician Liam Lawlor was sent for another spell in prison for failing to co-operate with the Flood Tribunal's investigation into planning corruption around Dublin, I wouldn't be surprised if a bit of that kind of 'flexibility' wasn't welcomed in my corner of Kerry.

One planning fiasco that probably had nothing to do with corruption and everything to do with bureaucratic incompetence has been brought to my attention by Tom Barrington. The old Royal Irish Constabulary barracks at Cahersiveen, now a heritage centre, looks like a child's picture of a gothic European castle. With its turrets it is at once arrogant and ridiculous and no doubt did little to improve the image of the RIC with the local population when it was built at the end of the nineteenth century. Barrington informs me that the design was intended for a fortress to be built in the north-western province of India. In his usual understated, dry way Mr B observes that there is presumably a barracks in the rugged mountains of modern Pakistan that was designed to sit by the banks of the Valentia River amid Kerry's more gentle hills. Now that would be worth seeing.

Leaving the mad barracks behind me I follow Barrington to another spot, one which ties more explicitly into my McCarthy heritage, Ballycarbery Castle. My guide is, as ever, very explicit in his directions. 'Cross the bridge. A little way up, to the right ... follow the road from the bridge a little way. At the T junction turn left. After about a mile, at Kimego school, turn left for Ballycarbery castle ...' Although now a ruin it's plain that the fifteenth-century castle must have been an outstanding edifice. Set on a slight rise it has commanding views across the waters of Valentia River and harbour to distant mountains and across Doulus Bay to the Atlantic. According to Barrington an earlier castle on the site was likely to have been the seat of the ancient kingdom of the Corcu Duibne which covered the entire Dingle peninsula on the north side of Dingle Bay and part of this peninsula, the modern barony of Iveragh, on the south side.

At the very beginning of the thirteenth century the southern part of that kingdom was overthrown by the MacCarthys, who established a principal seat here. This was in the good old days when, though trying to defeat or come to terms with the Anglo-Norman colonizers from England, the Gaelic Irish families were still busy fighting for each other's land. One of the MacCarthy leaders of the time was Cormac Fionn. He died in 1248 after establishing the dynasty of MacCarthy Mór. The MacCarthys seemed happy to fight their neighbours, even their cousins, as well as the Anglo-Normans, forming alliances and breaking them with a conscienceless élan. They were to establish territories and a power base during that period, which while subject to losses and gains and submissions to the Anglo-Normans would survive for three hundred years.

From the mid-fourteenth century the O'Connell family were the hereditary wardens at Ballycarbery and its predecessor, but though vassals of the MacCarthy Mór, they were not always as subservient as they might have been. It was the overlord's right to have his children fostered by his subject families. When one MacCarthy Mór sent a cradle to the O'Connells as a sign to send for a child to foster, O'Connell cut off the head of the messenger and sent it back in the cradle.

Friar O'Sullivan in his *Ancient History of the Kingdom of Kerry* recounts a more convivial tale.

> . . . two brothers of the gentlemen of the Connells, who lived in Ballycarbry Castle, in Ivrah, which was divided among them, the lower rooms and apartments to the eldest, the upper to the youngest, at a time that MacCarthy More and his lady, with their attendants, took a tour to said Ivrah, who had put up first with the eldest of said two brothers, where they were splendidly entertained the night and next day, at which time the youngest invited them to dine the day following, which MacCarthy More promised; but the eldest brother being very much dissatisfied and jealous thereat checked his brother for offering the invitation, but the youngest stiffly insisted on the promise he had, upon which there happened a hot dispute, which MacCarthy's lady quelled by promising that MacCarthy and she would dine with him having dinner ready earliest next day, so that said brothers parted in peace, each of them earnestly preparing to have that honour. But in the beginning of the same following night the eldest, in the lower rooms, as aforesaid, expecting to disappoint the brother in the upper of either fire or water, ordered all the doors and passages leading from said rooms not only to be locked, but also a guard to watch and prevent any attempt of opening the same, which the younger brother discovered, and could not otherwise remedy but by ordering all his pans and pots to be filled with Spanish wine, wherein all his meat was boiled over as many fires of liquorish as were requisite, so that, unexpectedly, he had dinner ready much earlier than the

eldest brother, and thereby the honour and pleasure of having MacCarthy More and his lady to dine with him.

The Friar gives no record of what the food tasted like but I imagine everyone left the table somewhat tired and emotional. Alcohol consumption appears to have been as notable a feature of life in the fifteenth and sixteenth centuries as it is today. Tadg II MacCarthy Mór, King of Desmond (and nephew of the founder of the MacCarthys of Ardcanacht), was, according to ancient books, a very heavy drinker indeed, outdrinking all his Irish and English neighbours. He died at Ballycarbery in 1428, though whether his demise followed a feast of meats boiled in wine is not known.

Donal IX MacCarthy Mór, the last King of Desmond, who also had a problem with the drink, mortgaged Ballycarbery to Sir Nicholas Browne for eighty pounds in the late 1500s. The castle ruins stand in splendid isolation, and while redolent of its former glory on the sunny afternoon of my visit, it looks as though the next great westerly gale could tear it free of the ivy that grows over much of it and reduce it to a pile of thousands of rocks. It must have been a remarkable place in its day. The outlook, even from the lower regions that are all one can now safely reach, is impressive. In its heyday it must have bellowed power and style to all those who saw it. There are no fences warding the public off, and its vast vaulted cellar still serves as a cattle byre. I find one staircase that I can imagine the elder O'Connell brother furiously barricading to thwart his junior's culinary plans and as I picture the scene I feel sure Barrington would share the joke.

Even late on a drizzly afternoon it isn't difficult to find the site of the Kilmichael ambush. Once through Macroom, I career on beside the River Lee and then cross it on a wide stone bridge.

There, on a tight bend, is a sign 'Site of ambush 9km'. It is still half light when I reach the spot. A large stone edifice, erected in 1966 and unveiled by a priest, looms over the road. A few steps lead up to a platform in front of the granite wall with words carved in Irish and English. A simple wreath of evergreen leaves bound with an orange, green and white ribbon lies there, limp and wet on the cold stone. A small noticeboard and a relief model of the site stand on the ground a few yards away.

I had been reading about the War of Independence when I suddenly realized that today is the anniversary of the ambush. For some reason I felt a pressing need to be here at this wild spot in County Cork, as if I'd get a better sense of the struggle that the Irish were waging at the time. On a December day in 1920 thirty-six members of the IRA attacked two lorries carrying a patrol of eighteen 'Auxiliaries' heading back to their base at Macroom Castle. The Auxiliary Division of the Royal Irish Constabulary had been hastily recruited from mid-1920 onwards as IRA raids became more effective. Many members were veterans of the First World War and soon had a reputation for drunkenness, brutality and acting outside the control of the establishment in Dublin. Like the RIC, the 'Auxies' were nick-named the Black and Tans because of their uniforms which consisted of khaki trousers, dark green police jackets and black belts. As often with matters of Irish history, the various sources I've read give wildly differing opinions even on this. You might imagine the very basic issue of paramilitary uniforms would be an uncontroversial subject. Not at all. Some sources say that Black and Tans was a general description for both the post-January 1920 RIC and the Auxiliaries together, while others argue that it applied to just the RIC. Some say they had khaki jackets and green trousers, not the other way around, while yet others have it that they had all-khaki uniforms with black belts and green hats. Quite a few people suggest they were named after a famous Limerick pack of hunting hounds.

Tom Barrington has, as ever, a detailed, though somewhat roundabout, explanation of the nickname. Being the devoted researcher that he was, he doesn't limit himself to covering only the sagas and history from the earliest times, a difficult enough subject to understand and communicate, but he also studies the county's physical form, its flora and fauna. In a couple of chapters entitled simply 'Things' he covers the gamut from beehive huts and Celtic crosses to geological history, from soil, plants and gardens to fishes and animals. In this last category he includes the extinct and the thriving, everything from toads to slugs and donkeys to dogs. It is in this section that he imparts his account of the hated paramilitary unit's name:

> In Kerry there are two breeds of dogs special to the county – the
> Kerry beagle and the Kerry blue terrier. The beagle is . . . tan
> coloured and black. This dog may originally have been a small
> Irish hound crossed with Spanish and French hounds . . . The
> breed was specially developed from the end of the 18th century
> at Scarteen, Co Tipperary, origin of the famous hunt, the
> Scarteen Black and Tans who gave their name to Lloyd George's
> militia.

Both the RIC and the Auxiliary recruits were poorly trained and often ill-disciplined, many RIC veterans having left the force because of social stigmatization as well as the growing risk of assassination – the former encouraged by Eamon de Valera, the latter by Michael Collins.

The ambush was the work of the West Cork Flying Column of the IRA. Like their enemies, the men lying in wait had little training – just one week. They had a rifle apiece and thirty-five rounds of ammunition. Their officer, according to the notice, also had two Mills bomb grenades. Scouts alerted the main ambush party to the approach of the small convoy of 'Auxies' and the IRA officer stood in front of the first truck, dressed in an IRA jacket, prompting the trucks to stop and investigate. A grenade was thrown into the first truck, followed by a hail of bullets. Some occupants of the second truck got out and a battle ensued. When the surviving Auxies threw down their rifles, a few IRA lads stood up assuming triumph was theirs, only to be gunned down as the enemy took out their pistols. The IRA officer then ordered all his men to open fire and not to cease until he ordered a stop. Result: three IRA dead against eighteen Auxiliaries. Reading these details as daylight fades adds to my sense of the event as I learn that the attack was carried out at dusk. The chill wind has me hunching my shoulders and tugging my cap down to shield my face from the hardening rain. Squinting into the half-light it is easy to appreciate that this is perfect bandit country, an ideal site for an ambush. An army could be hidden out there in the black and tan colours of the early autumn landscape, waiting for the order to open fire.

A light suddenly appears off to my right and almost has me moving for cover behind my car but it is just someone turning on a porch light a few hundred yards away. The house is old enough to have been there eighty years earlier and I wonder if the inhabitants had known what was going to happen and if they listened to the sound of gunfire. It doesn't look like prime farm-land, a hard place to earn much to live on. Certainly it would be a bleak place to die.

Reading of the struggles against British rule and the sub-sequent horrors of the Civil War in T. Ryle Dwyer's *Tans, Terror and Troubles*, I am pleased to find some light relief. In 1914 there was a big parade of Irish Volunteers in Killarney. The local lads were the only ones fully armed, marching with rifles and fixed bayonets. The Kalem Film Company had been filming around Killarney and the guns had been used in various scenes in which members of the Killarney Volunteers were extras. When filming was completed the American producer was happy to leave the guns behind.

There's nothing humorous at Beal na Blath, another bleak spot in County Cork. On a large raised plinth of red-painted brick stands a stone cross behind light grey railings. The figure of Christ crucified is carved on it and a man's name in Gaelic, Miceál O Coileán, and the date of his death, 22 August 1922. There is nothing else; no explanation of what happened here, no dramatic rendering of the actions of a few heroes against the many as at Kilmichael which I passed this morning. No relief map showing where the ambushers lay in wait and no green and white tourist signs carefully guiding you here, just a little old sign in the nearest hamlet indicating 'The Michael Collins Monument'. It was here that Michael Collins, the Big Fella, hero of the war of liberation and negotiator of the Anglo-Irish Treaty that brought in the Irish Free State was killed by his fellow Irishmen and former comrades, led by Eamon de Valera.

It is a gloomy and lonely spot, the sky thick with a cawing murder of crows, and a rocky bluff rising from the road behind the monument. Scrubby woodland and furze bushes line either side of the road which narrows and turns sharply, obviously a good spot for the ambush. A tattered wreath, a plastic rose and some withered twigs of holly are tied to the railings. For many, Collins's death was a tragedy. Not just because he'd been a hero in the war against the British but because he had a vision for the new Irish state, one that looked forward. He aimed to build a modern society with modern social policies rather than con-centrate on creating an Ireland, rural, Irish-speaking and Catholic, based on an idyll that may never have existed.

God knows what civil war must be like, the impossible personal, intellectual and moral choices people have to make. A very lonely and sad time for everyone, with friend set against friend, brother against brother. Maybe I shouldn't be surprised to find such a monument left unannounced, swept, like other uncomfortable matters in modern Ireland, under the carpet. Perhaps in its simplicity this is a more honourable monument than those adorned with heroic inscriptions stating, 'Pray God that Ireland in her hour of need will always have sons like these to fight and die for her.'

In Tralee a large National Graves Commission monument rears up at the very centre of the town. Atop a sturdy stone and marble plinth a man in shirtsleeves carrying a pike stares steadfastly into the distance – well, he would be if there wasn't a department store across the road. The plinth carries dedications to the heroes of all the risings against the English and quotes from Robert Emmet and other luminaries. Whilst I'd go along with the view of many modern historians and commentators that misty-eyed romanticism is no longer necessary to Ireland, I wouldn't deny a nation the right to celebrate its heroes; the freedom they fought to gain is just eighty years old after all. However, when reading about Emmet, executed in 1803 for leading a failed uprising in Dublin, it strikes me as ironic that the man whose words are etched in stone is now seen as an unrealistic if noble dreamer.

Behind the pike-bearing stalwart on his plinth, at the far end of Denny Street, stands the Thomas Ashe Memorial Hall, headquarters of the county council. Thomas Ashe, born a few miles from Inch near Lispole, was a key figure in the Easter Uprising in 1916, who died the following year through medical neglect after being forcibly fed while leading a hunger strike in jail. The Memorial Hall replaced the original County Hall which was burned down in 1920 while the town was under siege by British forces trying to win the release of two constables who had been kidnapped by the insurgents.

A thin man in shabby clothes, shapeless overcoat and a huge number of badges pinned on his shirt front emerges from a side road. He's singing occasional verses from Republican fighting songs, shouting a few words, then weaving about, more or less on the spot, awaiting the next breath of the muse to overtake him. He doesn't look drunk, just beyond the normal pale.

Celebrating those who struggled against British rule is fairly safe and perhaps serves to override the bitter memories of the time when victory had been achieved over the colonial power and the Irish turned to fighting themselves to determine how their newly won independence should be managed.

Though the pain of that time is much diminished, there are still latent memories of it, especially in the south-western counties of Cork and Kerry. According to Barrington, 'The civil war was fought in Kerry more bitterly than anywhere in Ireland.' He tells of awful massacres where the Free State government troops adopted hated British practices like blowing up anti-treaty, Irregular prisoners around a landmine. In an area where even today, as I've learned from my own cousins, people can speak of generations past with an intimacy and knowledge of detail that is surprising, perhaps one should expect that the bitterness of civil war would linger. Barrington writes, 'In general, the majority of the people of Kerry sympathised, at least, with the Irregular side.' He goes on, 'These memories, particularly of the civil war, for long nourished a tradition of violent revolutionary politics in Kerry, a tradition still not wholly spent.'

I'd been confused one day to hear a neighbour refer to members of the current main opposition party, Fine Gael, as 'the feckin' Blueshirts' but I am now beginning to understand the reference. The Armed Comrades Association, or National Guard, a fascist-style organization of ex Free State army servicemen, was formed in 1932 in reaction to the unexpected victory of de Valera's Fianna Fáil party in the general election of that year. It didn't last long, most members quitting its increasing extremism (and their blue shirts) to form Fine Gael. Although the direct link between the Blueshirts and modern political affiliations ended seventy years ago, it is still a stick with which to beat them.

The Blueshirts' last hurrah was a six hundred-strong outing in 1936 in support of Franco's Nationalist forces during the Spanish Civil War. The story is an intriguing, ironic and typically Irish one. At the time when the movement was losing backing for its domestic politics, its support for the fascist Franco was in keeping with the attitudes of the Catholic bishops, most newspapers and political parties. They saw the Spanish conflict as one between the forces of communism and Catholicism. Despite much pressure, the Fianna Fáil government remained neutral.

For a long time there's been a general and widespread distrust of the modern Sinn Féin and IRA and they've had muted support in Ireland south of the border. Many people, while sympathizing with their fellow Irishmen fighting in the north, are unhappy with the idea of Sinn Féin becoming a major player in the Republic. However, Barrington's point that violent revolutionary politics is not a spent force in Kerry was brought home to me on various occasions by people's reactions to stories of the machinations of the local Sinn Féin organization. The press has been reporting allegations that members were acting as vigilantes, beating up and driving out drug dealers, for instance. The tone in the papers is one of condemnation, yet many people see it as a positive move in the face of the Gard's apparent inability to address the problem.

Politics aside, I had been surprised to learn from Maureen Fitzgerald that only a little while ago the IRA had been very active in the area.

'The IRA used to train on the beach,' she had told me.

'What, the dunes here at Inch?'

'Yes!' she laughed, delighted with my surprise. 'I'd go down on the cob, the horse, to count the cattle and the sheep, it would have been around nineteen sixty-five when the troubles were bad up in the north, and I cut across the dunes to the strand. They'd be there with the bundles of guns on their backs, heading for the training place further down. They'd come from maybe Tralee and Blennerville or different places. We'd hear them training away, the shots going, and we were scared for our lives!'

'Did James MacCarthy have anything to say about it?'

'Sure we'd be talking about it and he'd say, "Say nothing!"'

Maureen had told me that James had a few caravans that he used to let out and that one time a couple of them had been rented by seven or eight men.

'It was the time of that big robbery, I can't remember where it was, but a lot of paintings had been taken from some big house and the police were searching every caravan site in the country. The sergeant from Annascaul came at just half seven in the morning and the IRA men were already down training in the dunes. I didn't tell him they were down there. He went away but he said he'd be back again. "Oh, mother of God!" I thought. A car was coming out from the beach and he got stuck so I went down and towed him out. "Look," I said, "I don't know and I don't want to know a thing, but the sergeant was here." Well, do you know, he went down again and collected his men and they loaded up and were gone! Later a detective came from Tralee and they dusted the caravan for prints. I didn't say that I knew them. Well, I didn't! Sergeant O'Leary, he's retired now, used to come to the house often with the summons because James was a Justice of the Peace and James would have to sign them. And when the detectives were here that day the sergeant was saying, "Oh, it looks so bad, I was in Annascaul and I knew nothing!"'

Pat Foley subsequently confirmed Maureen's account of the IRA beach parties. 'Oh sure, we all heard the gunfire. Everyone just ignored it.'

Pat also told me that during the days of the Maze Prison H-block hunger strikes, black flags were tied to all the telegraph poles from here to Castlemaine. One time he was in a shop in Tralee when some men came in with a flag, saying to the shop-keeper, 'You'll be putting this in the window for the parade, won't you now.'

Fidelus is pouring tea for me and her brother Anthony one day in her kitchen when Bridey Flynn appears at the door.

'I've to get some fags for that woman!' she says, referring to her sister Mary. Visitors are always dropping by at Foley's. During the day the kitchen is often busier than the bar.

Bridey stops for tea. When I'd come to Inch with my family in 1980 we'd visited a woman called Bridey McKenna McCarthy who'd worked with James, but I couldn't remember where she lived.

'Over at Cromane,' advises Bridey. 'We were very good friends, she worked with James for twenty years.'

Fidelus asks if she is still alive.

'I haven't been to her wake!' replies Bridey giving the younger woman a look as if to say, 'Are you mad?'

The talk turns to how people used to have bigger families and that they all lived together, packed into tiny one-up, one-down houses.

'There were fifteen Moriartys in their house once,' Bridey tells me. 'They had animals living in the next room and sheep coming into the kitchen. But none of them suffered for it,' she insists and, nodding her head, says emphatically, 'They were as healthy as stones.'

*

I'm lost. Using the Ordnance Survey map to take a more scenic route I've gone 'off Barrington' and ended up by a row of bungalows on a small road by the sea. Spotting a woman in her front garden I stop the car and walk over to ask for directions, hoping she won't give me the 'if I wanted to get there I wouldn't start from here' line.

I needn't have worried. The old lady is all smiles and says that in fact I haven't gone far wrong and that the town is less than a mile away hidden by the low, tree-covered hill where the road bends.

'You'll come in for a cup of tea so.'

To be honest I want to get on but it seems rude not to accept.

In the hall there is a row of black and white photographs, old family groups and one of a couple.

'Is that your family?'

'Yes, those were my parents,' she says, pointing to the couple. 'Wasn't my mother pretty?'

'Why yes she was,' I say looking closely at the photograph.

'Not like me, ugly! With my harelip. My dad always shooed me out of our grocery shop if there were any customers about. He could never bear the sight of me.'

'Oh, I'm sure not,' I say. True, the woman's lip is noticeable but hardly unbearable.

'"That deformity" he called it, he was ashamed of me,' she says regretfully.

Bad enough for anyone to feel embarrassed by their appearance, perhaps especially a young girl, but to have your father making you feel a freak must have been dreadful. The woman, who tells me her name is Patricia, takes me through to the kitchen. While she makes a pot of tea and puts out some fruit cake, I tell her a bit about myself and my experiences in Ireland and find myself talking about my mother and how I wish I'd had a chance to get to know her better when I was older.

Patricia says that she has some memories of her mother but not many. For the last couple of years of her life, the mother was in a nursing hospital outside town so the daughter only got to see her for a few hours at the weekend. When her mother died, Patricia was almost ten. Her father's behaviour grew worse, he hardly spoke to her for weeks, just grumbled if the food wasn't on the table when he came through from the shop. ' "Is there no use to you at all?" he'd say and then, soon after Mother died he stopped me going to school. "What good will it do you? Who'd be interested in your learning?" '

She'd read a great deal anyway, going to the library early so there wouldn't be many people about. The winter was best, she said, because the afternoons were dark and she could move about unnoticed. 'Not that people were nasty, it was just I thought I was horrible because of what my dad said.'

She says she longed for a best friend but could hardly get to form an acquaintance let alone a friendship until much later in life. Then, when she was in her mid-twenties, her father developed a heart condition and needed her help more and more in the shop. 'I was nearly thirty when I began coming out of the shell he'd made me wear.'

I try to imagine what it was like, youth effectively gone and brainwashed into thinking that you look like a monster. You have to care for your persecutor and do the work he said you weren't fit for. Suddenly Patricia had to go out into the world and learn the ways of it. Happily she'd found that she had a good business head and was soon running the shop very successfully and looking after her invalid father. He was always critical and at best would keep quiet in the face of her obvious achievements with the shop.

'Eventually he died. God forgive me, but I couldn't feel sorry, it was as if I had a chance to live for myself at last.'

She enjoyed working in the shop even more now there was no

glowering presence in the back room and business was good. Most of her customers had grown up in the town, some had been at school with her and though she hardly knew them intimately there was already a connection. Gradually she made some friends and enjoyed a social life which revolved around the church.

She now lives on the outskirts of the town in a small bungalow overlooking the water.

'So you sold the shop and came here to retire.'

'I had no shop to sell! He left the business to his brother's son. Even after all the years I'd made that place hum with success he never changed his will. My cousin let me keep it until I retired.'

Understandably her father's betrayal still wounds her, perhaps as freshly as when she first heard his will read. She stares out of the window for a moment or two. Her expression is inscrutable and I can't tell if it is sorrow or anger she's feeling. After a while she clears her throat, looks at me from the corner of her eye, then carries on.

'If it hadn't been for Aunty Bridget leaving me some money and the little I could set aside when I was running the shop, I could never have bought this place. Thank God property wasn't so expensive round here ten years ago.'

'Before all the blow-ins started coming!'

She smiles and nods. I realize I've been sitting with Patricia a long while and should be getting on. As she shows me out she pauses by the old family pictures again.

'Sometimes, you know, when I look at his face, it's almost as if it twists into a sneer like it used to. Then he looks as ugly an old bastard as I ever did!'

Four glum-looking characters are standing with collecting boxes outside Inch's little church when I arrive just on 9.30 a.m. on a cool and drizzly Sunday morning. About to put my hand in my pocket for the week's good cause I look at the words on the box and am surprised to see that they are collecting for Sinn Féin. I don't feel like making a political contribution on my way into church but I later learn that all political parties have a right to collect like this occasionally. Mike Courtney and two or three other men are standing in the porch. If I didn't know that men often lurk just outside the door, or at the back of the church, I might easily stay with them, thinking there's no room inside. It seems odd, to go to church and not actually to go in. I guess they chat a bit, though standing just inside the door as I do, unable to spot an easily occupiable pew seat as the place is almost full, I hear no murmur of chat until very near the end of the service. The congregation is a pretty good mix of men, women and children – plenty of familiar faces.

In his sermon Father Crean talks about us all needing a North Star to guide us through our lives. To make his point he uses a fairly rambling story about a pregnant woman who finds a focus and reason for her life through the birth of her child. It sounds more like a message he might have preached before the referendum on abortion than an illustration of Jesus as the North Star who would guide us through the bad times to God.

Once or twice I've been given the impression that people aren't wildly keen on the priest's sermons and now I notice a couple of cuffs being discreetly raised to check the time. Whether or not Father Tom is the sort of bright light that the Church desperately needs at the moment to inspire the youth to come to church and indeed join the priesthood I would not know, but whatever he's doing, he's still getting a good attendance.

As communicants file up for the sacrament in this simple building – a ceremony I've known all my life – I have the sudden feeling I'm witnessing something much more ancient than mere

Christianity, something atavistic and pagan. I've sometimes sat in churches trying to imagine what it would have been like in earlier centuries, when services were held in Latin and hooded priests ministered to princes and peasants, but never before have I thought of druids in church. It is as if the world has shifted and while things look the same I've moved into another 'dimension': there is something about the movement that seems so automatic, somnolent. Of course the whole thing is hardly lively in the absence of music and with Father Crean whispering about the Spirit and letting it into your heart.

Outside I meet up with my cousin Mike Kennedy.

'I wasn't quite sure where that sermon was going,' I venture.

'It was going for fourteen minutes,' he replies and asks me back for a cup of tea.

# CHAPTER TWELVE

'WE'LL GO BACK IN,' SAYS PHIL. 'YOU'LL PERISH OUT HERE.'

The dawn is very cold but my head is buzzing with the sights, sounds and smells in the small barn. The phone had rung at 5 a.m. At first I thought it was the alarm going off as I clawed up from a deep sleep. Stephen was on the line.

'Courtney's here, we have a cow calving, maybe here in half an hour. You said you'd like to see it.' Then I heard a voice in the background, his mother's I guessed, and he continued, 'But 'tis early, don't come if you'd rather wait. There'll be others.'

'I'll be right down.'

The sky was clear with a crescent moon still lighting the waters of Castlemaine Harbour as I staggered about in the morning chill getting into warm clothes and wellington boots.

Phil had been up to check on the cow at three and then again at six before Mike went off to work in Dingle. Stephen pulls on overalls and a woolly hat and we cross the yard. It is still dark but light is creeping into the east beyond MacGillycuddy's Reeks. The cow and a heifer, also close to calving, have been moved into a quieter shed away from the rest of the herd. 'They like a bit of quiet when they're ready,' Phil explains.

The two animals are chained by their necks to the stalls and each turns a bright eye towards us as we open the door and enter the small barn, the air overly sweet with the smell of straw and fresh dung. I'm still only half awake and everything seems so strange to me. Too strange perhaps. I suddenly notice strings of something I can't identify, especially through half-closed eyes, hanging from the cow's rear. Things are definitely about to happen down there.

'Shall I put my overalls on, so?' It isn't really a question from Stephen, more a checking off the list of things that need to be done. Phil has a bowl of water, soap and towel ready.

Stephen washes his hands then gently feels around inside the cow, nodding and telling me that the *crúbs* are in the right place, beside the head.

'Croobs?' I ask.

'That's the Irish for front legs.'

The heifer looks on confused and agitated, but the cow is lying down; she's more relaxed having been through it all before. This is the first time I've been present at a birth. Stephen, Phil and the animal are doing fine but *I'm* not. I find myself staring into cobwebbed corners of the cowshed, trying to think of anything except what is going on beside me. Stephen fishes around with bits of rope and wrestles with a heavy metal instrument he calls the 'jack'. Soon he has the ropes looped round the *crúbs* and is cranking away – the miracle of birth is happening. Now I am transfixed and when the small beast finally emerges and is gently laid on fresh straw to be nursed by its mother, I am surprised to feel so moved.

After the birth Phil says I look as if I need some food – I am pale but I think this is due to latent queasiness rather than lack of breakfast. On the way back to the house she shows me an adjoining shed where the calves will be kept until June and the weather improves. 'They'd die of pneumonia up on the hill,' she explains. A two-day-old calf is learning to drink from a bucket. We go on past the milking parlour.

'Now it's all mechanized,' says Phil, 'but when I was a twelve-year-old at home in Limerick, we used to milk by hand sitting on a little stool.'

Phil prepares me a full Irish breakfast, showing me frozen 'beestings', the first milk from a mother, which is full of anti-bodies, and telling me about times when things went wrong and the vet had to be called in. Then she hurries off to help Stephen with the second delivery while I eat, rather slowly.

A storm rages all through the night and the morning news on the radio reports that power lines have been brought down all along the west coast. Eight thousand homes in Kerry are with-out electricity. So far I'm OK but I check to see that I have some candles in case the power is cut that evening. Down at the beach I think I've come across a scene from the *Quatermass Experiment*, a flipping, flopping flotation of foam. With the full moon, the big spring tides bring the crashing waves close in to the café and there is more debris around than usual. The wind gusts up strongly to tear off candyfloss bundles of foam from the main body, which push around my legs before rushing away into the dunes. The place is another world and though the storm is furious the temperature is mild. This foaming at nature's mouth is fascinating and the overcast sky has a luminosity that makes the world seem bright, but lit as though from somewhere deep within.

By the time I get back to the cottage, light is breaking through the clouds and I watch the wind set the spray on the harbour's surface whirling and whirling into wild eddies, like ice skaters spinning on the spot. For a few minutes I stand outside the front door and lose myself in this wonderful space, a fusion of reality and fantasy where dance and music, the landscape and the wind all become one meshed, swirling entity.

Back inside I go straight to the photographs on the mantelpiece and stare again at my family. I want to tell them what a powerful effect this place is having on me, how free the great space outside makes me feel and how although I am isolated I don't feel lonely, that in a way I have them with me to share it. My parents would have loved it here; it is like so many of the cottages we stayed in on holidays, places to see, walks to take and of course all the cousins who are coming out of the woodwork.

One of the pictures shows my father and Terence sitting chatting on the terrace at home. I don't know how they got through those terrible years, desperately trying not to give in to their worst fears about what had become of me in Lebanon and facing the worst as my mother's health continued to decline. Terence has told me that at times, apart from the demands of work, he needed to escape to London just to take his mind off the sadness that they were all trying to deal with and overcome.

Together he and my father continued to look into the family history as a displacement activity, to try to focus on a broader picture than their current reality. I've found documents and notes which show them exploring other branches of the family tree. I get the impression that this wasn't so much a structured project as something to dip into when they had time or needed a break from the other stresses in their lives.

Having their unfailing support must have been vital to my mother as she not only agonized over my disappearance but had to deal with great physical pain and face the inevitability of an early death. Terence told me that in the last couple of years of her life, when she was still strong enough to go out, it wasn't so much her agoraphobia that constrained her but the fact that she couldn't bear the pity she saw in people's eyes when they spoke to her. I still feel a responsibility for that and I'm trying to dispel the image of my mother wanting to get out, struggling against the phobia that hemmed her in, and then, having managed it, being defeated at the point of reward by finding that the smiling faces of those she met were clouded with gentle frowns and expressions of commiseration. 'Even going to the butcher or baker', Terence recalled, 'could be terribly distressing for her.' How tragic that the well-meaning, supportive concerns of others could actually undermine and limit one's capacity to live.

A few days after coming home from Beirut I asked Terence if my mother had left me a last letter, a note, or even just some words to pass on.

'No, she didn't,' he said. Then, seeing the hurt in my face, he went on, 'She thought about it, we talked about it, but she just couldn't bring herself to do it. It would have been admitting defeat.'

Although I accepted this, a nagging feeling of distress stayed with me. Now, though, I think I can accept it fully and appreciate more deeply her remarkable courage and the way she fought to show me her love.

The sky is changing constantly, from light to dark to light again, reflecting my journey between joy and sorrow. Thinking of my mother leads me on to reflecting on the women I have met here. In many ways they seem to be a lonely breed, often carrying an air of melancholic resignation, demonstrated in the way they often sigh as they speak.

One night leaving the pub I passed an elderly woman sitting right beside the door. Once or twice during the evening my eye had been drawn to this lonely-looking figure. She'd come in with an elderly man, who I assumed was her husband, and they'd sat next to another couple. The man, however, had positioned himself at the end of the table with most of his back to the woman, excluding her from the conversation, while she perched on her chair close to the door and the draught. The fact that she was sitting in a crowd made her isolation all the more poignant.

I head over to the shop in Annascaul for milk and the newspapers and drive straight into a flood near the turning for the beach. There is a warning sign but the windscreen wipers are barely keeping up with the downpour so that by the time I can read it, it is too late. That I am only half seeing what is going on reflects many of my impressions as an observer. Only half the picture is apparent to me. Something right in front of me might be in focus but I can't be sure of what is happening on the periphery. Perhaps that's how the nation lives too – unable or unwilling to see things clearly.

I emerge from the flood and drive on.

# CHAPTER THIRTEEN

TO BE HONEST I CAN ONLY UNDERSTAND ONE WORD IN THREE, probably less. At times whole paragraphs pass over my head, totally incomprehensible. In all I spend an hour or so sitting at the bar in Foley's with this intriguing, lovely man called Dan. What I do gather is all interesting. There's something of the imp about this man, in both his puckish manner and his looks. His cropped greying hair shoots out of his head in every direction and his whole scalp ripples back and forth as he speaks. He wears grey slacks and a green sports jacket over a diamond-patterned red shirt. Dan builds chairs with rope seating in the traditional style like the ones in the pub lounge.

We talk about hardship and the example of Tom Crean the Antarctic explorer – no relation, as far as I know, to the current parish priest. This Crean, who came from Annascaul, served both on Scott's ill-fated expedition to the South Pole in 1910 and subsequently on Shackleton's 1914 attempt to cross the Antarctic. Crean was one of five men who joined Shackleton to make the extraordinary eight hundred-mile passage in a whale boat through terrible storm-driven seas to South Georgia in search of assistance for the rest of the expedition stranded on

Elephant Island. When he left the icy wastes he settled back at Annascaul and opened the South Pole Inn. Having travelled so far in the face of such enormous odds, Crean's end was ironic. He died en route to the hospital in Tralee before he could be treated for appendicitis.

Dan finds my accent as difficult to follow as I do his and so we watch each other closely as we speak. Nevertheless we develop an understanding during this short, intense conversation. Commenting on life's hardships, Dan says that to his way of thinking the horrors carried out by the English in Ireland were just an example of the terrible actions that human beings seem unable to desist from, adding, 'The Irish have been as cruel as anyone else.'

We talk of the positive effects of fear, how it can stimulate our minds and energies, and how we relish having dealt with it. I tell him that in captivity I was initially paralysed at times by a fear of fear itself and how I worked to overcome it and look it in the face. Suddenly Dan hooks his hands onto the bar edge and recalls Brian Keenan's words at Dublin Castle after his release.

'Hostage is a man hanging by his fingertips.'

I'm amazed his memory is so sharp ten years after the event and regret that he has to go off to meet a customer.

Parking in Cork city centre proves to be as challenging as deciphering Irish history. I know I'm getting near to where I need to be, the Cork Opera House, it's just the one-way system keeps diverting me. I end up in a back street and squeeze into a spot that doesn't look too illegal and go off in search of some fast food before attending a rendition of the great saga of Oisín by the Siamsa Tíre Theatre Company.

The National Folk Theatre of Ireland, Siamsa Tíre, was set up in 1974. The brainchild of Father Pat Ahern, the theatre aims to maintain and develop Irish folk culture, using music and dance to portray folk tales and elements of Irish rural life. Clearly the company's contribution is taken seriously as they are performing tonight at Cork's brand new opera house. I almost walk past the glass-fronted structure because I'm looking for a grand old stone-fronted building.

I've heard about the troupe from Pat and Máire whose two girls, Clíodhna and Ailbhe, and younger son Donnchadh are all involved, or hoping to be involved, with the company. There are only about half a dozen professionals in the group, the rest are made up of part-time adult members and youngsters who are studying the music and the dance.

With traditional music and songs and some stirring, Riverdance-style, high-energy, boot-stomping dancing, the company tells the tale of Oisín, the young hero of the Fianna, being whisked away to the Land of Eternal Youth, Tír na nÓg, by Princess Niamh of the Golden Hair.

The audience, made up mainly of families, children, parents and grandparents, is totally engrossed. As am I. But there are a couple of moments when I find myself, in a very un-PC way, thinking that the great warrior and hunter Oisín has a rather silly grin and hairdo. And there is something in the way he moves on the slower numbers that makes me think he might be happier staying with the chaps of the Fianna rather than going off across the sea with a princess who looks as though her mind is preoccupied with tweeds, twinsets and gardening.

My mind wanders from the proceedings on stage and I recall a story about my father having to leave a theatre in the middle of a ballet performance once. Instead of classic drama, my mother, brother and he had found themselves watching a modern dance interpretation performed by a group of men in tights with tassels dangling and twirling around their private parts. Never before known to succumb to giggles, my father went under in a big way. When other dance enthusiasts began to turn round to see what was causing an entire row of seats to shake violently, my mother and brother decided to get him upright and help him to the exit. The concerned faces of those around them suggested that they thought the poor man was suffering a life-threatening fit rather than desperate mirth.

A rapid-fire dance of great intricacy and power from the Fianna men brings me back from the brink of my hysteria. Realizing that only four of the entire cast are professionals sobers me; this is a very polished production altogether. Although this re-interpretation of the old saga, indeed the emphasis on the traditional styles of music and dance, might fall under the mantle of romanticization that some Irish find irksome, threatening to turn their country into 'Theme Park Ireland Inc.', I'd say that the work of Siamsa Tíre is an important cultural asset.

There is one moment when the entire audience begins to giggle. Oisín, as I had suspected all along, pines for his chums of the Fianna and decides to go back to see them. He leaves Niamh mending the lawnmower (no not really) and promises to return as soon as possible. He is warned that if he dismounts from his magical horse he'll never be able to come back. The trouble is that when he trots expectantly into the old hunting grounds he realizes that while time has been standing still in the Land of Eternal Youth, Ireland has advanced some three hundred years and his mates are all long gone. He rides about mourning his old friends and thinking of heading back to the wife when he comes across some men trying to heave a great rock into the back of a cart. As he leans down from his saddle to help them, his reins break and he falls to the ground.

At this point in the production there is a gasp from the audience. Oisín lies for what seems an age behind a rock. We are just beginning to think something has happened to the actor, when his shoulders begin to move and gradually his head comes up, now wreathed in a wig of long grey hair over a 'very old man' mask which sadly isn't terribly convincing. Pathos turns rapidly to bathos.

Maureen Fitzgerald had told me that James MacCarthy of Inch was a fan of Irish football and a big supporter of the local team. He'd written to the local papers about it in 1919 so I hunt through the microfilm archive in Tralee library. There, on the front page, no less, of the 7 June 1919 issue of *The Kerryman* I find James's letter. He's announcing that the Inch football team has become affiliated to the County Board of the Gaelic Athletic Association, GAA, for the first time. I glean a little of the character of this distant cousin from the tone of his short epistle. He makes his announcement and then complains that the board has not yet drawn the Inch team and appears to think it is second-rate whereas in fact 'they have beaten several teams that hold a good reputation in practice matches'.

Nowadays there aren't enough young people in the immediate area to field an Inch side. Nevertheless Irish football and other Gaelic sports are followed with passion throughout the country. But its story, past and present, is as much about events off the field as those on. The GAA was founded in 1884 to counter the spread of English games which, it was feared, would destroy Irish morale. From the outset it attracted a great deal of nationalist, if not necessarily revolutionary, support. There were rules forbidding any member of the association to play 'imported games' and banning the police and armed forces from membership. The GAA garnered massive support and from 1913 Croke Park in Dublin was developed as the national stadium. Since 1922 the association had not in fact had anything to do with athletics and focused instead on Gaelic football and hurling. After independence the GAA played a major part in the sporting life of the south and among Catholics in the north of Ireland.

While the ban on playing 'imported games' had been lifted in 1971, members of the British armed forces or the police in Northern Ireland have not been allowed in under the GAA's Rule 21. The debate on Rule 21 has continued for years but comes to a conclusion during my stay in Ireland at a special congress of 301 GAA delegates from all over the island. An overwhelming majority votes for the deletion of the rule from the association's official guide. Not surprisingly the delegates from the five northern counties vote against the deletion. Government ministers in the Republic welcome the decision and praise the tolerance and generosity shown by the GAA. Having grown up with the idea that sport and politics should be kept apart, my reaction to all this is one of surprise that a rule that seems to be purely political has lasted so long in a sporting body. Many sportspeople and commentators obviously feel the same and mock the platitudes of southern politicians and the condemnations of Republican politicians in the north as failing to come out and acknowledge that the rule has been, as Emer O'Kelly writes in the *Sunday Independent*, 'a weapon of bigotry and political sectarianism and so unjustifiable in the first place'.

It is clear, however, that the GAA will remain a bastion of Irish nationalism. For one thing no one else in the world has taken to the delights of Gaelic football or hurling, but its place in the struggle for independence wasn't limited to a social and cultural coming together at sports clubs and grounds. The original (Irish) Bloody Sunday saw twelve people shot dead at a major Croke Park fixture on 21 November 1920. That morning IRA men had killed thirteen and injured six other men who were believed to be British intelligence agents. Auxiliaries sent to Croke Park to look for wanted men opened fire, possibly after being shot at themselves.

A couple of months after the deletion of Rule 21 the GAA

congress in Dublin overwhelmingly votes against letting other 'codes' (soccer and rugby) play at Croke Park. Since the stadium lies idle for most of the year and the GAA could earn substantial funds by letting other sports use the ground, I can't fathom this. The money might be used to develop Gaelic sport, but many within the GAA see the opening up of Croke Park as the thin end of the wedge, that grounds all around the country will inevitably have to follow suit. The GAA is worried that if soccer and rugby gain ever wider access, kids will turn more and more to those sports, soccer especially. Given the passion the games generate, I'd have thought they have a pretty strong future, so is this all tinged with a bit of cultural paranoia? Ireland's subsequent success in the 2002 World Cup can only have helped soccer's popularity. Once again it feels like the arbiters of authority are trying to hold back the tide of change.

This debate has another dimension. It is of course to do with a politician's pet project. Bertie Ahern, the Taoiseach, is extremely keen on building a new national stadium, Stadium Ireland, or the Bertie Bowl. The previous year's GAA congress failed to allow other codes into Croke Park by just one vote. At that point they were facing a reduction in government funding if they didn't show willing, particularly as Croke Park might then be used as a venue for the joint Scottish-Irish bid to host the Euro 2008 soccer championship. Just before the vote they were told that they'd get the funding anyway. Government critics argue that Bertie had guaranteed the funds to ensure his scheme would keep going. Whether this is true or not, I have to admit that unlike the wilful idiocy of the Millennium Dome in London, Stadium Ireland, financial arguments aside, has its merits and a good part of the soccer-loving public quite justifiably feel their sport should have its own national stadium anyway.

My copy of *The Kerryman* informs me that the West Kerry Senior Gaelic Football semi-final is scheduled to take place at Páirc An Ásaigh in Dingle on Sunday afternoon. During Saturday evening I learn from Radio Kerry that due to the appalling weather the Páirc is in no fit state so battle will be joined at Castlegregory instead at the same time, two thirty. Full foul-weather gear is essential as I scuttle to get into the shelter of Castlegregory GAA's terraces. 'Terraces' is putting it somewhat grandly; it's more of a patio really. The Castlegregory team are taking on An Gaeltacht, the county champions from the west of the Dingle peninsula.

'It is three pound. Should be four, but with this weather I'll only charge you the three,' says the man at the gate as he hands me a sheet of paper naming the teams. Looking through the players' names, those of the Gaeltacht team in Irish of course, I realize that this, linguistically at least, is an international. Stiofan plays Stephen; Tomas tackles Tommy, and O Cinneide takes on Kennedy. It seems slightly odd that these lads who've grown up a few miles apart have the same names but spell them so differently.

I appreciate some skilful play but don't quite get all the rules. Barging, tripping, blatant obstruction and punching are kosher, but tugging at the shirt appears to be a definite no-no. Mind you, since the GAA was, as far as I can judge, established to keep politics in sport, a little bit of argy-bargy is only to be expected. The conditions on the pitch are daunting. Howling wind, which some of the players use to stunning effect to bend their high punts and score goals, and a sodden pitch make running and passing difficult. Every few (three?) paces the player must drop the ball and kick it back to his hand again, bounce it or pass it on. Bouncing is the least favoured option as the ball mostly makes a lot of splash and no bounce from the wet turf. Passing can be by means of a kick or by punching it out of one hand with the other. Fifteen players spread out to mark their opposite numbers and there is no discernible offside rule. All in all it's a mix of rugby and soccer, with no clear way of stopping muddled, messy bits of play, no rucks yet quite a lot of physical contact.

At half time a very dapper little man, in his early sixties by the look of him, emerges from the crowd and with notepad in hand starts talking on his mobile phone. He is giving Radio Kerry's listeners the half-time report. He has one of the sing-song, soft Kerry accents that seem to go with the older generation. I hear him saying, 'Despite high wind and rain, the lads from the home team are playing their hearts out against their powerful opponents from An Gaeltacht...' The wind starts howling around him, setting his notebook flapping wildly, and he moves out of earshot for some shelter.

Beyond the ground, sheep run about on the dunes and a farmer and his cattle walk through the rain to meet each other. A trio of horsemen appear on the crest of a sandy hummock, look at the masses huddled in the stand and against the perimeter wall, then turn to ride off in the lee of the dunes. Across the dunes I can see waves breaking in Tralee Bay and on the far shore a cloud of rainbow sits like a fireball, or a drop of diesel oil on water picked out in bright sunlight, over the village of Fenit.

The little harbour at Fenit is home to the *Jeanie Johnston*, a replica of one of the ships that took famine victims to America. The ship is far from complete and wildly over budget. The financing, which needs ever more wads of Kerry County Council's money, is causing enormous consternation in the local political and public arenas. Some feel the project must be supported, even if it might end up costing millions of euros more than forecast, as it will be a valuable tourist asset to the county. Others argue that enough is enough and that those responsible for failure to meet targets should be brought to task. It is also criticized as being another 'theme park Ireland' project, seeking to make profit out of tragic events in the country's past. The council has voted to keep the building programme going and all hands are crossing their fingers that the ship will make it to and through its sea trials. While I appreciate the arguments against pouring more public funds into her, when I get over to Fenit and see the *Jeanie*, the sailor in me is delighted that the handsome ship might make it to sail the seas as her original had done.

In the second half at Castlegregory the home team, 'Come on, lads!' continue to play their hearts out but to no avail. The An Gaeltacht boys in red and white mash the little fellas in their yellow and green strip. The champs make champ of the opposition. Once or twice I ask a neighbour what the score is. On the third occasion he looks confused and a bit embarrassed and mumbles, 'I've lost track a bit myself, y'know.'

I work out that kicking the ball over the crossbar between the high, rugby-style posts is good, but not as valuable as putting it in the back of the soccer-style net. (The local papers subsequently report that An Gaeltacht won with a score of 3–8 against Castlegregory's 0–13.) As far as I can make out, the home crowd are neither surprised nor depressed. Gamely they cheer, 'Come on, Colm!' when the Castlegregory number 15 gets the ball and there is only mild frustration when he passes it to a Gaeltacht man. 'That was shit, Colm!' Given the appalling weather it is a good and loyal turnout from both camps. As we stream out of the ground, through puddles and mud, friends greet each other as diddle-ee-dee music struggles from the PA system.

There is a cool, light breeze when I take the air late that night. But the skies have dried and cleared and stars are out to help the full moon turn the waters of the harbour silver. The heavens and the far shore, both dark blue, are dotted with lights and it is quiet, save for the grumble of the stream beside the house. The sharp night air is spiced with pungent peat smoke and the moon above is like a giant football punted into heaven.

One of the Castlegregory players was Pierce Ferriter, named, I assume, after the soldier and poet Piaras Ferriter who had become a folk hero of the rebellion which started in 1641. With his poetry Ferriter was continuing a long tradition of great families supporting and producing writers. The ancient Gaelic families had offered patronage to the bardic *fili* who recorded sagas and history to be passed down through the generations. Following the Anglo-Norman invasion the Gaelic traditions had lost influence but the fourteenth century saw Gaelic learning revive. Barrington notes that one Gofraidh Fionn O Dalaigh, 'sprung from the hereditary bardic family of the MacCarthy Mór', wrote very fine poetry that could appeal to both his Gaelic peers and the powerful English lords like the Earls of Desmond. The style of poetry, mainly highly polished courtly verses, developed as some of the Anglo-Norman families, such as the Desmonds and, in a lower key, the Ferriters, became ever more Irish. The genre of courtly poetry continued for two hundred and fifty years, according to Barrington, who notes that at the end of the sixteenth century Donal IX MacCarthy Mór, King of Desmond, first and last Earl of Clancarr, etc. etc., was writing in the same style.

The story of Donal IX was ultimately sad and rather pathetic. With his death a royal line that stretched back some twelve hundred years came to an end. Cousin Jean opens her account of his life with a description of Donal from William Camden's *Annals of the Affairs of England and Ireland During the Reign of Elizabeth*: 'He was a man eminent and of great power in Munster.' He was master, in name at least, of huge tracts of land in Counties Cork and Kerry, up to half a million acres in all, according to Barrington. Cousin Jean notes that he was 'reputed to have been extravagant and with a fondness for drink'. Barrington is more blunt, harsh even, displaying a puritanical side I haven't noticed before, calling Donal 'a dissolute and a drunkard'. As I'd found out when exploring Ballycarbery Castle, Donal was in the habit of mortgaging chunks of the family properties for cash to keep the parties going. He even mortgaged one of his daughters to the English Browne family. But for all his weaknesses Donal was acknowledged as a fine poet in the Gaelic medieval tradition, writing religious and secular verse.

A mile or so off the main N70 road between Killorglin and Killarney lies the tiny hamlet of Pallis, a corruption of 'palace'. This was the principal seat of MacCarthy Mór for three hundred years; now there are just a few modern bungalows and old stone barns. There is no one about when I visit. A couple of dogs appear and bark at me, lose interest and slope off. As I walk along the road the air is full of the smell of cow dung and the sound of birds gathering and singing in leafless trees that ring an old stone wall which perhaps once enclosed a grand house. The location is beautiful. To the south beyond the gentle slope of the hill, which levels out into a sedge grass flat that was once Donal's gallows field, clouds hang over snowy mountain tops and there is an imposing view up the Gap of Dunloe. It's no surprise to read that Barrington (recovered from his fit of prudery) loves this 'wonderfully beautiful place' and muses that it might have been here that Donal wrote some of his poetry. He quotes the last two stanzas of one of the poems:

I am a ghost upon your path,
A wasting breath,
But you must know one word of truth
Gives a ghost breath –

In language beyond learning's touch
Passion can teach –
Speak in that speech beyond reproach
The body's speech.

*(translated by Frank O'Connor)*

Some sources say there was once a castle here though others claim that the palace was never much more than a largish farmhouse. Whatever the architectural reality may have been, like my friend Barrington, I am moved by the exquisiteness of the place and can happily accept it as a likely place for old Donal IX to haunt. Majestic and poetic, you could believe, if you were a little tipsy, that it was the home of a great lord still. A little over a century after the death of Donal IX the Gaelic way of life was gone. The swansong for the great families, O Sullivan, MacCarthy, O Donoghue, was written by Egan O Rahilly, who came from a hereditary bardic family. He died in 1728 and in his last poem scanned:

Now I shall cease, death comes,
    and I must not delay
By Laune and Laine and Lee,
    diminished of their pride,
I shall go after the heroes, ay,
    into the clay –
My fathers followed theirs
    before Christ was crucified.

*(translated by Frank O'Connor)*

*

The book I'd been reading is still in my hands when I wake up. I'd gone to bed at eleven o'clock and must have closed my eyes almost immediately to sleep like a raft of lumber floating down a wide river.

Phil and Mike Courtney appear with a sprig of shamrock to wear in my lapel the next day, St Patrick's Day. Legend has it Ireland's patron saint chose the shamrock as a symbol of the Trinity of the Christian Church because of its three leaves joined by one stem. Having heard on the radio that there is a nation-wide shortage of the plant I am very grateful to my landlords for their kind gesture. Apparently many of the streams beside which shamrock used to flourish have been poisoned by all the chemicals running off farm land.

All talk is of the St Patrick's weekend and the television news reports on how it has become a major event all around the world. Most of the people calling in to a radio chat show say that rather than being in Sydney, New York or wherever and getting caught up in a festival of faux 'Oirishness' – and drink too much, they'd prefer to be at home with family – and drink too much.

Bertie Ahern, looking like the cat that got the cream, is all over the news bulletins visiting the White House and handing an enormous bowl full of shamrock to President George W. Bush. The President looks somewhat baffled by the gesture and, uncertain what the strange foliage might be, says, if my lip-reading isn't playing tricks, 'Thanks a million for the parsley, Bernie, and will you come bomb Iraq with us?'

St Patrick wasn't the first Christian missionary to Ireland and he didn't convert the whole island at one visit. Nevertheless a legend to this effect built up from the seventh century onwards in the grand old Irish way with history. This came as no great surprise to me, but I am shocked to learn that he didn't drive snakes out of the country either. RTE Radio One has a special St Patrick's Day broadcast which comes from the reptile house at Dublin Zoo. An academic from UCD points out that Greek historians and other early sources talk of Ireland as a snake-free zone long before St Pat first put a wary foot on Irish soil.

I'm flummoxed by the way the expert keeps switching to Irish, thus losing me altogether. The interviewer brings him back on line from time to time but then he wanders off again, like a poorly tuned radio drifting between stations. I won't be alone in my frustration. According to the 1996 census around one and a half million people class themselves as Irish speakers, but that leaves more than two million who have no fluency in what is supposed to be their alternative national language. Although the number of Irish speakers has increased by a million or so since just after independence in 1926 (in 1861 there had been more than a million Irish speakers), the current figure is hardly a ringing endorsement of the policies put forward by the founding fathers of modern Ireland, particularly Eamon de Valera. The hope had been that, starting with compulsory Irish in the classrooms, independent Ireland would re-create itself as a Gaelic nation. Sadly this didn't work very well and compulsory Irish on the school curriculum is now widely seen as having damaged whole generations of kids going to school in the 1940s, 1950s, 1960s and early 1970s. Not only did many children not take well to the arduous task of learning this difficult language, after school they couldn't use it in conversation with parents who spoke only English. One newspaper report argues that there are still thousands of people who are illiterate thanks to being forced to learn a language they couldn't use at the expense of a language they had to use. Their broader education was also damaged since the absolute requirement to pass in Irish in order to get a school leaving certificate meant that science, arts and business-related studies had to be ignored. Not only did this affect individual children but many believe that it meant Irish commerce had to make do with poorly educated employees and the civil service might have to take on the second-best applicant because their Irish was better than another's.

There are some strong Irish-speaking enclaves, particularly the *Gaeltacht* areas like the one to the west of Inch on the Dingle peninsula, and there are state-funded Irish-speaking radio and television stations, but maintaining the language still has to be done in the face of the widespread use of English and a desire to learn other European languages.

When Bridey Flynn was talking about a neighbour one day – Mike Daley – she pronounced the name 'Daily' first, then said, 'Oh no, you're meant to say it Dawley, aren't you, or is it Dawlig, I can't remember now!'

Mike Courtney said that he'd been taught entirely in Irish but that after leaving school he'd forgotten it all. He said he didn't mind it but that it just wasn't used at home and so his knowledge of it had withered away. Others have turned against the language altogether, blaming it for holding them back at school.

Ireland's independence came too late to resist the incursions of the English language in the twentieth century. Before the era of mass communication the linguistic dreams of the founding fathers might have been attainable.

I hear no Irish spoken when I join the crowd waiting for the St Patrick's Day parade on Denny Street in Tralee. First up are members of the Army Reserve marching smartly along. Then there's a snake with six legs, which looks more like a caterpillar to me, being chased by St Patrick on stilts (perhaps out of fear of being bitten).

A scout troop and judo school go by. Shamrock is everywhere on lapels (including mine) and many heads have large green hats on (not including mine). People stand on the pavement or on doorsteps as the parade makes its way past the doors of the Tralee Youth Club, Finucane Insurance and Auctioneers, the Southern Health Board, the Imperial Hotel, the Kerry Rape and Sexual Abuse Centre and the Tralee Beauty Salon. A man in a smart suit and raincoat, wearing a stetson, comes down the middle of the road with a monkey on a lead. I can't imagine what he is up to until I hear a mother explaining to her little boy, 'He's from the circus.'

Sure enough the circus is in town and we are treated to heavily made-up girls on elephants, a camel, horses and black men dressed as extras for a Tarzan movie. Things become a little more Irish in flavour with a whole string of girl pipe and drum bands wearing orange capes and hats. They look very neat and smart with their squeeze-boxes, pipes and drums – so pretty and serious. Their leader, a middle-aged man, barks instructions at them, 'Second march ready now!' while blowing the time with his whistle. A mixed band comes by playing 'The Belle of Belfast City', with one boy looking around, grinning at his mates on the pavement as he whacks away randomly at his xylophone. A float that consists of a rather beaten-up little sailing boat with people in fancy dress on board puzzles me until I hear two men laughing to each other and saying, 'There she blows, the great ship *Jeanie Johnston*!'

Finally that greatest of all Irish stars, Elvis Presley, comes by on the largest float, singing 'The Wonder of You'.

The whole event is very amateur but for an outsider that only adds to its charm. The local press isn't so easily impressed. In its next edition *The Kerryman* reports negative reactions from local councillors and members of the public alike. Certainly without the visiting circus it would have been very tame. One of the final floats is the most hilarious. The Kerry Society for the Prevention of Cruelty to Animals has two sheep and three lambs fenced in with chicken wire. Inside the cage with them, sitting on a smart garden bench, are two elegant, elderly ladies waving graciously to the crowd.

At supper that night Bridie Foley is also waving her hands, but with passion, and her fist bangs down on the dining table as she states vehemently, 'A nation without a language is a nation without a soul!'

There is quite a big party at Pat and Máire's, with John, Fidelus, Máire's sister Anja, her husband and a crowd of children. We're talking about language and Anja has been expressing her doubts about the real value of Irish in the modern world. She isn't arguing against keeping the language going, just wondering about the viability of the aspiration. Her question and Bridie's passion sum up a major challenge facing modern Ireland. Tied to the desire to nurture the language is the concern that other elements of traditional Irish culture, literature, drama, song and even music might fade away too. Not that this is likely in the Foley family. When the meal's over Clíodhna, Ailbhe and Donnchadh sing a song in Irish. For all I know they might be reciting the telephone directory but listening to their young, pure voices making music with this special language I can fully appreciate Bridie's passion and pride. Whatever they do with the Irish language, may the custom of singing, in the pub and at family gatherings, never die. There is an atmosphere of generosity and powerful intimacy in the room as Fidelus then Pat take their turn to sing. The last song comes from Bridie and we all join in the chorus of 'The Kerry Dancers':

> Oh! The days of the Kerry dancing,
> Oh! The ring of the piper's tune,
> Oh! For one of those hours of gladness,
> Gone, alas! Like our youth, too soon.

# CHAPTER FOURTEEN

AS I AM WASHING UP ONE SUNNY MORNING THE WATER FROM the tap dies from its customary gush to a mere trickle. Surely St Brendan's well doesn't need live rain to keep it going, there must be enough water on the hillside to keep it supplied for months. I hurry down to the Courtneys to seek help and Phil and Peter come back up to the house with me to check the taps, the shower and the lavatory in case there's a blockage. It's a classic scene, none of us has much of a clue about plumbing but we all suddenly develop determined ideas about what the problem could be. None of them gets us anywhere. We have a quick look at the water tank on the kitchen roof. From the bottom of the ladder Phil gives Peter instructions:

'Peter, take the lid off the tank.'

'Peter, be careful not to lose the clips, we don't want the lid blowing off in a storm.'

'Peter, check the pipe coming in.'

'Peter, check the pipe going out.'

We can't identify the problem, the tank appears to be in good order, so we decide we'll wait for Mike, who installed the plumbing, to return from work.

Mike appears that night with Stephen and we climb back onto the roof.

'Stephen, take the lid off the tank so I can have a look.'

'Stephen, give me the pliers.'

'Stephen, give me the screwdriver.'

My only duty is to hold the torch, which I do as an increasing drizzle mocks our struggles with my domestic drought. Mike discovers that the outlet from the tank is in fact blocked and has it cleared. Thinking all is well, we climb back down and go back inside to try the taps. Nothing. The rain is coming down fast now so we abandon plumbing for the day.

Phil and Peter are back in the morning and we study the various pipes coming through the wall behind the boiler in the kitchen to see which might be the one from the tank on the roof. Tentatively I loosen the nuts of a join on the most likely-looking culprit. For a moment there is nothing, it's dry, damn it. But then there's a gurgle followed by a rush of water. An airlock must have formed when we were working on the roof the night before. Now it is free and St Brendan is happily back on tap.

Bits of wheels, horseshoes, nuts and bolts, broken tools and bicycles are everywhere; I've never been in a place of work where the floor was so comprehensively littered. I'd only managed a glimpse inside Florence O'Sullivan's forge the first time I dropped round but now I can appreciate the chaotic interior in detail. Not that it bothers Florence in the least; he's been here all his working life so this is organized chaos. Stopping by to say hello I find him hammering away in the back of the shed. There's little light but I can just make out curious figures and letters written on the walls. Florence explains that these are the records of the brands for various sheep farmers. 'A farmer can usually identify a given sheep from a hundred others,' he tells me, 'but they need to brand them in case of a dispute with another farmer.'

Nowadays he uses readymade horseshoes but in the old days he made his own.

'Would you care to see how it was done?' he asks in his shy way.

The door bangs in the wind as he lights the fire with a bit of paper and a match and switches on an electric fan which coaxes the flames under the small chips of coal. The smoke billows and the sparks leap up the blackened chimney that his grandfather had built. Florence's family originally came from the Ventry side of Dingle, left for England at the time of the famine and returned to Castlemaine before setting up shop in Boolteens.

As he's got the fire going he says he'll finish a bit of work he's been doing for someone's gate and I watch as he hammers a bit of iron into a decorative 's' shape. That job done he takes a plain little bar of metal and begins heating then hammering, heating then hammering it until the horseshoe shape emerges perfectly formed and he takes up a punch to hammer the holes through for the nails. When he's satisfied with his work he dips it in a bucket of water, observing, 'That water's supposed to be good for curing warts!'

A few days later I'm back as he'd said a couple of horses were due in to be shoed. The morning is warm and sunny as the two horses, a brown and a grey, stand patiently, reins held by their owner and his daughter. They're from Tralee, the man tells me, and explains that most stables won't do hot-shoeing any more, preferring the easier method of nailing them on cold. 'But that way they're not so well seated and don't last as long as when they're put on hot.'

Florence, bent double over an upturned hoof, murmurs to the horse, 'Be nice now.' He cleans the hoof with pincers and a file. He disappears into the darkness of the shed, emerging a few minutes later with a red-hot shoe. There is a hiss as he presses it onto the hoof and the air is filled with smoke that smells of singed hair.

The dustcart pulls up. 'Hello, John Francis,' says Florence. The man watches for a minute or two then moves on.

A van emblazoned 'Burke's Butchers' arrives with a delivery for Florence who takes his meat into the house with two horseshoes in his other hand.

For long minutes the road is deserted and the only noise comes from the cawing of crows and the tapping of hammer against nail.

'That's a good horse, that's it.'

When the shoeing is done, we chat for a while and Florence shows us the wagon wheels he is making for a jaunting car that would be used over at the Gap of Dunloe near Killarney.

We tell the man and his daughter about our family connection and Florence jokes, 'Yes, the trouble all started about a mile from here at Ardcanacht!'

The language of Tory middle England is often the language of rural Ireland. 'Bring back the birch' or, if push comes to shove, the hurling bats, is a quietly approved way of dealing with growing youth crime. While no one likes the idea of vigilantes they feel that something needs to be done to curb crime. The Gards are on the run and there are no-go areas in Tralee, I'm told, which is shocking. Typical comments will be, 'There's too much political correctness, in the old days the Gards would give a young fellow a thump to remind him what was what! And in the schools the mother will be there, shouting at a teacher if they give a child a minor slap; "I know my child, I know my child," they say, "Little Mikey would never have done that!"'

The idea that in some places there might be underlying social reasons that push kids off the straight and narrow – poverty or generations of unemployment, for example – are given a passing nod but no real credence. But on the other hand there's general agreement that it would be pretty hard for the youth of today to get any inspiration to good citizenship from the national leaders of Church and state.

One truly disturbing development is increasing racism. *The Kerryman* reports that Tralee is earning a reputation as one of the most racist towns in Ireland. Foreigners living in the town say that they are regularly insulted on the streets and often fear that the abuse will turn physical. This is disturbing to learn, but at least there is some comfort in the widespread condemnation of such attitudes and the setting up of groups to celebrate Kerry's growing cultural diversity. But more than once I've heard people complaining about immigration along these lines: 'I'm not a racist, but I tell you when they come here looking for a soft touch, B&B and spending money, well! It's not all of them, like, some come here and work very hard to send money home, build a house for their family. If they can do that, fair play to them, I can respect that. But those Romanians! When you go to the Caribbean you learn what racism is all about, I can tell you.'

Just as in the UK, there's a growing paranoia about asylum seekers. With the worries that the economy is at least slowing down there are fears that there won't be enough jobs to go round and there are rumblings in the papers against foreign workers. Some people, including one or two politicians, have been running off at the mouth about the country being overrun by economic migrants. This seems to go in tandem with a growing resentment of the EU and a clear desire among many voters to try and keep it and the potential new and poorer states in Europe at a distance (despite the fact that Ireland has benefited enormously from EU membership and handouts over the past years). In reality the latest figures show that while there was a big jump in asylum claims between 1998 and 1999, the figure has now dropped slightly to a national level of just over ten thousand for the year. In Kerry there are only 370, the majority from eastern Europe and a few from Africa and Asia, seeking asylum among the county's population of 126 thousand. Whilst there are unpleasant overtones in some quarters, there are also people seeking funds to set up centres to help asylum seekers in Kerry and a column in *The Kingdom* newspaper makes the point that it's a bit rich for the Irish, who have made homes in countries all around the world, especially in times of famine, persecution and economic hardship at home, to be pulling up the drawbridge against others who've found themselves in a similar plight.

A very good session on Gerry Ryan's morning radio show has a ghastly spokeswoman from some organization that has been leafleting against asylum seekers in the Dublin area. She is a real screecher but completely loses out to a representative from a race relations body and an Asian doctor, a longtime Irish citizen. The woman accuses Ryan of being entirely biased and trying to twist her words but he keeps very quiet during the three-way argument and simply says at the end, 'You [the audience] are not stupid. I think you know exactly where this lady was coming from.'

In the next news bulletin we learn that Mohammed Ali's grandfather was Irish and that his great-granddad was a plasterer in County Clare. So that's nice.

Stormy weather is back and raging like a monstrous orchestra, the higher notes of the tree-tearing wind accompanied by a deep tone like rumbling stones from the blast across the chimney's top. The paper draught-excluder across the fireplace in my bedroom crackles back and forth like a flap opening and closing over a tracheotomy. When I open the front door, the breath is sucked from my body. It's hard not to think that there is some alien force out there. But where is it going and why? What is the purpose of this Herculean energy?

Just up behind my house there's a plot of land for sale, which belongs to the Kennedys. There used to be a house up there and you can still make out some of the ruins. Mike Courtney reckons the old house was built in 1839, the Year of the Big Wind. So dramatic was this storm that a book has been written about it which includes reports from the newspaper of the time, the *Kerry Evening Post*, for the week of 5 January 1839:

In Killarney and its neighbourhood the hurricane raged with terrible fury. The town sustained much damage and many houses were shattered. Mr. James Goggin's chimneys were blown into the street, and caused that gentleman and the whole neighbourhood much alarm – Mr. Michael McCarthy had a similar cause of terror, the roof of his house being laid quite bare. The windows of the Victoria Hotel were shattered to pieces and many aged trees . . . were laid prostrate, in every quarter and in all directions.'

Even Donal IX's beautiful haunt at Pallis wasn't spared.

The house of an opulent farmer, named John Sullivan, at Pallas, near Killarney, was blown down, and having taken fire, was totally consumed together with a valuable haggard [hawk], three cows, and twenty firkins of butter destroyed . . .

And in Galway:

Seven lives have been lost, and there are four lying dangerously wounded. From eleven o'clock at night to five in the morning the streets were impassable, as slates and stones were flying in all directions in rapid succession, chimneys falling, the roofs of houses giving way, windows smashing, men, women and children screaming and crying . . .

At the house a couple of hundred yards from mine, the story was that the wind blew out the earth that served as mortar between the stones of the walls. The west wall of the main room was lined with an old-fashioned dresser and, as the wind burst through, all the plates were hurled off the shelves. I can imagine such a scene all too well on a night like this and the other nights when I've sat up in my bed waiting for the windows to blow in.

Pat Foley stops by one evening with a couple of books he thinks I'll find interesting. While we chat I point to the picture of the Sacred Bleeding Heart of Jesus and say that I've seen one in nearly every house I've visited. A few years earlier, he says, there would have been pictures of the Pope and JFK, likely taken from the newspapers and framed, up there alongside the Son of God.

'Did people go off JFK when the stories of his sexual philandering came out?'

'That came after he'd gone and people would say, "Sure, he was only human." It's a bit like Charlie Haughey, a great politician who may have gone wrong in some ways. People in this area and especially around Dingle still revere Charlie.'

Haughey is a clever man; in 1970 he was dismissed from the Fianna Fáil government of Jack Lynch following the 1970 Arms Trial in which he was accused of conspiring to import arms. He went to ground, building a personal power base around the country. In 1979 he became party leader. Pat remembers playing in the field across the road from the pub when two big Mercedes pulled up outside the pub. It was

Haughey and his entourage. He stopped and had a drink with the locals.

The apparent indifference of the Irish to the alleged corruption of public figures has perplexed and depressed me. The final programme in the television series *Seven Ages*, which has been reviewing the history of the state, gives me some insights into this and other issues that have cut across the probably romantic view that I brought with me to Ireland. A deep cynicism is perceived to have taken hold of the Irish at the end of their state's first century. While that perception doesn't alleviate the irritation that they have such an apathetic attitude, it does make some sense of it. And the cynicism isn't universal or completely anaesthetizing. I've seen flashes of anger from Máire and Anthony, for example, about Liam Lawlor, and from Phil about the way in which money has been spent on the *Jeanie Johnston* project. I know how hard these people work and appreciate how angry it makes them when the taxes they pay are squandered.

Alongside the cynicism there is confusion. Since the Church has lost its position as the respected moral arbiter following the revelations of sexual abuse, paedophilia and the apparent collusion of the establishment with some of the perpetrators, there is no clear alternative system of morality for people to turn to. One contributor to the programme says there is a need for a 'concept of common citizenship'. Former President Mary Robinson says that Ireland's strength has always come from the margins and that the Irish need to look there for inspiration again and be on the side of the marginalized, both at home and in the developing world.

There is widespread disappointment that during the years of the Celtic Tiger not enough has been done to address the growing gap between rich and poor. But at the same time commentators note that there has been a dramatic change, within one generation, from a culture of overriding, sometimes stifling, duty to family to the supremacy of the individual's desires.

After an end-of-year budget in which he seems to be giving something to nearly everybody, Minister for Finance Charlie McCreevy is being labelled a wizard on a par with Harry Potter. But the government is facing a massive deficit, due to falling revenues from income tax and VAT caused by the economy slowing down, by expenditures to counter foot and mouth and by the loss of tourism as a result of the disease and 11 September. Unless the economy really powers ahead, McCreevy may be setting up the country for a massive financial shortfall at the end of next year. So disaster could loom and RTE's economics correspondent George Lee appears to be taking more than usually morbid pleasure in pointing out the weakness in the minister's plans.

Lee is one of my favourite figures on Irish television. I've nicknamed him 'Hangman' because of the melancholic joy he seems to derive from telling us that the economy is going down the pan. One night he reported on the property market. Following a big boom in prices, it had become more difficult than ever to get on the housing ladder. George ended his report with the line, 'Some people would find this repulsive.' I like this bluntness, a trait displayed by a number of Irish broadcast journalists who appear far more subjective than their British counterparts. 'Hangman' is the scouring pad on Ireland's Teflon politico/economic scene. He shares Jeremy Paxman's outrage but lacks the elegant, world-weary studio manner of his English counterpart. George is barely controlled passion: raging outside the ministry, bank or wherever in his gumboots in the rain. Our intrepid reporter really got his depressed dander up when a series of disasters with flagship Irish companies caused the international business community to look at the Irish stock exchange with concern. For all that the Celtic Tiger had achieved, there were concerns that the Irish weren't quite mature enough to deal with the real world. One case saw a Nick Leeson/Barings-style scandal rock the Allied Irish Bank. An employee at AIB's American branch was found to have lost around sixty million dollars in dodgy share trading. G. Lee was ecstatic as he announced, from beneath his umbrella outside AIB HQ, eyes glinting with a hint of mania behind his spectacles, 'Heads will roll.'

His monotone delivery did little to disguise a licking of lips.

When the dust of budget day has settled most people put doubts about the long term to the back of their minds, hoping that the economy will do well enough to avoid disaster. Self-interest, as usual, wins the day and the majority, except the very poor, seem happy enough. But the issue remains: to what extent is the community responsible for the individuals within it? How caring should it be?

My cottage has become a real home. Although I'd never felt nervous in any way about being here on my own I had felt quite lonely and uncomfortable for a while. But now, as well as knowing my neighbours, there is the secure familiarity of the commonplace, the utensils and cupboards I use, the settings for the oven, the satisfying ritual of fire-laying and collecting peat from the shed, that give me a real sense of belonging. Perhaps, too, I'm feeling more at home with myself.

So it's odd that when I go for a walk through the dunes at Inch one evening, anxiety descends on me. Images of un-exploded IRA munitions blowing me up or of the marsh swallowing me, a whole set of hitherto unthought of and there-fore unexpected fears engulf me as I meander through the hummocks of sand and grass. I'm beset with unexpected dreads. It's as if something inside me that I can't identify is casting about for an outlet.

When I see rabbits scuttling, startled, for their burrows, their white tails bright in the failing light, my nerves loosen up. The dunes are so extensive, it isn't until you are in among them that you realize their scale. At something like a thousand acres I imagine whole brigades of IRA men could train unnoticed and not even trespass on a golf course, should one be developed. But what would become of the solitude and peace of the spot?

As I wander through the dunes in the fading light, my mind begins to break free of the vague quagmires lurking in its corners and I'm conscious of a growing feeling of clarity. My stride lengthens as I cut through the sandhills to the shore and back towards the house lights dotted across the hillside at Inch.

This final section of my walk, an easy stroll along the strand, abruptly turns grim when I pass close to the carcass of a seal. Its head, or rather its brain and eyes, have been pecked clean by birds and there are myriad claw marks scarring the sand around the head, which is now no more than an outline in red on the sand. The body is quite untouched. The wind hardens as I walk on and the rain comes spitting after me from the sea, the impact of the drops so sharp that I cannot at first be sure whether it is rain or sand that is snicking, nagging at me like vicious doubts. My jeans and jacket are quickly soaked but rather than hurrying on I come to a stop.

'Oh my God!'

I don't want to think it, have never dared say it, but now it's in my mind and if I can't express it at this moment then probably I never shall. I've told myself that I haven't been able to read my mother's old letters in case I find her critical, in case I find her less loving than I remember, than I want. But now it rings clear in my mind that I know that can't and won't be the case. The fear is that I'm not going to be able to bear that love because of my feelings of guilt. Yes, I feel guilty about not having been a better son and, however innocently, putting her through such agony in her already desperately painful last years, but that isn't what really worries me. I fear that once I let my guilt out she'll be so distressed that she won't be able to forgive and love me again.

In my cell after I learned of her death, I remember being overcome with fear that my home would have changed for ever. How could my father and brother be coping? I just couldn't imagine home existing without my mother there. Over time my subconscious absorbed the new reality, that she wasn't there, and I was convinced that Terence and my father would be managing, practically at least, very well. When I came home this was evidently the case and my worries on that score were finally eased. But now they've come back to me. As I began the process of readjustment to the real world, a process that would take longer than I'd anticipated or was actually conscious of as it played itself out, I was sitting alone at my father's house one day and the words fell out of my mouth: 'It's easier she's not here.'

How could I think like that? Loving her so much, knowing how much she loved me and how she'd fought to be there to express that love again, how could I deny her in that way? Aware of how much she had suffered through her illness and my disappearance, how could I, even for a moment, push her away because I thought I had too much on my mind to be able to address her worries too?

'I am so sorry.'

I'm not sure how long I've been standing as these terrible, shameful memories go through my mind. Perhaps only a minute or two, but now I am so cold, with the wind cutting through my wet clothes, that my legs, face and hands are almost numb. I turn to face the wind for a moment and feel those hard drops biting at me again. Finally I turn towards home.

Over a couple of days I begin to feel better again. Looking at my mother's picture, she has obviously not changed, but now I've told her the worst. It is a relief. On Saturday night I am looking forward to going down to Foley's. My pleasure at having become part of this community is again running strong but I'm missing Anna and want to be with her.

Sitting at the bar I mention this to Bridget Fitzgerald who says she is looking forward to her boyfriend coming over in a couple of weeks.

'Ah well,' I say, 'I suppose absence makes the heart grow fonder.'

'It does,' she says, nodding firmly. 'You have to go away to come back.'

Also at the bar are Ann and Barry, my English blow-in friends. We get the giggles early in the evening – that is at about ten o'clock – when the musician, a solo artist with a full sound combo machine/backing track set-up, starts warming up. Emmanuel is a lovely guy and a good musician but we know he gets nervous before a gig and for a long time he seems content only to graze his guitar strings occasionally and leave the 'backing group' to do its thing. After what feels like a very long time he's clearly decided he's ready to go for it with an Elvis cover. He gets as far as, 'Wise men say only fools rush . . .' when the power goes and his 'band' disappears into an aural black hole. The electricity failure is only momentary but it is spooky and it saps Emmanuel's confidence. Understandably he takes a while to get it back together again.

Barry and I are beginning to shake uncontrollably, danger-ously close to terminal laughter, imagining the poor fellow's distress if the computer on his sound machine has gone back to its default setting of tunes and rhythms, none of which he knows, reducing his artistic input to an occasional spot of humming.

By the end of the evening Emmanuel is happily in full swing and has everyone up dancing. Please God, though, I never, ever want to hear 'Obladi-Oblada' again. Ever.

# CHAPTER FIFTEEN

JUSTIN OF CLASH ARRIVES AT WATERSIDE JUST AS I DO. HE'S BEEN brought down from Annascaul by his sister Mary and her husband who are visiting from Dublin. Mary had run the London marathon for me as part of the campaign for the hostages yet plays down this enormous effort, saying it had been good fun too. My thanks for such a generous gesture feel inadequate.

Mike, Justin and I set off to meet some cousins. It's an exciting moment and anticipation is running through me. I've been lucky so far to discover these new relatives and luckier still that we have been getting on so well. Now we're off together to look up more family. One or two Mike or Justin have met before, others we'll all be meeting for the first time. On the way we pass the old National School at Keel which is now a private home. It had been lived in by a man believed to be a key figure in the local IRA. Once a neighbour was chasing a dog that had been worrying his sheep and, shotgun in hand, he followed the animal down the small riverbed that runs very near the house. The dog went into a growth of gorse and stayed put. The neighbour decided to blast the dog out with his gun. When he raised the weapon to fire, two men emerged from the bush saying, 'Don't shoot, we're Special Branch!' They were Irish police keeping watch on the comings and goings at the house.

As we drive on we celebrate the extensive roadwork being carried out between Inch and Castlemaine. Mike, who used to work as an engineer in the roads department before going into planning at the county council, says he can't remember the last time the road had been properly resurfaced like this.

At a place called White Gate Cross Roads which, as Mike and Justin happily point out, has no white gate, we turn off towards the River Maine. I've been down this road a couple of times to walk beside the slipway on the river bank. This time, though, we turn off to visit the remains of the old church and graveyard. Justin has been here before with his father and knows that Justin MacCarthy of Inch was buried there. He tells me that Justin of Inch was the last MacCarthy buried in the family vault; his son James was buried at Inch, in the cemetery across the road from Foley's Pub. At his father's funeral, James had told the local builder to close the little mausoleum off as there was no room for anyone else to go in it and to erect 'a bit of a chapel business on the top'. Chapel business or no, we can't distinguish it from a number of other edifices, but there is an elegant memorial to Justin's sister-in-law Anne, wife of Jeremiah (the father of the railway builders). This marble cross with a dove and a swirl of carved flowers around it had been commissioned by her sons after their return from southern Africa.

Heading on towards a place called Ballyfinnane, we stop to say hello to Florence at the forge in Boolteens. He is as busy as ever but is intrigued to hear of our mission to see other cousins, the 'crowd back there' as he calls them.

Standing outside Liam Hickey's nursery at Ballyfinnane, we chat about family connections. Liam and his sister Noreen tell me that their mother, Nancy, who has been dead for six years, was a daughter of Garrett, one of the six brothers who'd gone to Rhodesia at the turn of the last century to build railways. Justin of Clash had told me on the drive over that he'd once visited the place and met Nancy who'd had a biscuit tin full of cuttings about me. 'Oh yes, he's one of ours!' she'd affirmed.

There is confusion all round as to how they had concluded that I was related to this branch of the MacCarthy clan. Justin says that an Irish journalist had turned up at some point asking if we were related. Why he might have guessed at the connection remains a mystery. Justin could only say that he had no idea. He'd looked at the family tree with his sisters and their best guess had been that I was descended from one of the brothers of James of Inch. For some reason suspicion fell on the one called Florence, who'd had to clear out when he'd got a local girl with child. My head was reeling. All these convolutions to get nowhere near the truth!

Leaving Liam and Noreen we three go to church, or at least to the car park of the church at Currans a few miles away. This name I know well from the old pedigree which records that a Justin (I'm not making this up) MacCarthy who was born at Ardcanacht in 1762 died at Currans in 1835. The car park is deserted when we arrive but another car pulls in shortly and a couple emerge. A tall, elderly man wearing a flat cap introduces himself as Wayne. No, he doesn't really; he's another Justin of course. To keep it clear in my head I dub him Justin of Cliddaun (where he lives). He has white hair and rather protuberant ears and I wonder at the age of this shy, gentle man, especially when I realize that he is the son of one of the six railway-building brothers. With him is his much smaller wife Maureen who exudes a lively enthusiasm.

Introductions are made and it amazes me the way they immediately grasp how Mike and I fit in as distant cousins. As we
talk, another car pulls in and another white-haired man
approaches, who is also rather shy. This is Billy Walsh, brother
of Dan, the retired policeman I'd met in Cork with Cousin Jean.
We talk for a while before going to Justin and Maureen's farm at
Cliddaun. The large farmhouse with its extensive outbuildings
had been built by Justin's father James with the money he
brought back from Africa. The farm is now run by Justin and
Maureen's son, another James.

As Maureen prepares tea we are taken through to the living
room to see a picture of the railroaders' mother, Anne, whose
grave we had just visited at Keel. She has a very determined face
and it comes as little surprise to hear that whatever her sons
might have been up to with the Moonlighting campaign against
the English landlords, she used to move pistols around for the
organization, taking them in and out of Tralee, tied under
the tails of her donkeys.

I begin to notice that many of these stories are prefaced with
the phrase, 'There's a yarn that . . .' So there is room given for
doubt; after all, none of this has been written down as a historical
record. However, if two of her sons had to skip the country
because of their involvement with a Moonlighters' attack on a
land agent in Castleisland, then they may well have got their
inspiration from this tough-looking mother.

As we sit in the large kitchen eating the cakes and buns with
which Maureen has covered the table, I sit back and listen. For a
while the talk is about farming and the latest developments of
the Kerry Group, the pros and cons of its transforming from a
farmers' co-operative into a public company. Justin of Clash and
Billy Walsh reminisce about voting against the start of this
change some years earlier at a conference in Tralee. Then the
conversation takes us further back in time to the 1930s and de

Valera's economic war with Britain. As with so many things Irish, this 'disaster' of a policy which cost the farming industry dear before it was resolved after six years seems as fresh in contemporary minds as something that happened in the past decade. Of the present company only Justin of Cliddaun might have been alive at the time and then just a boy. But again, as with the grasp of family connections, stories told around firesides and kitchen tables have kept memories in sharp focus.

Maureen's son James searches for various newspaper cuttings, books and a copy of the family tree while she bustles around the table with a teapot asking, 'Shall I hot that up for you?' He returns with a family tree that traces us all right back to Milesius, whose sons were supposed to have conquered Ireland and are credited with bringing Gaelic culture with them. Although modern history and archaeology put the Gaelic invasion at around 100 BC, their sagas say they arrived around 1700 BC from Spain. And that is what this family tree happily maintains.

I notice Maureen smiling at me.

'Is your head spinning, John, with all this family history?' she asks.

I have to admit it is but that I'm hoping to gain courage from the family motto that appears on the pedigree: *Forti et Fideli Nil Difficile*, To the Strong and Faithful Nothing Is Difficult. Trying to put a perspective on ancient tales of Gaelic invaders, on yarns of Moonlighters and railway builders, on memories of economic warfare and the present state of agriculture in Kerry is all too much. I so wish that my parents and Terence could be here to share all this with me. They would have other questions to ask.

As the conversation goes on around me in my cousins' kitchen, I think of the family photos back at my cottage. I can only feel sorrow at the way events have so confounded our family life. One can forever be saying 'if only' and 'it should have been like this' but we have to make do with what there is. There is no chance to relive these moments; as the cliché has it, life isn't a rehearsal. And although I miss having my immediate family around me I console myself that I am surrounded by family, even if they are people I have only just met. They are warm-hearted and welcoming individuals with whom I am comfortable and feel a kinship.

I warm to young James and his humorous take on life.

'I'd only come back to run this place for a couple of years,' he says. 'That was twelve years ago! They always said those brothers came back from Africa loaded down with money. Well, I'll tell you, I've seen none of it. I've looked through every nook of the place and believe me there's no treasure, no gold or diamonds!'

Billy has a copy of an old sepia photograph that was believed to include the brothers at a ceremony on the railway in Rhodesia. Neither Billy nor Justin of Cliddaun can identify anyone in the picture but James points to one figure leaning casually against a steam engine.

'That's Garrett, it has to be! That's just how the Black Garrett would stand.'

'The Black Garrett?' I ask laughing.

James smiles. 'My cousin, old Garrett's grandson. I'm after calling him that because of his black hair. My other cousin Garrett has red hair.'

'And he's the Red Garrett I guess.'

'He is!'

We had been hoping to find Black Garrett and now, armed with detailed directions to his house, Justin of Clash, Mike and I say our goodbyes and move on.

The Black Garrett is greyer than his dramatic epithet suggests, but the moment he comes out of his house and leans against the doorway, I can see immediately why James had identified the man in the old photograph as his grandfather. And, having seen the brothers in a clearer, formally posed wedding photograph, it is obvious this man 'had the head of old Garrett on him'. His family still live at Farran though the old house that the railwayman owned stands decaying a few hundred yards from the modern home.

When we talk of his grandfather he laments that they'd never found any written records of his activities in southern Africa but he leaves the room for a moment to return with a shotgun that had been brought back from Rhodesia. 'The first hammerless gun anyone round here had seen.'

Black Garrett runs a plant hire business and comes across as someone who shares the adventurous spirit of his grandfather's generation. While appearing a rough and ready type he reveals a native wit that is at once informative and highly entertaining. Like many of his fellow Kerrymen he has a natural ability for yarning and states his views with strong arguments and language. He expresses his disgust with the ongoing revelations of the Church's failure to deal with those priests involved in abuse, and when it comes to politics he is just as outspoken. 'They should clear the whole fecking lot out and start again. They're a disgrace, only interested in looking after themselves!'

His upper body sways as he waves his arms and moves his head sharply up, down and around for emphasis. As a contractor he has a good deal of contact with local politicians and his account of the activities of some of them, encouraging additional work, at the council's expense, for their friends, or ensuring that their own families get the pick of some council contracts, is at once hilarious and disheartening. When I ask if the tribunals investigating corruption in high places don't show that the nation is at last coming to terms with this sort of problem, he tosses his head and tuts, 'It'll take a lot more than that!'

I like Garrett a great deal and while I'm sure he gives as good as he gets in his wheeler-dealer world, his clear blue eyes, set among the wavy grey hair and thick beard, speak of an innate honesty of spirit that would make him a valuable friend.

I still find it hard to work out anyone's political affiliations. Probably this is because people here are canny about them in any case, but the fact that they swing over the history of modern Ireland with such abandon, moving from the war against the Black and Tans to the Civil War and on to the IRA hunger strikes of the 1980s and then glide into the activities of the likes of Charlie Haughey often leaves me struggling to keep up. As I strive to tie the historical threads together, the nuances of anecdotes that might give a lead on their political leanings pass me by.

There seems, though, to be a curious mixture of respect and disdain in so much that is said that I can't tell where loyalty might lie. While Garrett is critical of priests who wouldn't say a Mass for an IRA man on hunger strike he is also mocking of the fact that some forty 'green heroes' apparently came forward to claim a state pension for an action against the British in 1921 in which only ten people actually took part.

One of his daughters appears with glasses and whiskey. As the Black Garrett reminds us of the massive anti-malarial whiskey intake of the railway builders, I can well imagine this MacCarthy, who is so at ease with himself, leaning casually like his grandfather in the picture, holding court in a bar. It's a surprise when he says he never touches a drop.

Back at home, sitting at the table looking out across Castlemaine Harbour to MacGillycuddy's Reeks still quite clear in the evening light, I start adding in the new connections I have learned on the family tree. It's dark outside by the time I've finished, and it seems as if I've written the name Justin a hundred times. As I'm putting the papers away I notice the old pink folder containing my mother's letters.

Why not? I think. I've revealed my worst thoughts and actually feel better for it. And I'm nearing the end of my stay, my period of solitude and reflection. If I don't read them now they might go back into the loft at home and become an emotional 'no-go area' again. During my time at Inch I've come so much closer emotionally to my mother and these letters are the most tangible and personal link I have with her.

A feeling of excitement and anticipation comes over me as I sit on the sofa and spread out the contents of the file, surprised that there are so many letters. I pick one out at random, from January 1978, my second year at university.

She starts 'My Darling John' and goes on with some news from home; my student grant has arrived and she's paid it into my bank account, she asks if the snow is bad in Hull, down in Essex some of the roads had been blocked, she reminds me that bacon sandwiches make a good snack. I'm smiling now and then my grin broadens when I read, 'I hope you can read this, I can't, because I can't find my glasses!' Then, just before she signs off 'loads of love, M', she writes, 'Please <u>communicate</u> with us in some form or another.' I feel myself go cold and numb, overwhelmed with all the old guilt that I must have seemed a thoughtless son.

I'm about to put the letters away again but instead reread this one and this time it reveals to me how loving she was and confirms what I knew, that when I was away I wasn't always good at keeping in touch with home. That's all. I decide that rather than reading the whole lot now, I can let this first taste sink in while I sort them all into chronological order. It's classic displacement activity but in fact it has a positive effect, in that the process lets me acclimatize to the idea gently, letting me appreciate how often she'd written – once a week. Soon I realize that I don't have all the letters, but certainly a great many and in one case a whole year's worth.

At the back of the folder I find a couple of letters and some postcards from my father. They are more humorous and affectionate than I would have remembered them. One card sent to me at school while he's on a business trip to New York says he's sorry to hear I've got the flu but hopes I'll be better soon and that he's looking forward to seeing us all the weekend after next. He ends the card with the puzzling code, 'ITMTRMTB dear John EYAF'. It's not until I read one of the letters that I remember what this means: 'In the meantime remember me to be ever your affectionate father'. He'd come across this sign-off in a biography and then adopted it himself. I like this little flourish. It comes at the end of a brief note saying all at home are glad to hear 'that you are safely returned to terra-firma' after I'd completed a parachuting course at school. Across the top of the page he's written 'Up the Airborne', in which he served during the Second World War, and congratulates me, 'Very well done dear lad. The first jump is always very frightening.' Other cards came from places in Europe and Australia and they remind me of the enthusiasm he had for visiting new places and meeting new people. Other letters talk of developments at home and, again with an almost boyish enthusiasm, of plans for future holidays.

Finding these few dispatches from my father is an unexpected bonus and boost. Now that I've ordered them into piles I can look at my mother's letters without the old, awful anxiety. Just looking at the familiar copperplate, slightly sprawling handwriting brings her, the way she spoke, back into sharp focus. I look at her photograph, which I've propped up next to me, and smile as I think, We'll read these through over the next few days.

# CHAPTER SIXTEEN

I NEED A SPECIAL ADAPTOR FOR ONE OF THE WHEEL NUTS BUT can't find it. Instead of bringing balm, the warmth of the day is only serving to heat my irritation as I fume with my attempts to change the flat tyre on my car. 'Bloody car! Bloody, bloody Irish and their bloody potholed roads!'

I'm trying, unsuccessfully, to get through on my mobile to what looks like the nearest (nearest being a relative term and meaning, in fact, the next town) Renault dealer when a man walks past.

'Excuse me. Do you know anything about Renaults?' I ask.

He isn't sure and says he'll try the garage. He dials and gets through straight away. 'Hello, how are yeh? Can I speak to Patrick? Tell him it's Liam.'

'You know someone there?' I ask, surprised.

'Patrick. He's in sales.'

And Patrick's on the line and confirms that I need a special nut and that it should have come with the car but they do have them in stock if I can't find the original. So it looks like a cab ride fifteen miles each way but at least I know that I'll have a car that can move again. I thank Liam who heads off to his car. Then I remember that there are some storage compartments under the seat. Sure enough I'd put the nut kit in there. I shout to Liam that I've found the nut and he gives me the thumbs up. A minute or two later he pulls up in his car to see if I can get the nut off all right. As he asks, the nut comes free. Seeing that all's well he smiles and drives off.

'Bye, Liam, thanks a million!'

'Good luck, John.'

Such kindness, and for a total stranger, transforms the heat of my frustration and anger with the car into a warm glow of well-being and oneness with my fellow man.

Coming out of Tralee library that afternoon a wonderful thing stops me in my tracks: the year's first sniff of freshly mown grass. For me it has always been a signal of hope, that the good times are just around the corner. It's a lovely evening, cool but above all fresh with the promise of spring.

Back at Inch I have to go down to the beach. Any tension and tiredness in my body disappears as I pace along the sand. The crisp, fresh evening air fills my lungs and the faint fireball of the sun setting through a haze, with the mountains sitting humped in pure white cloaks of cloud, fills my vision. I wander a little way into the dunes and find the peace there in seconds. The sound of the waves rolling in far away across the beach dies to a whisper as I move deeper into the wildness of the tiny, sandy mountain range.

Walking back along the beach I meet Dora McCarthy, a neighbour but no relation, whom I'd met briefly at the Stations Mass at Foley's. Standing there, taking in the beautiful evening and the expanse around us, a fisherman or two tending their lines which stretch way out into the surf, we chat about the weather improving and with it our moods. Smiling, she says she's feeling better because with the warmer weather and the efforts of her physio her back pains are much improved. She talks about her hopes and fears for her children, a boy and a girl who are playing nearby, and how she worries that sometimes she might be too protective of them. A natural enough worry for any parent but I didn't know that Dora is bringing up her kids alone. Her husband, 'My lovely husband!', had died a few years before.

At the car park I meet Maureen Fitzgerald, coming or going from a walk. Every time I go down to the beach and into the dunes I remember her words about the peace you can find there. When I tell her this, she looks out over the water with a contemplative air and sighs. 'Ah, 'tis beautiful!'

I notice again the way she has of looking at you when you've asked a question, as if she is weighing you up as well as her answer. But the scrutiny of her eyes, set in a rosy face with high cheekbones beneath short hair, is not at all aggressive, nor defensive. It doesn't feel judgemental. Maureen had not told me anything of her private life but in her quiet way, within the sympathetic aura which she shares with others of her neighbours, I have felt the space to be myself.

There may be horrific things going on in this world and in this country but in truth I have met only great kindness and openness, a real welcome. People look at me but don't seem to judge. Giving people the benefit of the doubt might be seen as a weakness, but it can be a strength too. The poet Brendan Kennelly spells this out in an interview he gave to Jimmy Woulfe for his book *Voices of Kerry*:

I think you have to assume in creation that people are more or less the same; socially they may be more deprived or privileged. Or they may have more or less talent or intelligence. But having said that, there is another kind of equality which dominates the moment of encounter. And it is extraordinary the way people can smell condescension off you if you happen to think that person is not as well educated as you are, or whatever . . . There is no room for snobbery or condescension, because both these things are simply, as I would see them, they are denials or disfiguration of intelligence. And as far as I am concerned, one of the most important things in life is to be intelligent and good humoured, and if possible graceful. It's one of the most beautiful words of all, grace. I am not particularly graceful in carriage, but it is a quality I love in people. I met a lot of that in Kerry, particularly among the older women and among some men. It is a quality of reticence; of standing back and looking at the world. Of not judging it too quickly. Of giving people the opportunity of presenting themselves to you on their own terms and of you not wanting them to be what you wanted them to be, but of accepting them for what they are.

Driving back in the rapidly failing daylight, I can't believe my eyes. I'm facing east but I think I'm looking at another sunset. Then I realize it is a fire. I speed home anxious that I'll find the cottage in flames. But no, high up on the hillside between Pat Foley's house at Ballinagroun and the Courtney place at Caheracruttera there is a ring of fire. Looking through the binoculars I can see flames leaping high around a large dark centre. No doubt a farmer is burning off dead grass, but it looks like a giant search party, or siege fires around a fort; great leaping flames on a still cool night. Turning my back on the fire I look out across the harbour towards the lights of Cromane. The moment of panic over the fire has given way immediately to viewing the place as a sanctuary again.

The postmistress at Annascaul is engaged on one of her interminable phone calls when I go for some stamps. As ever the conversation seems to involve her striving to talk her interlocutor through some tricky procedure or endeavouring to understand some convoluted schedule or logistical process that they want her to fulfil. In the quiet of the post office I feel almost as though I am intruding on a very intimate conversation. In her little booth she might almost be a priest in the confessional.

'I'll have to go now, OK, call me back in ten minutes then,' she says before coming with a smile to serve me.

Headlines on the front page of the *Irish Times* speak clearly of how elements of the Irish social landscape are changing. '"Substantial" disposal of weapons by IRA' reads one, and below it, 'Inquiries will be given necessary information, archbishop promises.' The fact that the IRA has destroyed some arms hardly indicates that the peace process has come to a successful conclusion and indeed in some circles the action is seen as a cynical move to give Sinn Féin a more positive image for upcoming elections. And reading the details of the statement by the Catholic primate, Archbishop Brady, following an extraordinary general meeting of the Irish bishops at Maynooth, it emerges that the bishops will be handing over to the state inquiries into clerical child sex abuse 'the information they consider necessary'. The attitude that they have the right to determine what the people should know is still painfully obvious.

While these headlines aren't announcing a brand new Ireland, they do indicate, to my perhaps over-optimistic mind, that brighter days are on the horizon. It is intriguing that the institutions that have been so important in creating and defining independent Ireland are themselves now being forced into the modern world in which many of their countrymen have been living for a good few years.

The IRA might have had support only in limited quarters for a long time, but the Church's esteem and authority has been left largely unchallenged. Now there is a growing perception that it is on the run, that it will have to change dramatically if it has any chance of once again becoming the nation's spiritual and moral home. The most dramatic example that the writing is on the wall for the authoritarian Church comes at the bishops' meeting at Maynooth College. In what journalists describe in awed tones as 'unprecedented scenes in the college's 200 year history', a victim of clerical child abuse, Gerard Kelly, stood in the path of the Papal Nuncio, Dr Giuseppe Lazaratto, and spoke directly to him. On the radio news a reporter explains how the press corps stood silent as Kelly, with dignified determination, effectively forced the Pope's envoy to stand still and hear what he had to tell him about the abuse he suffered as a child in an industrial school. It is clear from the reporter's tone that he believes he has witnessed something of great significance. Watching the event on the television news that lunchtime, and seeing the Nuncio's shock and disbelief that someone would not automatically stand aside in deference and would even dare to speak out at him, I too have the sense of witnessing a watershed, the moment of revolution when something unassailable is revealed to be powerless.

Strolling among families walking and playing on the beach, I think that perhaps Ireland is not only shaking off the depression of gloomy winter weather but also anticipating confronting and dealing with the murky moral issues that have beset it. People seem relieved and happy that the Church is on the back foot.

Going through some papers at the cottage, I come across the notes that Father John J. óRíordáin had given out at his talk on Celtic spirituality some months before at Killarney library. In the current climate I find the brief final section, 'Faith and Institution (Cycle of Growth and Decline in Faith)', just about sums up what is happening with the Church. He describes a cycle of six stages:

The Preacher arrives to announce the Good News, the People respond in Faith to the Message, there is a human need for some organization so inevitably the Institution emerges, the Institution expands and devours the Faith, the Faith weakens, the Institution collapses. And the cycle starts all over again with the return of the Preacher.

People want to have the Church working for and with them in their faith again, not clinging on pathetically to the shreds of its former power. More than once I've heard the saying, 'The people have got to take back their Church!' It is clear that clergy, from the local priest up to the archbishop, will be working out notice unless they start delivering.

'They will have to put their house in order,' says Donal Sheehy as we sit on the high stools in Foley's Pub with our pints of Guinness. Talking of the latest revelations about abusive priests, Donal voices what many suspect: 'Do they go for that work because they want to do those things?'

Speaking in his slow, methodical way, he tells me that in earlier years he was much involved with athletics in the area. There had been a priest whom he liked very well until he found out that he had been abusing young girls of thirteen or fourteen all the while.

'I was horrified. I liked the man. I talked to him and found him sound. Then I learned what he'd been doing. And it was horrible!' He is looking earnestly into my face. His pale face topped with grey hair and his eyes, bright and beady behind his spectacles, all reflect his deep shock.

'Now that people feel free to talk about corruption in the Church, maybe they will begin to address the horrors that go on in some homes?' I venture.

'Ah yes, there was that man sent to prison for abusing his own daughter. Yes, that's another taboo we'll have to deal with.'

A neighbour comes in and sits on the far side of Donal and the talk turns to the recent performance of the local football teams. They speak earnestly as all fans do of the strengths and weaknesses of the players and their management, ending a critique of the wasted talents of such-and-such a player with a firm, 'Am I right or am I right?'

The bank and hedge along the road at the bottom of the field below my house are being dug away by the road-working team that have been making their way along from Castlemaine. Getting out of my drive and onto the road is going to be much easier, and safer too. Mike Courtney is inspecting what the team have done to his field when I drive down to try out the new exit.

'They ought to have elections more often!' he jokes.

Down at Foley's, Anthony is talking with Fidelus and they tell me about a friend's wedding they've been to at their 'home place above in Meath', on the other side of the country.

'It was awful,' Fidelus says. 'When the priest asked, "Do you take this woman to be etc. etc.," the groom said, "Can I ask the audience?" We all sat there not knowing where to look. I thought it must be some joke they'd worked out and that when the priest asked her she'd say, "Can I phone a friend?" But there was nothing! The priest looked furious. I don't know what the poor woman can have thought.'

'The eejit bridegroom ought to take himself off into a small room for a while and have a long talk with himself,' Anthony comments.

He makes me laugh telling of his troubles the night before. He'd been away from home working and staying up near Limerick during the week. He'd got back to the house he was staying in at two in the morning to find himself locked out, so he'd had to drive the two hours back to Inch. With heavy stubble on his face it has to be admitted that he looks a bit rough. But for his smiles and laughter he could seem menacing. When he asks for a coffee to help him keep alert on the drive back to Limerick, Fidelus says she hasn't any. 'I was drinking too much of it and it was after giving me the shakes,' and she waggles her hands about for emphasis. 'Anyway, it's bad for the skin too I'd say.'

'Oh, I don't worry about that,' laughs Anthony, stroking his spiky chin. 'I use Oil of Ulay!'

We talk about the latest happenings with the Church and how it must change to survive. Fidelus says that all sorts of regulars in the bar have been suddenly venting very strong feelings about abuse committed by some clerics and about the arrogance of the Church as a whole. 'One man was almost frothing at the mouth he was so angry! He wanted to shoot those bishops. I started wondering if they'd got at him.'

She says that she lost the focus of her faith after her young brother Dennis died and that she finds it more comforting when she is back at the 'home place' to go and sit by his and their father's graves and pray and talk to them. As she speaks I'm aware again how her openness about the difficulties she's faced in grieving have helped and encouraged me to talk about mine and work through the process.

In the still of dawn, a rolling birdsong calls me outside – it sounds like a big creature but for all I know it is a wren. Then I hear Inch's backing track again; so strong and insistent is its deep base hum, it makes you think it must be some giant electrical installation, but it is only the waves breaking on the beach two miles away. This is the most beautiful morning I have seen at Inch. As the sun comes up to the south and east of me, beyond the distinct and distant silhouette of MacGillycuddy's Reeks there is a purple blush in the sky and the white clouds begin breaking up and thinning around the mountain tops, leaving little puffs of misty cloud along the Cromane shore. Everything takes on a pink hue, the water, the sky, even the hedgerow, all echoing the vividness of the pink-wash walls of the old wash-house at Bridey Flynn's campsite in the field across the road. By seven o'clock the air is alive with birdsong, lambs' cries and the lowing of cows and their calves.

Mid-morning the postman arrives. 'Hello, John. Beeyootiful day! Let's hope this weather stays with us now!'

Having gone through the day's post, it feels like a good time to sit and read my older correspondence, my mother's letters.

Almost immediately I feel a weight lifting. Mostly the letters are fairly short notes, often ending with an exclamation that she's just noticed the time and that she must dash for the post. In fact at the end of the very first letter, written when I was fifteen, she finishes, 'I had intended writing much more than this but I have left myself short of time.' After just a few letters it is obvious that sending my brother and me away to school had been a terrible wrench for her. 'I am <u>longing</u> for the end of term when we can all be together again,' she says and goes on, 'How are the exams going, my love? I have been thinking about you every day.' Clearly our being at boarding school wasn't something that my parents would have wanted had they not believed it would be good for us. Whether or not it was a real benefit ultimately I sometimes question, but I find myself smiling as it occurs to me that had I not been away at school I wouldn't have these letters.

I am surprised to find that she was always encouraging my plans – rarely fulfilled in those years – to go travelling with friends. For some reason I've had it in my head that she'd gently tried to dissuade me, hoping that I wouldn't go, so that I could spend holidays with the family. While this was undoubtedly true on one level I discover advice like 'when you're camping I've heard it's good to put a newspaper under your sleeping bag, like a tramp', and on another occasion she has made a whole load of phone calls exploring the possibilities for me to work abroad in a hotel one summer.

Having thought that we didn't talk much and that somehow my parents were always disappointed in me, a letter wishing me well in my A levels gives me a fantastic lift. 'I hope your little cloud of depression will lift soon, my love. I used to have little times like this when I was younger but they soon lift and all is bright again. Whatever you do don't worry about your A's . . . You can count on our support . . . have no fear that if you don't make it to Oxford [where Terence was studying] that we will be disappointed, for we certainly will not . . . we only want you to do what you want.' She ends the letter, 'Keep smiling!'

Her letters are full of bits of news about the goings-on at home. In a way the details are mundane but I devour the reports of new curtains, even a new boiler, or the fact that she is looking forward to showing off her new dress. There's gossip about who she's been seeing and what she's done, and there are stories, like the drama of an exhaust pipe falling off the car, which aren't quite concluded as she has to dash off to the post box. Her courage in dealing with the agoraphobia shines through in places. At the end of 1976 she writes to say she has nearly finished a course of sessions with a counsellor and that 'I am feeling much better, have been into Dunmow today!!' And despite the phobia she is taking degrees at the local polytechnic, sometimes going to London with friends, though this becomes rarer in the later years, and taking part in the campaign against the expansion of Stansted airport. In the very last letter I have, during my finals at Hull, she writes, 'We went to the Chelsea Flower S on Tuesday last and felt quite o.k. I was very bucked.'

As I read on I hear her voice more and more clearly and having her 'read' to me is soothing and magical. And memories of laughter and running jokes come back to me. In one letter she addresses me 'Darling Tottenham Court Road' and signs off,

'Your very loving Wimpole Street'. I can't for the life of me remember what this was all about; had we been playing Monopoly, or Mornington Crescent? Neither sounds right so perhaps it was just some daft joke between us at the time.

My heart is soaring as her words take me back into the home and family that nurtured me and sustained me through difficult times. One phrase seems to sum up all the letters and brings her closer than ever: 'The role of mother is my favourite part, for one likes to feel needed . . .' I find myself sobbing over the way she signs off, 'your ever loving mother' or 'your very loving mama'. But then my sobs turn to laughter as I notice how many times she apologizes for her handwriting, blaming either a new pen or poorly prescribed glasses.

The anxieties that have kept me from reading the letters for so long now seem ridiculous. I suppose by not addressing them I'd let them build up into a form of neurosis and in the process almost managed to forget how close we had been. Having found so much joy and love, feelings of guilt and anger are put in perspective; all that is now in another place. I look at her photograph and start thinking about those times and our lives then. Although I wish that we could know each other now, the pain of that wishing is eased because, at last, I can see that we had known each other then.

Through the windows and door the warm breeze carries in the birdsong. My heart, like the house, is open.

My time at Inch is coming to an end and as I go around the little house that has been home to me, packing up and cleaning, I find I am sadder to be going than I would have thought. Home in England is tugging hard on my sleeve yet I know I am going to miss this house and the people of Inch. The rain and wind have come back but, though storms are forecast, the ferry to England will be sailing on time.

Last night I had a dream in which I was with my mother when my father died. We were weeping together when Terence came home and we had to break the news to him and then we all wept together. I didn't awake with any sadness; rather I was filled with a sense of relief and fulfilment. Perhaps this was a further step towards resolution; I'd had a chance to grieve with, and not just for, my mother. Now I can go home with my relationship with my family home and especially my mother firmly re-established. Now I am able to pick up my parents' pictures, hold them side by side and love them back, content to know how much they loved each other and their two boys. I can talk to them and have those conversations that I've missed for so long.

Over the following days getting closer to mothers becomes something of a theme. As I meet friends and say goodbye, we talk about the weather and news as usual, and they ask me how I've enjoyed my time in Kerry. When I tell them about reading my mother's letters, they in turn share conversations that they've had with their mothers or older women friends. It seems these women, too, are reflecting on their lives and wishing that they'd been more supportive – in the difficult teen years, when the daughter's marriage wasn't going well, or the kids were driving them mad. They wish they hadn't been so harsh on their husbands, their children and on themselves. Resolution appears to be in the air, and once or twice I ask, 'Why do you think they're suddenly saying these things now? Is it because of what's been happening with the Church?'

'Oh yes, definitely I'd say.'

I wonder if, just as the people as a whole are taking back the Church for themselves, these elderly women will be taking back their lives which they've run according to the strictures of an institution that has been in many ways, and particularly in its social/sexual attitudes, suddenly revealed as profoundly flawed.

But modern Ireland has only existed for eighty years and,

with the benefit of hindsight, it is possible to appreciate that it was founded on an essentially backward-looking vision at the beginning of a century that would see probably the most dramatic social and political changes of any period in the world's history. The Irish have perhaps tried too hard to keep one foot in the past. Now they are realizing that their institutions must evolve to keep pace in the twenty-first century.

'We wouldn't want you to go without a proper goodbye!' says Fidelus, announcing she is cooking supper for me and some friends who are coming in for a final drink. I feel torn; on the one hand I'm looking forward so much to being home but on the other I don't want to leave the community at Inch which has become an important part of my life. Foley's Pub, imbued with the generosity and affection of Fidelus and John, will always be my local, I hope, a place where I'll be welcomed, looked after and encouraged to take a seat at the bar with the other locals. Painted up on the wall of the café at the beach are a couple of lines, inspired I suppose by the American poet Robert Frost: 'Dear Inch, must I leave you? I have promises to keep. Perhaps miles to go to my last sleep.' I've no doubts I'll be returning to dear Inch before any thoughts of my last sleep.

I chat with Fidelus and John and savour my last few pints of Guinness. Donal Daly comes in, then Paddy and Mary O'Brien. Bridget Fitzgerald is there too, as is Martina. Otherwise the pub is fairly quiet, with Fidelus's reggae playing in the background as we sit and sip, gossiping like any group of friends in the pub.

When I started out for Inch I'd wanted to see how real the *craic* was. Would the magic of the Irish pub scene with its music and humour retain its appeal over a six-month stay? It has, showing that beyond mere entertainment it is an important and valuable part of Irish life. But there is a paradox too. The Irish drink far more than their European neighbours and with terrible consequences. The ability to dodge difficult questions with humour and wit, and sometimes plain weakness, has left many individuals and some institutions in terrible straits.

In many ways Ireland has proved to be an even more confusing and contrary place than I'd thought it might. When I set out on my journey I never anticipated finding so much sorrow, hearing so many stories of personal tragedy and public corruption. The undercurrents of Irish life have proved far darker than I had imagined. As I've tried to get under its skin, Ireland has got under mine, irritating, charming, depressing and exciting me by turns.

In many ways I can see parallels between my own private journey to grieve for and reconnect with my mother and the journey the Irish people are making as they deal with difficult issues and emotions from the past and present. With communities like that at Inch with its kindness and humour – and its faith – it is more than possible that the nation will emerge refreshed and ready for the future.

Not only have I made friends in Inch, but I've met cousins who have given me a genuine and generous welcome as a distant but definite member of their family. And it is the sense of belonging, the importance of family life, that all these individuals have given me that has affected me most profoundly. It may not be something that is unique to the Irish but they do have a special gift of welcome. The openness of others, who at first were strangers, has encouraged me to be open with them in turn as we've become friends. And by answering my questions about themselves they have helped me ask and answer questions about myself that I needed to resolve.

The fishing boats are out in force in Castlemaine Harbour as I drive east along its shore for the last time. At Boolteens I toot the horn when I glimpse Florence O'Sullivan, just inside the doorway of his forge, deep in conversation with a customer. An arm waves as I pass.

All the belongings from my home in Inch are packed into the back of the car. No longer do the boxes of family papers and letters hold any mystery or nagging doubts in my mind. When we'd first sifted through them a year or so ago Terence had quoted the line from *The Go-Between*. 'The past is a foreign country: they do things differently there,' and indeed at the start of my sojourn in Ireland I feared that I would always be cut off from my immediate roots and from the person I had been. Travelling through my personal history has proved less fraught than I'd imagined. The roads back to my family home, far from being impassable, have opened up.

All too easily the past can be distorted by selective memory. That 'past' becomes a 'reality' which in turn can distort the present, affecting our interpretation of the world around us and circumscribing our reactions to it. I had let frustrations and resentments with my parents become confused with my feelings of guilt, and had built a barrier over which I could no longer see my family life for what it really was. The past changed into a territory that was unfamiliar to me.

Whilst exploring the landscape of Kerry and living in relative solitude at Inch, I have been given that rare chance to step aside from the mainstream of my life and work my way through the barriers that had come to stand around my old home. At last I have escaped from the muddled outlook on my early life. Alongside winning a clearer perspective on my own history, I have had the chance of surveying my temporary homeland.

For the founders of modern Ireland the past was not a foreign country at all but the place they believed was home. Eighty years on, forging a future based on an idealized and over-romanticized vision of the past is widely recognized as a flawed venture. In the blinkered desire to make an idyll work, there was an inherent risk that too much would have to be swept under the carpet; failing institutions would have to be propped up, their weaknesses plastered over. Having one eye always looking back has meant that at times the Irish lost sight of the way the world was changing and their need to adapt with it.

At Castlemaine I turn onto the main road and head south for Cork and the ferry. Suddenly overwhelmed by a feeling of optimism and eagerness to be home, I accelerate out of the village, recalling the line I'd heard one night in Foley's Bar.

'You have to go away to come back.'

# BIBLIOGRAPHY

Barrington, T. J., *Discovering Kerry*. The Collins Press, Cork, 1976.

Connolly, S. J. (ed.), *The Oxford Companion to Irish History*. Oxford University Press, Oxford, 1998.

Curtis, Edmund, *A History of Ireland*. Methuen, first published 1936.

Cusack, Mary Frances, *An Illustrated History of Ireland*. First published 1868; reprinted Senate, Twickenham, 1998.

Dwyer, T. Ryle, *Tans, Terror and Troubles: Kerry's Real Fighting Story 1913–1923*. Mercier Press, Cork, 2001.

Foster, R. F., *Modern Ireland 1600–1972*. Penguin Books, London, 1988.

Foster, R. F. (ed.), *The Oxford History of Ireland*. Oxford University Press, Oxford, 1989.

Kavanagh, Patrick, *Selected Poems*. Penguin Books, London, 1996.

King, Jeremiah, *County Kerry Past & Present: A Handbook to the Local and Family History of the County*. First published 1936; facsimile edition, Mercier Press, Cork, 1986.

King, Jeremiah, *King's History of Kerry*. 'The People' Printing Works, Wexford, 1912.

MacCarthy, J. (ed.), *The Last King Donal IX MacCarthy Mór*. The MacCarthy Clan Society, Kanturk, Co. Cork, 1996.

MacCarthy, Samuel Trant, *The MacCarthys of Munster*. First published 1922, The Dundalgan Press, Dundalk; new edition edited by Terence MacCarthy, 1997; facsimile edition, with an introduction and commentary by Terence Francis MacCarthy, Gryfons Publishers and Distributors, Little Rock, Arkansas, USA, 1997.

MacDonogh, Steve, *The Dingle Peninsula*. Brandon, Dingle, 2000.

O'Sullivan, Friar, of Muckross Abbey, *Ancient History of the Kingdom of Kerry*. Edited with preface and notes by F. Jarlath Prendergast, O F M; originally published by the *Journal of the Cork Historical and Archeaological Society* 1898–1900; reproduced on the MacCarthy Clan website.

Smith, Charles, *The Ancient and Present State of the County of Kerry*. First published 1756; reprinted Mercier Press, Cork, 1969.

Woulfe, Jimmy, *Voices of Kerry*. Blackwater Press, Dublin, 1994.

Yeats, W. B., *Selected Poems*. Penguin Books, London, 1991.